THE POLITICS OF MATERNITY CARE

THE POLITICS OF MATERNITY CARE

Services for Childbearing Women in Twentieth-Century Britain

Edited by

JO GARCIA, ROBERT KILPATRICK,
MARTIN RICHARDS

CLARENDON PRESS · OXFORD

Oxford University Press, Walton Street, Oxford OX2 6DP

Oxford New York Toronto
Delhi Bombay Calcutta Madras Karachi
Petaling Jaya Singapore Hong Kong Tokyo
Nairobi Dar es Salaam Cape Town
Melbourne Auckland
and associated companies in
Berlin Ibadan

Oxford is a trade mark of Oxford University Press

Published in the United States
by Oxford University Press, New York

First published 1990
Reprinted 1990 (with corrections), 1991

British Library Cataloguing in Publication Data
The politics of maternity care: services for
childbearing women in 20th century Britain.
1. Great Britain. Welfare services for pregnant women
I. Title   II. Garcia, Jo   III. Kilpatrick, Robert
IV. Richards, Martin, 1940 Jan 26–
362.8' 3
ISBN 0–19–827287–1

Library of Congress Cataloging in Publication Data
The Politics of maternity care / edited by Jo Garcia,
Robert Kilpatrick, Martin Richards.
p.   cm.
Includes index.
1. Maternal health services—Great Britain—History—20th century.
2. Obstetrics—Great Britain—History—20th century.
I. Garcia, Jo, 1950–. II. Kilpatrick, Robert. III. Richards, Martin.
RG964.G7P65 1990   362.1'982'009410904—dc20   89–15959
ISBN 0–19–827287–1

Printed and bound in Great Britain by
Bookcraft (Bath) Ltd, Midsomer Norton, Avon

Contents

List of Contributors

Rosaline Barbour	MRC Medical Sociology Unit, University of Glasgow
Jennifer Beinart	Wellcome Unit for the History of Medicine, University of Oxford.
Rona Campbell	Department of Social Administration and Policy, University of Ulster at Jordanstown
Ann Cartwright	Institute for Social Studies in Medical Care, London
Vanessa Coupland	Child Care and Development Group, University of Cambridge
Lyn Durward	Maternity Alliance, London
Ruth Evans	Mind—the · National Association for Mental Health, London
Sally Garforth	National Perinatal Epidemiology Unit, University of Oxford
Jo Garcia	National Perinatal Epidemiology Unit, University of Oxford
Josephine Green	Child Care and Development Group, University of Cambridge
Ann Jacoby	Institute for Social Studies in Medical Care, London
Robert Kilpatrick	Wellcome Unit for the History of Medicine, University of Cambridge
Jenny Kitzinger	Child Care and Development Group, University of Cambridge; now at the AIDS Media Research Project, Glasgow
Jane Lewis	Department of Social Science and Administration, London School of Economics and Political Science
Alison Macfarlane	National Perinatal Epidemiology Unit, University of Oxford

Ann Oakley	Thomas Coram Research Unit, University of London
Elizabeth Peretz	Wellcome Unit for the History of Medicine, University of Oxford
Ann Phoenix	Thomas Coram Research Unit, University of London
Shirley Prendergast	Child Care and Development Group, University of Cambridge
Alan Prout	South Bank Polytechnic, London
Margaret Reid	Department of Community Medicine, University of Glasgow
Martin Richards	Child Care and Development Group, University of Cambridge
Sarah Robinson	Nursing Research Unit, Kings College, University of London
Wendy Savage	The London Hospital
Eckart Schwarz	The Clinical School, University of Bristol

Introduction

BIRTH has a very special social and emotional significance for women and their partners, and it is therefore not surprising that its conduct remains a matter for public as well as professional interest and discussion. Indeed, in the last twenty years, obstetrics has often been cited as an important example of over-medicalization and the unnecessary, and perhaps dangerous, over-use of technical intervention. It is also a part of medicine where questions concerning choices about care have been to the fore, and there have been continuing arguments about the extent to which women can, or should, have control over what happens to them. This book stands both as a reflection of these debates on British maternity care and as a contribution to them.

There is sometimes a tendency for questions about medical care to be seen as technical matters to be decided only by those with specialist knowledge. Medicine is, of course, a body of technical knowledge, but its practice involves choices which are made in the light of this knowledge. This is true not only at the individual level, when, for instance, a pregnant woman seeks advice from a midwife or doctor, but also collectively, when decisions are being made about the kind of service to be provided—for example, the extent to which care should be concentrated in large hospitals rather than smaller local units, or the way in which a unit or a domiciliary service should be staffed. This means that questions about the nature of care and how it is to be provided and funded are as much political as technical. The public as well as the professionals who provide the service are, or at least should be, involved in the debate and decision-making.

Looking back, the 1950s seems like an age of innocence in the development of the National Health Service in Britain. Science appeared to be marching hand in hand with clinical skills and was making many diseases things of the past. Of course, cures were not available for everything, but it seemed only a matter of time before what had been done for infectious diseases could also be achieved for the more intractable problems like cancer and heart-disease. The Health Service had brought this new style of medicine within the reach of all. While there might be a lingering backlog of neglect and poor investment, here, too, time and the post-war economic recovery would soon allow the remaining problems to be cleared away, or so the argument ran.

However, while belief in the idea of the National Health Service remained unshaken (at least until the new political climate of the 1980s began to turn selfishness and ability to pay into social virtues), doubts began to arise about modern medicine and the ability of science to provide magic bullets for all ills—doubts which were fed by episodes like the thalidomide tragedy and the stubbornness of the non-infectious diseases in the face of the offerings of the pharmaceutical industry. Another characteristic of the period was a dismissal of the role of public health and its downgrading in relation to 'scientific' medicine. This led to what many saw as an over-concentration on hospital services at the expense of those in the community. Concern also grew over the manner and style in which medical care was being delivered. Queuing in the general practitioner's waiting-room or in a hospital out-patient department could at least be eliminated by providing more doctors and organizing proper appointment systems, but there were also complaints of another kind that seemed to indicate that all was not right in the relationship of doctor and patient.

Interestingly, one of the first places within medicine where these concerns surfaced was obstetrics; and by the early 1960s they had become sufficiently serious for the Ministry of Health to issue a policy statement entitled *Human Relationships in Obstetrics* (1961). It is this debate about the relationship between childbearing women and the professionals who provide their care—its future development as well as its history—that is the central theme of this book. How has maternity care in Britain come to be organized in the way that it is? How does it affect those most closely involved—mothers, their partners, and babies; midwives, general practitioners, and obstetricians? Why are there continued tensions between mothers and these professionals? As the historical chapters in this book will make clear, criticism of maternity care is not a new phenomenon but goes back at least to the turn of the century when the present organization of professional services began to take shape.

Before going on to outline the scope of the book, there are some general points that should be made. First, perhaps, is the question of whether maternity care is special or whether the issues with which we will be dealing are general to the whole of medicine. The answer would seem to be that both have some truth: the provision of any kind of medical care involves a relationship between professional providers and the receivers of treatment, so that maternity care is bound to share some characteristics with medicine as a whole. This means that to view it in isolation would be misleading to some extent. For instance, while some features of hospital ante-natal care may be special because childbearing women are involved, the experience will also have much in common with any hospital out-patient clinic dealing with men, women, or children and all kinds of medical conditions or problems.

There are, however, some features which make the delivery of babies rather different from, say, the provision of treatment for victims of a road accident. While initially at least the accident victim is likely to be grateful for whatever help he or she can get, the delivery of a baby is not usually a medical emergency. The mother, together with her partner, is likely to have thought about her delivery and have hopes and fears for it. She may well have strong feelings about how it is to be conducted, where it is to take place, and who is to be present. She may not see herself as a patient nor the occasion as primarily a medical one, but rather as the entry of her child into the social world of families and friends. But the extent to which maternity care has special features that mark it off from medicine as a whole may have been reduced as maternity care has become medicalized and a matter for obstetric control. Such control has shifted the focus of birth from the social and emotional to the physiological and medical.

Many of the chapters in this book have as an underlying theme the notion that having a baby is an integral part of the life of the mother. Birth is often a central moment in her life and is above all a social event, involving as it does both a change in her social status and a reordering of a whole range of social relationships. It is an event about which the mother may have many fears and anxieties as well as positive feelings. While some of these may touch on matters that are at least partly medical—will the baby be well, will the pain be bearable, will effective pain-relief be at hand—these concerns in themselves do not make the birth a medical event.

Most mothers travel hopefully, trusting that medical intervention will not be necessary but wanting it on hand in case it is. As has been pointed out so often, pregnancy is not an illness and labouring women are not patients—in clear contrast to accident victims. As several of the chapters in this book make clear, the health-care system usually operates from the opposite assumption—that all pregnancies are pathological until their normality is demonstrated after the event. So the professionals tend to be pessimistic travellers, assuming the worst until they are proved wrong by a safe arrival. The approach of care-givers must, of necessity, differ somewhat from the views of the women they look after, because of the need for a degree of detachment from the emotional and very personal event of birth, and because the hospital setting of most maternity care tends to reinforce the 'illness' view of childbearing. However, there is a very sharp distinction between the traditional approach of attending and supporting women, and the position of those who set out to 'manage' labour and delivery—a position which is central to recent developments in obstetrics, as Schwarz points out in his chapter on obstetric textbooks (see Chapter 3 below). Of course, care-givers, like mothers, vary in their views, but as Wendy Savage confirms in the book's concluding chapter, it is the conceptual issue of how delivery is approached that is at the centre of much of the current debate. This professional tendency to regard birth in terms of pathology and illness can be interpreted as the way in which the professions—both medical and midwifery—manage their own anxieties. Research which has applied insights from psychoanalysis to institutions like hospitals suggests that this management of anxiety may be a very important, but unspoken, feature of their organization, and explains some aspects of their bureaucratic structure and practice (Menzies Lyth 1988).

Gender has a particular significance in maternity care, not only because of the obvious point that those who give birth are women, but also because the two professions involved in providing care are almost entirely divided by gender. The implications of this divide are discussed by some of the contributors to this book in their exploration of the uneasy and changing relationship between midwives and doctors. Are midwives, because they are almost all women, more likely to share the perspectives of those for whom they care? This question is not addressed directly here, but it is a part of the puzzle that several of the authors seek to solve.

Another key element in the debate about maternity care is the role of technology. In common with other branches of medicine, obstetrics has seen many new techniques come into use in recent years. What makes new technology a special issue in maternity care are the widely differing perceptions of the appropriateness of these new techniques. For instance, while the use of electronic monitoring of the fetal heart-rate is the subject of strong argument, in another field of medicine, such as adult intensive care, the use of such a device is seen by most care-givers and recipients as appropriate and necessary. There is a tendency in the maternity field to use the word 'intervention' with the sense of 'inappropriate interference', and also to exclude from consideration some older techniques which do involve intervening but which are usually used by midwives, such as inhalational analgesia or the Pinard stethoscope. The differing views of obstetric and midwifery techniques also reflect the shift in the boundary between the obstetrician's concern with the abnormal and the midwife's with the normal. Once all deliveries come to be seen as potentially abnormal—and so appropriate for obstetric intervention—midwifery techniques become a mark of the benign and the normal, especially for those who may wish to oppose obstetric control. But imposing these value-judgements on technology can stand in the way of a considered view on the benefits and disadvantages of different forms of care.

Technology is not simply a matter of nuts and bolts and transistors. Technological innovation also consists of a conceptual change. One that will concern us in much of this book is the shift towards the *management* of labour from the earlier idea of support and assistance. Again, these concepts have a special significance in maternity care. While few would argue about such an approach to the care of the seriously ill, there is certainly not universal agreement that labour and delivery are processes to be managed. Technology is created to fulfil perceived professional needs, and embodies the assumptions that those who create it may have about its use. Recent obstetric technology has been produced within the prevailing assumptions about appropriate care—that women should labour in hospital and, usually, on a delivery bed. For example, the design of most monitoring devices assumes their use in hospital rather than at home, and many of the devices employed in labour can only be used when a woman is lying in bed. The development of ways of monitoring aspects of labour or of pregnancy with devices that can be easily transported, so that they can be used by midwives at home or in local clinics, is a welcome departure from these narrow assumptions and, indeed, marks a return to an earlier era. In the 1930s a gas-and-air machine was developed specifically for use by midwives in the home; among other requirements it needed to be small enough to be transported by bicycle.

Although the contributors to this book are diverse in their backgrounds and perspectives, some common themes are apparent. The first concerns the wider social needs and circumstances of childbearing women and their partners. The experience of childbirth is influenced not only by the nature of the health·services, but also by a wide sweep of social and economic policies and attitudes. As Jane Lewis points out in the first chapter, women's organizations concerned with maternity in the early part of this century campaigned on a wide range of issues, including health care, benefits, employment, and family finance. Elizabeth Peretz, in her study of local maternity care in the inter-war period, looks at some of the difficulties that women faced in obtaining maternity care that was within their means. These themes are taken up again, towards the end of the book (Chapter 14) by Lyn Durward and Ruth Evans. They discuss the very diverse pressure groups that are currently concerned with maternity, some of which increasingly include in their campaigns the social and financial problems of parents and children. These authors examine the varied roles of pressure groups in the present political climate.

In another chapter concerned with the political and social setting of maternity care, Ann Phoenix puts the childbearing experiences of black women in the context of a racially discriminatory society and health service, and looks at some of the stereotypes which get in the way of good care. She also discusses the campaigns that have been set up to tackle the issues involved, such as Training in Health and Race and the organizations concerned with sickle cell disease. Margaret Reid, in a chapter on the new and rapidly expanding programmes of fetal diagnosis and screening, draws attention to the moral and social dilemmas that parents may face either when they seek screening or are offered it because of risk factors of which they may not be aware. This seems to be an area where the development of technology is running well ahead of our understanding of how to deploy it. As there are no treatments currently available for the conditions that are being diagnosed in pregnancy, all that can be done is to offer parents the possibility of an abortion. So legislation and social attitudes towards abortion and towards provision for the handicapped have an influence on parents' decisions and on the deployment of these procedures. Future technological developments in this field seem especially likely to increase the dilemmas that parents will face.

Another possible consequence of the growth of pre-natal screening is a shift in the roles of the different professions in pregnancy care, since the use of fetal diagnostic techniques is largely a matter for obstetricians rather than midwives. What was once a central position for the midwife in the care of pregnant women is likely to be further diminished. These roles, and the relationships between the key professions, provide the second major theme that runs through this book. Sarah Robinson deals historically with the development and regulation of the midwifery profession (Chapter 4). She documents the legislative and institutional processes that began to form the profession in the earlier part of this century, and describes how subsequent changes in the provision of maternity services affected the midwife's role. She also looks in some detail at their present position within maternity care

and at recent changes within midwifery. Eckart Schwarz
(Chapter 3) describes the development of the concept of
obstetrics as revealed by textbook writers in the post-war
period. He illustrates a shift from a view of obstetrics as
intervention in time of crisis to a wider brief which includes
the surveillance and management of normal pregnancy and
birth.

A rough index of the growing role of the obstetrician is
provided by the change in the place of birth from home to
hospital. Rona Campbell and Alison Macfarlane describe the
rapid growth in hospital delivery rates that occurred in the
late 1960s and 1970s, and examine some of the debates about
the desirability of the change. To some extent one must look to
a much earlier period for the roots of these developments. Jane
Lewis and Sarah Robinson both comment on the rising
proportion of hospital births in the inter-war period as it
relates to the themes of their chapters, and Elizabeth Peretz
notes that there was considerable local variation in the trend
towards institutional birth during these years. Concern about
maternal mortality in the inter-war years (discussed by Jane
Lewis), led, among many other things, to the creation of the
College of Obstetricians and Gynaecologists in 1929. This
undoubtedly strengthened the position of obstetricians in
relation to general practitioners and midwives. Similarly, the
setting-up of the system of confidential inquiries into maternal
deaths also led to a shift in power, since it was the obstetrician
who carried out the main part of the inquiry and, often, the
practice of midwives and general practitioners that was the
object of scrutiny. Growing obstetric power confirmed and
extended the role of the obstetric hospital in the overall
maternity-care system. However, as Elizabeth Peretz reminds
us in Chapter 2, the 1930s saw the creation of a national
service firmly based on domiciliary midwifery care and
general practice. In order to understand the major shift in
direction that maternity care took after the war, further
detailed research of the kind described in her chapter is
needed on hospital and general-practitioner obstetrics before
and during the Second World War.

It was not until the National Health Service was set up in
1948 that the predominant view became one of a national

service with the consultant obstetric unit at its heart. The textbooks analysed by Eckart Schwarz clearly document the conceptual shift that the obstetricians brought about in hospital care as the NHS developed. In the early post-war period, care for the mother and baby without complications was a midwifery matter. By the 1970s there was a tendency for obstetric responsibility to be extended to all mothers, and a consequent reduction in the scope of the midwives' role. However, the practical application of the ideas that Eckart Schwarz describes was not uniform, and responsibility for decision-making and policy formulation in maternity care varies markedly between hospitals in Britain (Garcia and Garforth, forthcoming).

The profound changes in the role of the midwife which arose from the move into hospital and from the changes in obstetrics are discussed by Sarah Robinson in Chapter 4. By the end of the 1970s some have come to see the midwife as little more than an obstetric nurse, a very far cry from the autonomous practitioner with the black bag who cycled through the Oxfordshire lanes and served the pre-war maternity service that Elizabeth Peretz describes. But Sarah Robinson and Wendy Savage both point to some of the recent concerns and developments within midwifery which could be cause for optimism: schemes to provide continuity of midwifery care and to use midwives' skills more fully; the active involvement of midwives in research and in successful groups like the Association of Radical Midwives.

Jenny Kitzinger, Josephine Green, and Vanessa Coupland take up the theme of the relationship between midwives and doctors in Chapter 8, in their study of contemporary labour wards. They use interviews and observational data to explore the views of midwives on the boundaries of their practice and on the negotiation of day-to-day work with doctors. They also make the important point that we need to differentiate between the roles of consultants, registrars, and house officers and not treat all 'doctors' as a conglomerate category. The role of the other important professional group, the general practitioners, is discussed by Rona Campbell and Alison Macfarlane in the context of the debate about the place of birth. General-practitioner involvement has been a central

part of the discussions and disputes about the provision of
maternity care in different settings, and these authors examine
the stances of the three main professions in relation to safety
and choice about the place of care.

In their chapter about parenthood education in schools
(Chapter 7), Shirley Prendergast and Alan Prout point to the
messages about medical power and control that are conveyed
by class-room films about birth, and suggest that these may be
important in forming young people's views of childbirth. Thus
the shifts in the roles of the professions in maternity care are
made clear to the potential users long before most of them
encounter this part of the Health Service, and the image
young people have of birth is much more likely to be of an
obstetrically managed delivery than of supportive midwifery
care. The book concludes with an interview with Wendy
Savage about the future of maternity care and the roles of
doctors and midwives. She argues strongly for changes within
both midwifery and obstetrics as well as for a renegotiation of
their relationship, and sees a radical reappraisal of the way we
train both midwives and doctors as central to this change.

A third theme, which is discussed by many of the
contributors, concerns the views and experiences of those who
use the maternity services, and the ways in which change can
take place in response to parents' pressure groups and to
research on parents' views. Jane Lewis (Chapter 1), Jenny
Kitzinger (Chapter 5), and Jennifer Beinart (Chapter 6) all
address this theme from historical perspectives. Jane Lewis's
chapter includes a description of the Women's Co-operative
Guild which campaigned on maternity services in the early
part of this century and which conducted a pioneering survey
of women's experiences of childbearing. Jenny Kitzinger
examines the history of the National Childbirth Trust, the
largest British lay organization concerned with childbirth,
and traces the ways in which the Trust's attitudes towards the
professionals have changed since its foundation in 1956. In
her chapter on pain-relief in labour, Jennifer Beinart includes
a discussion of the role of organized lobbying for particular
forms of pain-relief and the important part this has played in
the evolution of services. She describes how in the 1930s and
1940s the call was for more of what would now be called

intervention, while in more recent years most lay groups have argued for less routine use of drugs for pain-relief.

Ann Jacoby and Ann Cartwright describe the more formal ways in which the views of service-users can be assessed (Chapter 13). This of course has taken on a considerable importance in the arguments about the kinds of care that should be provided, as each side tends to claim that their preferred option is what childbearing women really want. Ann Oakley and Martin Richards (Chapter 10) use data from such studies to explore mothers' responses to Caesarean section. Caesarean section rates are rising, and the use of this method of delivery is at the centre of many arguments about obstetric control. Given the wide variety of needs and preferences documented in these chapters, it seems clear that services should offer choices, and of course there are attempts to do this. However, policy and practice often diverge, and there seems to be a general tendency for the care offered in such bureaucratic institutions as hospitals to become routine and inflexible, again providing an example of the ways in which professional anxieties are contained. A major challenge for the future is to counter this so that the maternity services can meet the diverse needs of their users. Two other chapters report studies of specific aspects of care. Jo Garcia and Sally Garforth (Chapter 9) use interviews and observational studies of labour ward care to discuss the first contacts between babies and parents. Here again the relationship between the professions and the scope for, or lack of, flexibility in institutional care are central themes. The growing trend for fathers to be involved in maternity care, both ante-natally and in labour, is taken up by Rosaline Barbour (Chapter 11) who uses her recent observational and interview research to discuss this development. While many parents welcome this trend, it is not without problems, especially when it becomes a routine expectation rather than one of the available options.

This introduction should also draw attention to the limits of the coverage of this book. We have not set out to deal directly with the clinical aspects of maternity care, though inevitably elements of this are discussed. A striking recent development has been the growing volume of research on the effectiveness of aspects of care, and increasingly this involves the use of randomized controlled trials. One of the early advocates of these was Archie Cochrane, who pointed out in 1972 how little was known about the value of much of what constituted obstetric care. For a systematic account of the effectiveness of the elements of care, readers are directed to a book edited by Chalmers, Enkin, and Keirse (1989).

Our concern in this book is with *British* care and hence with provision within the National Health Service. However, we hope that much of the material will be of interest to readers in other countries with other systems of medical care; many of our themes apply to any childbirth situation and all have parallels in other systems of care provision. We decided not to include chapters on some important topics related to maternity, such as the new techniques for *in vitro* fertilization and other methods of assisted conception (Stanworth 1987), and more general issues in women's health (Graham 1984; Homans 1985), though several of our authors do touch on these topics. In spite of our concern that the wider social circumstances of childbearing women be taken into account when providing care, we have limited ourselves to maternity-health services and have not included material on social welfare, housing, or employment.

There are also some subjects which fall within our chosen brief but which we have not been able to deal with, for a variety of reasons. For example, we would like to see more research on the way in which maternity policies are developed and implemented at national and local levels, and on the practical roles played by different professions and by such local committees as the Maternity Services Liaison Committees. To some extent, the nature of maternity-care policies reflects the structure of the administrative system, but, sadly, as yet little work has been done on the administration of maternity care. The changing role of the paediatrician in the maternity hospital is another important development that we would like to have dealt with in this book but on which there is a lack of research. There is also very little systematic information about inequalities in maternity-service provision, either geographically or socially, though there is ample evidence of social inequality in mortality (Macfarlane and Mugford 1984). As Ann Phoenix points out, black women may not receive the sort of care they need, and, among others, the same is true of travellers, very young women, or those who are homeless. What is the potential for improving services to particular groups by local schemes, such as special ante-natal clinics for young women or such national programmes as the Asian Mother and Baby campaign? Another important theme that is worthy of further consideration is the role of research in changing maternity care; although research may often be motivated by a desire to improve services, we know little about its eventual effectiveness.

Maternity care is important because, as we know, women's experiences of care may colour their relationship with their children and have a critical bearing on their well-being in the weeks and months after birth. Unlike the situation in most of medicine, those who use the maternity services are, with few exceptions, fit and healthy, and they often have clear ideas about how they want their delivery to be conducted. This means that any underlying tension between provider and user is more likely to surface here than elsewhere in medicine. But while there are some special features of maternity care, the debates contained within this book may in many ways be seen as running through the whole of medicine. In this sense, maternity care is at the vanguard, where the engineering approach of modern medicine encounters the personal and emotional concerns of those it sets out to serve.

The editors would like to thank their colleagues, in particular Jill Brown and Sally Roberts at the Child Care and Development Group and Philippa Claiden at the National Perinatal Epidemiology Unit. Our thanks also go to the editorial and other staff at Oxford University Press for their sympathetic help and careful attention to detail.

References

Cochrane, A., 1972, *Effectiveness and Efficiency* (London, Nuffield Provincial Hospitals Trust).
Chalmers, I., Enkin, M., and Keirse, M. (eds.), 1989, *Effective Care in Pregnancy and Childbirth* (Oxford, Oxford University Press).
Garcia, J. and Garforth, S., forthcoming, 'Midwifery Policies and Policy-Making, in Robinson, S. and Thomson, A. (eds.), *Midwives, Research and Childbirth*, ii (London, Chapman and Hall).
Graham, H., 1984, *Women, Health and the Family* (Brighton, Wheatsheaf).
Homans, H. (ed.), 1985, *The Sexual Politics of Reproduction* (Aldershot, Gower).
Macfarlane, A. and Mugford, M., 1984, *Birth Counts* (London, HMSO).
Menzies Lyth, I., 1988, *Containing Anxiety in Institutions: Selected Essays*, i (London, Free Association Books).
Ministry of Health, 1961, *Human Relations in Obstetrics* (Central Health Services Council, Standing Midwifery and Maternity Advisory Committee; London, HMSO).
Stanworth, M. (ed.), 1987, *Reproductive Technologies: Gender, Motherhood and Medicine* (Cambridge, Polity Press).

I

Mothers and Maternity Policies in the Twentieth Century

Jane Lewis

PROFESSIONALS and policy-makers have always tended to abstract childbirth from the fabric of women's lives. Judgements as to the proper place of birth (home versus hospital) and the merits or demerits of increasingly 'high-tech' procedures (from episiotomies and inductions to ultrasound and amniocentesis) have been made in relation to whether they contribute to a 'successful' outcome, measured in terms of mortality and morbidity rates. As Hilary Graham and Ann Oakley (1981) have pointed out from their study of childbirth today, there is a considerable difference both in the meaning attributed to childbirth by women as opposed to doctors, and in their respective definitions of 'success'. To women, childbirth is a life-event rather than a medical event, while 'success' is measured in terms of personal fulfilment and satisfaction rather than statistical aggregates.

This chapter will show that there has always been a gap between the perceptions and demands of women in respect to maternity policies and practices, and what has been offered by policy-makers and professionals. However, women's views have undergone significant change over time; early twentieth-century women's groups campaigned actively for anaesthesia and hospital births. Such demands can only be understood in relation to the material circumstances of women's lives. It is interesting that the demand for anaesthesia came primarily from middle-class women, while the call for hospital births came mainly from working-class women, whose choice of help in childbirth was limited in the majority of cases to a midwife or 'handywoman'. A ten-day rest in hospital made sense in the context of the hard household labour performed by working-

class women who also underwent frequent pregnancy. After
the Second World War women's material circumstances
changed dramatically. Pregnancies were much more likely to
be planned, household labour to be easier, and a much larger
percentage of women to be in paid employment when they
became pregnant. Women's ideas about what they wanted in
terms of maternity practice changed accordingly. What has
remained constant is first, the way in which women's concerns
about childbirth and maternity have ranged much more
widely than purely medical matters; and second, the conflict
between their demands and the medical profession's preferences
and priorities.

Early Twentieth-Century Childbirth and the Women's Co-operative Guild's Maternity Campaign

In 1914 the Women's Co-operative Guild (WCG) asked its
membership—for the most part respectable, married, working-
class women—to write down details of their maternity
experiences. On the basis of the 386 replies it received, the
Guild concluded that:

During the months of pregnancy, the woman must learn by
experience and ignorance, usually being told that all her troubles are
'natural'. In order to scrape together a few shillings she often goes
out to char or sits at her sewing machine or takes in washing; she
puts by pence in money boxes, she saves little stores of tea, soup,
oatmeal and other dry goods; when times are bad she goes without,
providing for her husband and children before herself . . . Up to the
last minute before childbirth she has to wash and dress the children,
cook the meals she's sometimes too tired to eat, and do all her own
housework. At her confinement often only an untrained midwife is
available, who sometimes has to make use of a child's help . . . in the
areas where bad housing causes the family in hundreds of thousands
of cases to live in two or three rooms . . . privacy and quiet are
impossible. (Women's Co-operative Guild 1917: 1.)

The average working-class mother of the 1890s married in her
teens or early twenties, had ten pregnancies, and spent fifteen

years in a state of pregnancy and nursing, compared to the
four years spent thus after the Second World War. A vignette
from one of the letters received by the Guild translates these
statistics and the Guild's conclusions as to the conditions of
maternity into human experience:

I had been married eighteen months when I had my first baby,
when I had a trying time, it being only an eight-months baby. My
waters broke five weeks before, and caused what the doctor called a
'dry labour'. The baby only lived twelve hours. The second came
three years and nine months afterwards. I had a straight labour, but
I flooded afterwards, and if the doctor had not been there I should
have lost my life; it caused me three months doctoring afterwards.
The third one, which came two years and one month after, I had a
fairly good labour. Over this one my sufferings were mostly before it
came. I had varicose veins in the right leg right away and the
irritation was most distressing; I used to walk the bedroom most
nights during the last month. The fourth came two years and three
months after the third and the doctor put me an elastic band on my
leg, and that was better . . . Between the fourth and fifth I was four
years and eleven months and then the sixth I went five years and
eleven months and was forty-two when I had him . . . I had a good
husband but he never earned more than 28 shillings a week and I
have always had to work up to the last. (Llewellyn Davies 1915: 54–5.)

This woman also had a miscarriage, which again meant
calling in a doctor, something she could ill afford. Of the 386
women replying to the Guild, 348 had borne between them
1,396 live children, 83 still births, and 218 miscarriages.

Having babies in itself is not necessarily detrimental to
health, but in the conditions of the early twentieth century,
when housework was very much hard labour and money was
short, there is no doubt but that frequent pregnancy taxed
women's health severely. The members of the WCG, who
would have done quite a bit better than the very poor,
expected to have what they called 'womb problems' after
childbirth, most had varicose veins and swollen ankles, and
very few had a complete set of teeth. None of these was likely
to cause premature death. But taken together they added up
to a serious amount of ill health among working-class women
during the early part of this century. One leading gynaecologist
commented that 'it is probably not an overstatement to say

that about 60% of hospital gynaecology is a legacy from vitiated childbearing' (Young 1928: 967).

Working women's experience of wife- and motherhood was dominated by their responsibility for managing the family economy and solving the food/rent equation, which they often accomplished only by going short of food themselves. One investigation of family budgets in Lambeth just before the First World War showed many wives making do with what they called a 'kettle bender'—a piece of dry bread soaked in hot water—while husbands, who had to be kept fit enough for hard manual labour, sat down to a small meat ration and children to a meal that was neither as poor as that of their mothers' nor as good as that of their fathers' (Reeves 1913). Another inquiry into the conditions of families in Middles-borough reported that girls were more prone to illness as soon as they began to menstruate (Bell 1911). In view of the fact that we now know that healthy childbirth depends in large measure on a woman's diet throughout her life, it is perhaps not so surprising that early twentieth-century women experienced difficulty with their pregnancies. The threat posed to women's health by frequent pregnancies, and the financial stress imposed by each new arrival, were consider-able.

Compared with today, very few married women were employed full-time. Those who were, seem to have experienced high morbidity rates. From the start of the National Health Insurance scheme in 1911, the 10 per cent of married women who worked in full-time insurable occupations experienced much higher than expected rates of sickness. Government inquiries into the issue concluded that this was due to their ignorance of the principles of insurance and to 'malingering'. Women trade-unionists, however, pointed to the additional rigours of frequent pregnancy and hard household labour (PP Cd. 7686 and 7698; Whiteside 1987). Water often had to be drawn from a communal tap and then heated in a copper; clothes had to be pounded by hand in the 'dolly tub'; there were no modern scouring-agents or soap powders; and very few working-class houses had indoor lavatories before the First World War (Roberts 1985). A government return of 1914 showed that as many as 54 per cent of households in Hull and 15 per cent in Liverpool were still making do with privies of one kind or another (Local Govt. Board 1914).

The majority of working-class women who did not go out to work full-time nevertheless took on various forms of part-time work to supplement the family budget. Washing, mangling, and charring were the most common ways of earning a few extra shillings. Kathleen Woodward (1928: 12) remembered her mother's bitter complaints about washing: 'Wash, wash, wash; it's like washing your guts away. Stand, stand, stand. I want six pairs of feet and then I'd have to stand on my head to give them a rest.' Some of the most famous accounts of working-class life during the early part of the century made a point of commenting on the wife's apparent lack of leisure. Generally, women had much less opportunity than men for either reading or exercise (Rowntree 1922).

All social classes of women in late Victorian England shared the prospect of frequent pregnancies and painful childbirth, although from the 1870s to the inter-war period the middle-class birth-rate dropped steadily, and at a faster rate than that of the working class. Middle-class women could count on domestic service and could afford to pay for a doctor to attend them in childbirth. Nevertheless, it has been suggested that they experienced a very real tension in reconciling their prescribed role of 'angel in the home' with both the work of supervising a household staff on what was often a tight budget and undergoing painful childbirth (Rosenberg 1972).

By the time of the First World War there were calls from both working- and middle-class women for greater access to maternity beds in hospitals, albeit for rather different reasons. The WCG started its National Care of Maternity campaign in 1914, and produced several schemes for a national maternity service. Each successive proposal paid more attention to the need to provide' poor women with the best skilled medical assistance available. In 1914 the demand was for trained midwives; in 1917, for a trained midwife and easy access to a doctor, with specialist care and hospital accommodation where necessary; and by 1918, for a doctor to supervise every case and enough hospital beds to accommodate those living in poor home conditions (WCG 1915 and 1917;

Barton 1928). The Guild stressed both the unsuitability of working-class homes for childbirth, with their lack of running water and absence of privacy, and the need for working-class women to go into hospital for ten days in order to secure adequate rest. It also stressed the need for home helps so that women could go into hospital and not worry about how husbands and other children were faring. It was not until the 1948 report on Maternity in Great Britain that the medical profession made a coherent case for home helps (Jt. Com. of the Royal College of Obstetricians and Gynaecologists and the Population Investigation Com. 1948).

Middle-class women campaigned for more maternity beds because they wanted specialist care and because anaesthesia was more readily available in hospitals, although it was by no means routine (see Beinart, Chapter 6). As late as 1932, only 60 per cent of women giving birth at the Royal Free received some form of pain-relief. Judith Walzer Leavitt's research in the United States has demonstrated how, during the First World War, women campaigned strongly for access to 'twilight sleep', a mixture of scopolamine and morphine that altered consciousness in such a way that women did not remember pain or feel exhausted by the effort of labour (Leavitt 1980). The drug was difficult to administer safely and fell into disrepute on both sides of the Atlantic after several well-publicized infant deaths. In this country Marie Stopes, the birth-control pioneer, was among the first to be given the drug at the Twilight Sleep Nursing Home, after receiving assurances that there was no danger to the child. But for whatever reason, her baby died.

What is clear is that women of all social classes in the early twentieth century expressed fear of childbirth in terms of both the pain and the considerable chance of subsequent health problems. Their fears were real and arose directly from the conditions of maternity they experienced. When these are understood, their demand for hospital births becomes readily comprehensible.

Maternal Mortality and Maternal Health in the 1920s and 1930s

During the years before the First World War the attention of policy-makers and doctors, chiefly those in public health, was concentrated firmly on the problem of infant mortality, which still stood at 110 per 1,000 for the period 1911–15 (compared to 62 per 1,000 for the early 1930s). It was only as the infant mortality rate showed signs of a steady decline that attention turned to mothers rather than babies, focusing again on mortality rather than on the more general issue of women's health and welfare that was raised repeatedly by women's groups.

The first government report on maternal mortality appeared in 1924 (Campbell 1924). Between 1923 and 1936 maternal mortality was the only major cause of death of women aged 15–44 to show an absolute increase, never falling below 5 per 1,000, compared to 0.11 per 1,000 today. The publicity accorded to the high maternal mortality rate was disturbing to the government, first because it made efforts to raise the rapidly falling birth-rate difficult (politicians from all points on the political spectrum were concerned about the 1930s' predictions of a rapid fall in population), and second, because of the political embarrassment it generated. An unofficial maternal mortality committee organized by May Tennant, a superintending Inspector of Factories before her marriage to a Liberal MP, and Gertrude Tuckwell, a leading trade-unionist, was formed in 1927 to lobby the government on the issue and on the more general question of morbidity among women. The Ministry of Health later expressed irritation at the way its reports on maternal mortality were being used as ammunition by women's groups criticizing maternity provision.

Medical analysis of the complex causes of maternal mortality suggested that the answer was to hospitalize childbirth. In 1927, 15 per cent of births took place in hospital; in 1933, 24 per cent; in 1937, 25 per cent; and in 1946, 54 per cent. The conclusion of historians working in this country and in the United States has been that the quality of attendance in childbirth was the crucial determinant of

maternal mortality rates before sulphonamides became available in the late 1930s and blood transfusions in the course of
the Second World War, but that a safe attendant was not
necessarily to be found in the hospital (Devitt 1977; Loudon
1986). In fact, data on place of maternal death is difficult to
interpret. The hospital record was not good, but any home
deliveries developing complications would often be removed
to hospital and then the hospital would be recorded as the
place of death. From the evidence we have, it would seem that
there was massive variation in standards of care in hospitals,
from the very good to the downright poor. It is somewhat
easier to generalize about the middle-class nursing home,
which was a much more uniformly risky place to give birth in
the inter-war period. It seems clear that the hospitalization of
childbirth increased the status of obstetrics within medicine
(the British College of Obstetricians and Gynaecologists was
founded in 1929, becoming the Royal College in 1938), and
that this in turn reinforced the trend towards hospitalization.
One consultant congratulated the 1926 conference of the
National Association for Maternal and Child Welfare on
having 'travelled today very far from the old view that a
confinement is an interesting domestic occurrence which
should be celebrated in the family like Christmas or a
birthday party' (Eden 1926).

However, obstetricians also claimed that they were responding to women's demands for more access to hospital
births. The Professor of Obstetrics at University College
Hospital claimed that this demand was so great that if the
hospital did not expand its obstetrics unit, women would seek
attention in the poor-law infirmary rather than give birth at
home. Thus, if the hospital was to maintain its quota of
maternity patients, it had to increase the number of in-
patients (UCH Magazine 1930). There is no doubt that
women did want greater access to hospital beds, in large part
because they were told that hospitals were the safest places for
childbirth. To some extent, therefore, the campaign for more
maternity beds was provider-led. In terms of one of the major
reasons for women seeking a hospital confinement—anaesthesia
—there was no clear evidence against midwives using gas and
air in homes, but the British College of Obstetricians and

Gynaecologists and the BMA consistently advised against this (PRO MH55/625). In the case of maternity practice at University College Hospital, the increase in in-patient provision was matched by a cut in the number of district midwifery patients, effectively precluding choice as to the place of birth.

Even if professionals and women's groups could broadly be said to have shared a desire to see more hospital births, a gulf remained between the wide-ranging scope of women's demands for better maternity provision and the narrowly clinical concerns of doctors and government. First, the WCG's emphasis on the importance of home helps during childbirth never assumed a similar position of prominence on the agenda of obstetricians. The issue was usually mentioned in the national maternity schemes drafted by specialists, departmental committees of the Ministry of Health, and the BMA, but only under the heading of ancillary services. To specialists, the trained home help, with carefully defined duties, was primarily a means of professionalizing this aspect of maternity work and of superseding the undignified 'crude arrangements' that mothers made with 'gossiping neighbours' to help them during and after childbirth (PRO MH55/230). As Nancy Schrom Dye (1987) has commented in her work on the medicalization of childbirth in the United States, one of the most important aspects of medicalization was the change that occurred in the structuring of patient–doctor relations. Once the parturient woman was removed to hospital, she was also removed from the presence of friends, neighbours, and lay attendants, and medical authority became absolute.

Second, there was great resistance on the part of the Ministry of Health in particular to seeing the issue of maternal mortality as in any way a part of the larger issue of women's health and maternal morbidity. In 1932 Tuckwell and Tennant approached the Ministry to ask for an inquiry into sickness and disability among women. The Chief Medical Officer, however, did not believe such an inquiry would be ' "advisable" in the sense of being desirable from our point of view'. As he wrote in a departmental memorandum, the findings could only prove 'embarrassing' and 'could have but one ending, namely, the demonstration of a great mass of

sickness and impairment attributable to childbirth, which
would create a demand for organized treatment by the state'
(PRO MH55/262).

Third, the government also resisted the attempts of
women's groups to address the issue of the welfare of
childbearing women. The WCG and Tuckwell and Tennant's
maternal mortality committee insisted that a measure of
economic assistance for mothers was necessary if they were to
be able to guard their own health and that of their children
effectively. When the 1911 National Health Insurance Act
provided for the payment of a maternity benefit, the WCG
campaigned successfully to have it paid to wives rather than
to husbands. The Guild, the Women's Labour League, and
the Fabian Women's Group began a campaign for 'mother's
endowment'—what became family allowances—in the years
before the First World War. In 1910 the Fabian Women's
Group conducted an experiment in Lambeth, paying an
allowance to forty-two poor women whose husbands earned
'round about a pound a week', the usual wage for a labourer.
The book they published in 1915 showed how mothers tended
to be the ones who went without if the food/rent equation did
not balance, and provided evidence of the desperate need for
such an allowance (Reeves 1915).

During the inter-war years the campaign for family
allowances was taken up by single-issue lobby groups, and the
whole subject became embroiled in the nutrition debate of the
1930s. The BMA advocated a minimum daily intake of
calories and grams of protein that was higher than that
recommended by the Nutrition Advisory Committee of the
Ministry of Health, and the major issue became whether mass
unemployment resulted in malnutrition because unemployment benefit was insufficient to secure a minimum diet (Lewis
1980; Webster 1985). While family-allowance lobby groups of
the 1930s concentrated on providing evidence of child poverty,
the National Birthday Trust fund, under the leadership of
Lady Rhys Williams, undertook a campaign in 1934–5 to
distribute Brandox, Ovaltine, and Marmite to necessitous
pregnant women in South Wales. Lady Rhys Williams (1936)
claimed that as a result both the maternal and infant
mortality rates decreased. The suggestion of women's groups

during the inter-war years that poor health and even high maternal mortality rates should be linked to poverty was firmly rejected by the government and ignored by obstetricians, who confined themselves to clinical issues and argued that the hospitalization of childbirth was the only way to avoid maternal deaths.

Finally, women's groups were anxious to give women greater control over their fertility. Birth-control was a taboo subject before the First World War and barely respectable during the inter-war period. The WCG's letters about maternity revealed how many of the writers were completely ignorant not just about contraception, but about all aspects of female physiology. A very few letters contained oblique references to attempts at abortion. Unknown numbers of women resorted to one of the potions advertised in the newspapers of the day; or to lead plaster (before it was scheduled as a poison in 1917); or, as a last resort, to an abortionist (McLaren 1978). During the 1920s many women's groups came out in support of birth-control as a necessary part of any maternal and child-welfare policy, and as the natural complement of a measure of economic independence for mothers. The WCG was the first to do so in 1923. However, in line with its concern to increase the birth-rate, the government refused to countenance the giving of birth-control information through local authority clinics, other than to women who were ill with TB, heart-disease, diabetes, or chronic nephritis. The government did take up the issue of abortion though, largely because it thought that criminal abortion was inflating the maternal mortality figures. An inter-departmental committee was appointed to look into the subject in 1938, but could not see its way either to legalize abortion or even to make birth-control more widely available, fearing that such a step would adversely affect the already low birth-rate (Ministry of Health and Home Office 1939).

While it would be wrong to suggest that hospitalization— the most important step on the road to 'medicalizing' childbirth—was imposed on women without their consent, it is important to understand how women's support for this particular policy derived from the conditions under which the majority of them gave birth, and how much support was but one element of a much wider set of demands designed to improve the lot of mothers.

The Post-War Years

Today, women's material conditions have changed. The labour participation rates of married women have risen five-fold in most western countries, while the number of years spent in childbearing have declined dramatically and the conditions of domestic labour have improved. In these circumstances it is not surprising that many women are now asking for the right to have their babies at home. But late twentieth-century medical domination of childbirth has grown more formidable with its technological sophistication and the authority that it wields through the hospital. Early twentieth-century women's groups were content to exchange their power to determine the meaning of childbirth as a domestic event in return for increased safety and pain-relief. Women's groups today, as well as some sympathetic obstetricians such as Wendy Savage, have found great difficulty in reasserting women's rights to determine the conditions of childbirth. Some have sought to negotiate a way out of the dilemma by rejecting medical technology altogether, but this involves forgoing the access to medical care that was won so hard earlier this century.

While doctors concentrate on such developments as ultrasound and amniocentesis to ensure a successful birth, groups like the Maternity Alliance continue to define maternity policies more widely, campaigning both for the freedom to choose when and whether to become a parent and for more economic assistance for mothers (see Durward and Evans, Chapter 14). The maternity grant, first given under the 1911 legislation, became means tested in April 1987, and all the evidence suggests that Britain compares poorly with other European countries in the financial support it offers to women becoming mothers (David and New 1985; Roll 1986). Thus, while social policies have assumed wife- and motherhood to be a woman's most important role, the real needs of mothers have not been met. As Denise Riley (1983) has observed, it has been motherhood as a social function rather than the needs of individual mothers that have determined the behaviour of policy-makers. Such an analysis can also be applied to the medical profession's response to childbirth. Ann Oakley has described the process by which wombs have been perceived as containers to be captured by particular ideologies and practices (Oakley 1984). The gap between women's perceptions of childbirth and maternity and those of professionals and policy-makers remains as large as ever.

References

Barton, E., 1928, *The National Care of Motherhood* (London, Women's Co-operative Guild).

Bell, Lady F., 1911, *At the Works*, 2nd edn. (London, Thomas Nelson, 1st edn., 1907).

Campbell, J., 1924, *Maternity Mortality* (Reports on Public Health and Medical Subjects, 25; London, HMSO).

David, M. and New, C., 1985, *For the Children's Sake* (Harmondsworth, Penguin).

Devitt, N., 1977, 'The Transition from Home to Hospital: Birth in the United States, 1930–60', *Birth and the Family Journal*, 4, pp. 47–58.

Dye, N. Schrom, 1987, 'Modern Obstetrics and Working Class Women: The New York Midwifery Dispensary, 1890–1900', *Journal of Social History*, 20, pp. 549–64.

Eden, T. Watts, 1926, 'Midwifery in the Home from the Consultant's Point of View', *Annual Report of the National Association of Maternal and Child Welfare*.

Graham, H. and Oakley, A., 1981, 'Competing Ideologies of Reproduction', in H. Roberts (ed.), *Women, Health and Reproduction* (London, Routledge and Kegan Paul).

Jt. Com. of the Royal College of Obstetricians and Gynaecologists and the Population Investigation Com., 1948, *Maternity in Great Britain* (London, Oxford University Press).

Leavitt, J. Walzer, 1980, 'Birthing and Anaesthesia: The Debate over Twilight sleep', *Signs*, 6, pp. 147–64.

Lewis, J., 1980, *The Politics of Motherhood* (London, Croom Helm).

Llewellyn Davies, M. (ed.), 1915, *Maternity: Letters from Working Women* (London, Bell).

Local Government Board, 1914, *Return as to Scavenging in Urban Districts* (London, HMSO).

Loudon, I., 1986, 'Deaths in Childbed from the Late Eighteenth Century to 1935', *Medical History*, 30, pp. 1–41.

McLaren, A., 1978, *Birth Control in Nineteenth Century England* (London, Croom Helm).

Ministry of Health and Home Office, 1939, *Report of the Inter-Departmental Committee on Abortion*, (London, HMSO).

Oakley, A., 1984, *The Captured Womb* (Oxford, Blackwell).

PP Cd. 7686, 1914–16, XXX 1, Report of the Departmental Committee on Sickness Benefit Claims under the National Health Insurance Act.

—— Cd. 7698, XXX 551, Minutes of Evidence Taken by the Committee on Sick Claims under the National Health Insurance Act.

—— Cmd. 3584, 1929–30, XXV, Report by the Government Actuary on an Examination of the Sickness and Disability Experience of a Group of Approved Societies in the Period, 1914–27.

PRO MH55/230, J. Campbell to A. Stutchbury, 11 June 1920.

—— MH55/262, Sir George Newman to the Secretary, 26 Oct. 1932.

—— MH55/625, British College of Obstetricians and Gynaecologists Investigation into the Use of Analgaesics Suitable for Administration by Midwives, 1936.

Reeves, M. S. P., 1915, *Round about a Pound a Week* (London, Bell).

Rhys Williams, Lady, 1936, 'Malnutrition as a Cause of Maternal Mortality', *Public Health*, 50, pp. 11–19.

Riley, D., 1983, *War in the Nursery* (London, Virago).

Roberts, E. A., 1985, *A Woman's Place* (Oxford, Blackwell).

Roll, J., 1986, *Babies and Money* (London, Family Policy Studies Centre).

Rosenberg, C. Smith, 1972, 'The Hysterical Woman: Sex Roles and Conflict in Nineteenth Century America', *Social Research*, 39, pp. 652–78.

Rowntree, B. S., 1922, *Poverty: A Study of Town Life*, 2nd edn. (London, Longman, 1st edn., 1901).

University College Hospital Magazine, 15 (Aug. 1930).

Webster, C., 1985, 'Health and Welfare and Unemployment during the Depression', *Past and Present*, 109, pp. 204–30.

Whiteside, N., 1987, 'Counting the Costs: Sickness and Disability among Working People in an Era of Industrial Recession, 1920–39', *Economic History Review*, 40, pp. 248–56.

Women's Co-operative Guild, 1915, Annual Report, 1914–15.

—— 1917, *Memorandum on the National Care of Maternity* (London, WCG).

Woodward, K., 1928, *Jipping Street* (London, Longman).

Young, J., 1928, 'An Address on Maternal Morbidity from Puerperal Sepsis', *British Medical Journal*, 9 June 1928, p. 967.

A Maternity Service for England and Wales: Local Authority Maternity Care in the Inter-War Period in Oxfordshire and Tottenham

Elizabeth Peretz

SEVERAL models for the future of Britain's obstetric services were current in the 1930s, but only one of these was the hospital-based, consultant-led service that we know today. Lewis (1980) has explored the origins of this hospital model. This chapter looks at another model which became a practical reality after the 1936 Midwives' Act. The legislative background for this model is discussed in some detail by Sarah Robinson in Chapter 4. In its day, the service was important enough to be known as the National Maternity Service; it was run by local authorities and supervised by the Ministry of Health and the Central Midwives' Board. This service had as its backbone not the obstetric consultant, but the domiciliary midwife. In this chapter I shall be looking at two local authority schemes from the point of view of the nature, availability, and cost of maternity services. The two areas were chosen for their contrasting features, although both escaped the worst ravages of the Depression and both authorities had enough money to provide, at least in theory, an effective maternity service. So, taken together, these two schemes give some indication of the diversity of service existing across the nation, although they cannot stand as an adequate description of the whole service, which must await future research. This chapter uses local papers, reports, and minute-books to explore the strengths of the national maternity-service model in the chosen areas. The schemes were locally planned and run, but their standards were monitored by central supervision. Their strength lay in their flexibility, the variety of services they provided, and the continuity of care they were able to offer with other public health services, including the provision of hospital and specialist facilities for a minority of cases. They provided accessible council clinic facilities during a historical period when general-practitioner services were not free for most parturient women. Their flaw, from the mother's point of view, was that these services were not all free at the point of delivery; in fact they were only free for those who could prove their need under a means test. They were also liable to be cut or skimped by local authorities trying to save on the rates, or by ministry officials trying to save money. A by-product of these economy drives was the continued reliance on volunteers, with their frequently 'charitable' prejudices and inability to provide continuity of care. The chapter concludes by looking briefly at developments after 1939 in an attempt to explain the post-war retreat of the domiciliary midwifery service.

Pressures for a National Maternity Service

In Britain the inter-war years witnessed a great concern about the issue of maternal mortality, which contributed to pressures for the establishment of a national maternity service (see Lewis Chapter 1; Loudon, 1986, 1988). Pressure for this service came from a number of influential sources, both medical and lay. Jane Lewis has pointed to the struggle between the consultant obstetricians and the general practitioners of the British Medical Association, with their competing claims for the management of childbirth (Lewis 1980). However, many influential voices demanded schemes in which the majority of deliveries would take place at home in the hands of the trained midwife. In 1926 John Fairbairn, an obstetric consultant who was to become the second president of the College of Obstetricians and Gynaecologists, wrote in favour of a midwifery-based maternity service to reduce maternal mortality: 'attendance in normal labour can be left to the efficiently trained midwife with a medical practitioner at her call in case of need, and this requirement may be taken

as the basis of the work of the maternity service'; and: 'a
maternity service based on an attendance by a well-trained
corps of midwives under medical supervision with provision
for difficult cases is the one most likely to give the best results'
(Fairbairn 1926). In 1927, in an official report called *The
Protection of Motherhood*, Dame Janet Campbell, Senior Medical
Officer at the Ministry of Health wrote a plea for:

A complete Maternity Service, that is a service which secures every
woman such assistance as is needed to ensure for her a safe journey
through pregnancy. . . . such a service might well be based on a
scheme for improved domiciliary midwifery in which many normal
deliveries and all maternity nursing would be performed by
midwives, but always with the active support of the patient's own
doctor. (Campbell 1927.)[1]

In the inter-war period, voluntary groups were powerful in
the whole field of public health at both national and local
levels. They provided many of the services in infant and
maternal welfare. Lady Rhys Williams, who ran the National
Birthday Trust Fund which was dedicated to improving
childbirth for 'ordinary' women, was also secretary of the
Joint Council for Midwifery which helped bring the 1936
Midwives' Act into being. Jane Lewis discusses her belief that
the two most important safeguards for motherhood were a
good and well-trained midwifery service with specialist back-up,
and adequate nutrition for pregnant women (Lewis 1980). In
short, with few exceptions, there was broad agreement amongst
all authorities in the 1920s and 1930s, from the Ministry of
Health and the College of Obstetricians to the voluntary
organizations, the general practitioners, and the midwives, on
the ideal structure of a national maternity service. Such a
service should be based on midwife deliveries at home, backed
up where necessary by general practitioners or, in exceptional
cases, by consultant obstetricians. There were differences in
opinion between certain authorities as to just how many
deliveries should take place at home and how many in
hospital, but they were small differences. Home delivery by
the midwives was to be the backbone of the service. Hospital
care, supervised by specialists, should be available for

---

[1] For more information on Dame Janet Campbell, see Chapter 4 below.

teaching purposes and for those mothers for whom it was judged unwise to give birth at home, whether for medical or social reasons. Irvine Loudon (1988) has pointed out that this was the sort of model found in most European countries, with an especially strong tradition of home deliveries in Scandinavia and The Netherlands. But it was a model that was rejected in the United States, where, at least in the urban areas, hospital delivery was the rule, and where in the 1930s home delivery was already considered an anachronism, a poor second-best.

A National Maternity Service

The campaigns were successful, and by 1938 local schemes for maternity were well established throughout Britain and were held to be generally adequate. These services were based on local authority public health departments which were run by the Medical Officers of Health. All rural areas and county boroughs were expected to provide their own schemes for the maternity requirements of their districts. Background legislation, Ministry of Health memoranda and guidelines, and pressure group propaganda stressed that these services should establish an adequate domiciliary midwife service for all women, backed up by hospital and specialist care for those with abnormalities and those defined as 'necessitous'. Much of the legislation and Ministry of Health policy (communicated by memoranda to the public health departments) was aimed at making maternity safe by improving existing services. The Ministry said that a good maternity service should provide: trained midwives, supervised by inspectors; ante-natal care; post-natal check-ups; a system of referral to general practitioners or specialists as appropriate; abolition of unlicensed midwives and unlicensed maternity homes; a network of general practitioners or specialists to be called in by midwives in obstetric emergencies; and laboratory back-up. Although guidelines from the Ministry continued to shift and change, the backbone of this recommended structure throughout these years was domiciliary midwifery.

In our age of almost complete hospital delivery, it is hard to believe that only fifty years ago this system based on home delivery should have been regarded by some with national pride. It is easier for us to assume that all that was happening in the inter-war period was tending in the direction of the institutional alternative we know today. Two of the chapters in this book (Chapters 1, 4) describe the rising percentage of hospital births—15 per cent in 1927, 25 per cent in 1937, and 54 per cent in 1946—as important evidence that the trend to hospitalization was well under way in the 1930s. But the position was not so clear at the time. Most would have agreed that the hospital alternative was important for some births, with consultant care for referred cases, but that domiciliary midwifery was appropriate for the majority of births. The Midwives' Act of 1936 was seen as putting the finishing touches to a mature national maternity scheme based on midwives. Problems were perceived only where local authorities provided inadequate services, and these were dealt with by inspections, warnings, and the threat of grant-withdrawal by ministry officials. This last threat carried some weight. Local maternity schemes were funded partly through the rates, but partly from ministry grants allocated for five-year plans made by the local public health departments and ratified by the national officials. The Ministry kept itself up to date with local affairs by conducting nation-wide local authority public health surveys (Annual Reports of the Chief Medical Officer at the Ministry of Health; Bradbury 1987); the results of these were also used to push for reforms and improvements. These included recommendations to secure an adequate number of fully trained midwives, home helps, proper supervision, and good hospital and specialist back-up. There was no general scheme for an eventual hospital-based service.

One of the striking features of these public health surveys was the extraordinarily wide variation in the quality of maternity services across the country. It is often impossible to make useful generalizations about the maternity services in the country as a whole without adding the caution that local variations were far more important than national averages. For example, national percentages of trends in home births compared with hospital births mask dramatic differences between areas. The numbers of mothers having children in hospital were generally higher in urban districts than in rural ones. The flexibility of the system ensured this; more obstetric abnormalities, but in particular more 'necessitous' mothers living in unfit housing, could dramatically increase the number of hospital deliveries in one area compared to another. There were many other differences which can only be adequately studied locally. The two areas compared here have been looked at for the period from 1918 to the outbreak of the Second World War. Medical Officer of Health reports, maternity committee minutes, the report-books of local nursing associations, and local newspapers have been considered alongside the public records of the Ministry of Health to build up a description of these maternity services which is then put against a brief social geography of each area. While these two areas alone cannot stand for the whole country, their political, geographical, and social differences do provide a starting-point for exploring the strengths and weaknesses of the National Maternity Service.

Tottenham and Oxfordshire in the Inter-War Years

The two local schemes looked at here, in Oxfordshire and Tottenham in London, were both developed in fairly prosperous areas of Britain. There was poverty and unemployment, but not on the overwhelming scale experienced in the industrial areas of North-East England or in South Wales. During the inter-war period, workers in Oxfordshire increasingly turned their backs on agriculture to commute long distances to Morris's motor-works at Cowley. Oxfordshire was a county of scattered villages and hamlets, and small towns specializing in glove manufacture or blanket-making (Barnett House Survey 1938–40). Its population of 129,082 in 1931 was slowly rising; it had been 122,325 in 1921. The county of 637 square miles excluded the county borough of Oxford itself, which was in a period of more rapid transition (Census, 1921–31). In contrast, the county's social structure was that of an old-established landed and commercial 'gentry' and an equally old-established rural working population. The county council was dominated by the gentry and the small-town manufacturers and tradesmen (Oxfordshire County Council [OCC], Minute Books 1917–39). These were the people who made the decisions in Oxfordshire about what money to spend on public health, and on the maternity service in particular. They were the ones who employed the Medical Officer of Health who ran the county's public health department, and it was their wives who ran the volunteer charitable organizations of the county, amongst which was the Oxfordshire Nursing Federation (ONF) which employed the county's village nurse-midwives (ONF, Reports and Minute Books).

Tottenham, skirting the Greater London metropolitan complex, housed workers from all over London. The main industry within its boundaries was furniture-making. It was engulfed by built-up areas during the inter-war period, when it lost many of its big houses and gained some large model housing estates built by the London County Council and by Tottenham Urban District Council (Llewellyn Smith 1937; Annual Reports of the Medical Officer of Health, Tottenham). There were few large benefactors, and councillors were often tradesmen and trade-unionists, with a sprinkling of general practitioners and solicitors (Tottenham UDC/MBC, Year Books). The rising inter-war population was nearly the same as Oxfordshire's: 146,711 in 1921, and 157,772 by 1931. It escaped the worst of the Depression. It was spread over a compact four square miles, with easy access to neighbouring health facilities to augment its own. The council only took over responsibility for every aspect of its maternity provision after 1930; until then its midwifery had come under the public health department of Middlesex County Council. The powerful charitable organizations prevalent in Oxfordshire were significantly absent from Tottenham; the Medical Officer himself was the one who tried to keep a nursing association alive, and even he was unsuccessful until the later 1930s (*Tottenham Weekly Herald* 1919–39).

The Two Maternity Schemes in Action

The Ministry of Health requested maternity-service plans from all local authorities under the terms of the 1936 Midwives' Act. Medical Officers of Health were asked to draw up these plans, and they faced quite different obstacles depending on their region; some problems were geographic, some economic, some social, and some political. The Ministry was very keen on economy; on grounds of geography alone, Tottenham had the simpler and more economical task. The estimated cost for its comparatively elaborate maternity scheme in 1937 was £3,000 after receipts from mothers (£6,000 without receipts) (Maternity and Child Welfare Subcommittee [MCW] Minute Book 1937). Oxfordshire was more spread out and communications were more difficult, so that a service which in comparison to that in Tottenham seemed barely adequate—heavily dependent on charitable donation, and not generous in its allowances to mothers—was estimated to cost £6,000 after receipts from mothers and voluntary contributions to local nursing associations. Cars and telephones amounted to £3,400 of the cost of the completed scheme, estimated to be £13,714 before receipts (OCC, Annual Report of the County Medical Officer [MOH Reports] 1936). Geographical factors certainly played a large part in this difference. Tottenham's population and size meant that the Medical Officer of Health requested funds for sixteen midwives, although in the end the authority had to be content with an equivalent of eight; Oxfordshire in contrast had sixty nurse-midwives, which was probably the equivalent of thirty full-time midwives, but thirty persons could not have covered such necessarily large geographical areas. Both areas had an annual birth-rate of around 2,000 (Tottenham, MCW Minute Book, 1936; OCC, MOH Report 1937).

In Tottenham, everything, from home to hospital to clinic, was within easy walking distance. There were three ante-natal clinics held on different days and within the reach of all pregnant women. These were run by a woman specialist who practised during the rest of the week in London teaching hospitals (Tottenham, MOH Reports). Mothers who were referred to general practitioners or to the hospital either walked to their appointments or they could be taken in the council's ambulance in emergencies. There was full co-operation between the hospitals and the clinics. Most of this had been operating since the early 1920s, with encouragement from the councillors who voted in the necessary money. Once the midwives became the responsibility of the council, this system ensured great continuity for the mother and infant. In addition, there was an efficient back-up service of home helps and convalescent treatment paid for on a generous scale by the council, and a gynaecological clinic for longer-term problems resulting from pregnancy (Tottenham, MOH Reports). In Oxfordshire the Medical Officer had the nightmare problem of providing a maternity service for a population that was the same size as Tottenham's but was spread out over an area 184 times larger. He provided ten times as many ante-natal clinics as his Tottenham counterpart. Oxfordshire's once a month ante-natal clinics, begun in the mid-1920s after ministry pressure, were serviced by out-of-area general practitioners. Mothers could be referred to general practitioners or hospitals by health officials or ante-natal clinics, but they had to pay for these services unless they could prove that they were too poor to do so. For mothers in outlying districts these clinics were often hard to reach and might involve a long walk or the extra expense of a bus-fare. There were attempts to reach more women in need of ante-natal care in the late 1930s, when the general practitioners won the right and the fees to do ante-natal visiting themselves, and the clinics were disbanded.

Ease of access for the mothers was one consideration; another was adequate professional staff. By a judicious use of voluntary zeal and ministry grant, there was some semblance of a county-wide midwifery service in Oxfordshire by 1939. Most of the village midwifery was carried out by the ONF's nurse-midwives; only one of the sixty midwives operating in the county scheme was actually employed by the local authority in 1937. The ONF was the umbrella organization which co-ordinated the district nursing associations of the villages and small towns. These were voluntary associations dependent on voluntary contributions. The less well-off gave a few pence a week, while others gave large annual contributions.

They were dedicated to providing trained district nursing and midwifery, and were administered by the wife of a doctor, vicar, or landowner. A percentage of the associations' expenses was available from government grants channelled through the ONF. Where distances made it possible, several villages would combine to employ one trained nurse (ONF, Minute Books). Ministry officials were pressing about aspects of the maternity scheme which they found inadequate; in response, a specialist was engaged who had an appointment at the Radcliffe Voluntary Hospital and who would travel to attend in times of need; a back-up laboratory service was instituted, and an emergency flying-squad for county-wide obstetric care was in operation in 1939. Oxfordshire had no post-natal clinics, no gynaecological clinics, no convalescent homes, and no real home-help services.

A comparison of the Tottenham and Oxfordshire schemes as they were presented to the Ministry finds Oxfordshire lacking. A comparison of how the schemes worked in practice increases the distinction. After the 1937 plans, the situation was as follows. Midwives in Oxfordshire covered a large patch of ten to sixteen square miles, often on foot or bicycle. There was only one replacement nurse-midwife available for the whole county. Only the Inspector of Midwives and thirteen of the sixty practising nurse-midwives had cars or telephones in 1937 (OCC, MOH Report 1937). The emergency obstetrician was used on average less than once a year during the later 1930s, probably because of the size of fees and travel expenses asked for. The back-up laboratory service was hardly more than nominal, and was only used two or three times between 1937 and 1939 (OCC, Public Health Committee Minute Books, 1919–39). Large numbers of the ante-natal 'clinics' hardly deserved the name, being held in a makeshift manner once or twice a month in church halls, and their low attendance rates probably reflect their lack of popularity and inconvenience. In 1935 the average attendance at these clinics was 1.5 mothers per session. When the general practitioners won the right to run the county ante-natal scheme themselves (in their surgeries or mothers' own homes), this only increased numbers a little: in 1937 only one-quarter of all pregnant women in the county were seen ante-natally. General practitioners were the only doctors called in to help midwives in the Oxfordshire system. As part-time ante-natal medical officers for the county, they could refer pregnant women to the Radcliffe Hospital maternity department from early in their pregnancies; but this was only possible for the 25 per cent who attended for ante-natal care. As ordinary general practitioners, they could be called in by midwives to help in emergencies during delivery. In 1937, 55 per cent of the children in the county were delivered at home by a midwife, and in half of these deliveries the general practitioner was called upon, most usually to repair a torn perineum.

In Tottenham 53 per cent of all pregnant women attended the clinics in 1938, so there was a good chance of referral to hospital for special cases. After delivery, women were encouraged by the public health department to use the post-natal clinic to ensure they received care throughout the neonatal period.

Hospital Delivery

Unfortunately, there are no data on how many mothers elected to be delivered by their general practitioner, but there was a wide difference between Tottenham and Oxfordshire in the proportion of mothers who gave birth in hospital. Numbers were rising in both areas, from around 20 per cent and 9 per cent respectively in 1928, to 50 per cent and 10 per cent in 1938 (MOH Reports). Tottenham was therefore slightly higher than the national average quoted above (p. 34), and Oxfordshire considerably lower. In neither area was the hospital alternative seen as appropriate for all maternity cases. It was an expensive option for confinement; while a midwife could be engaged for as little as 10s. (50p) in some places (Lewis 1980), the general practitioner rarely cost less than £2, and the statutory week or fortnight in hospital cost between £4–£12.

The Consumer's Viewpoint

From the woman's point of view, costs, and the effect on the family budget, were very important considerations. In Oxfordshire, if a mother or her husband were part of the National Insurance scheme through their work, she could expect to get a 30s. (£1·50) maternity benefit. This could pay for a midwife, whose average fees in this area were 10s. (labourers' fees) in 1917, raised to 25s. for most people by 1936, with a little over to pay for baby clothes and other expenses. Having a doctor would already eat into savings. A doctor called in for an emergency could cost £2–£3; although this was paid by the county council in the first instance, the consumer had to repay later on. Analgesia was an unheard-of luxury (see Beinart, Chapter 6). But to be designated a special case by the ante-natal clinic was potentially a financial calamity. A case-history exists of one mother who applied for a grant to cover such expenses from the county council in 1934. She had to find a 3s. return fare for each ante-natal clinic in Oxford. She had to pay for twelve days in hospital at 14s. 1d. a day—a total of £8. 9s. 0d. (Annual Report of the Radcliffe Infirmary 1924; OCC, Public Health Committee Minute Books). Employing a home help in her absence ate up another 30s. Add to that the hidden costs of providing herself and her baby with respectable hospital clothes, and a clear picture emerges of a mother whose family could be going without food, adequate clothing, and warmth for the next year. She was successful in her claim, but few were in Oxfordshire. The schemes were expected to be self-supporting. Although they were run by the local council and supported by rates and government grants all over the country, users were expected to pay for everything except check-ups and advice unless they could prove real hardship. Oxfordshire County Council, as we have seen, was composed for the most part of traditional liberal or conservative gentlemen who seemed still to subscribe to the idea of the 'deserving poor', and were not disposed to give help lightly. In the last three years before the war, around 200 women from Oxfordshire were delivered in the Radcliffe Infirmary. The county council gave help in only two or three of these cases. It is unlikely that this reflected the real level of need. In 1937 less than 10 per cent of the fees payable to general practitioners for emergency midwifery visits was finally recovered by the county council from the mothers. In this case, the Midwives' Act of 1918 had left the council liable for these doctors' bills in the first place, although they were empowered to recover the fees later. Money was a major stumbling-block for mothers using the Oxfordshire maternity scheme, though there were other problems. The district nursing associations who employed the nurse-midwives had a great deal of power even after 1936. In April 1928 an inquest on a baby who lived only a few minutes was held in the village of Bloxham. It was said that she would have lived if she had had skilled help at the time. The nurse-midwife had been asked to attend, but had refused on the grounds that the patient was unmarried. It was the rule of the nursing association not to attend such cases without special permission from the secretary, which in this instance had not been obtained (ONF Minute Books). The Ministry method of maintaining the standards of midwifery was to demand that local authority inspectors should supervise midwives. One record of a failed inspection exists where the secretary of a local association objected to having her servants interfered with without her permission (Wellcome Unit, Oxford, letters in connection with the setting-up of the midwifery service by the OCC).

Tottenham mothers were in a better position than those in Oxfordshire: the council was sympathetic to their financial needs, had a more lenient means test, and paid out many more grants. As we have seen above, their scheme was cheaper to run anyway, so they may have felt that they could afford to be more lenient. Hospital costs were about 90*s*. on average, less than those at the Radcliffe; while midwifery fees were higher—42*s*. for a first child and 31*s*. 6*d*. for subsequent children. There were more generous allowances: the council would pay for a midwife to attend the mother of a family of four with an income of 52*s*. a week after rent. Wage averages may have played some part in this, together with rents. In Tottenham, 540 families from all social classes were assessed for the New London Survey: the average wage was over 80*s*. a week and only 15 per cent of the families earned less than 52*s*. a week. In Oxfordshire the University Social Survey showed that one-third of the work-force was still in agriculture and earned 36*s*. a week or less. These figures cannot give an accurate picture, but they serve to give an impression:

examining the number of individuals helped in any one year may reveal more. Families in Tottenham received more help than those in Oxfordshire. In February 1936, a representative month, the council approved four requests for free home helps, four for maternity hospital fees, and two for domiciliary midwifery fees (Tottenham, MCW Minute Books); in Oxfordshire in the same month no cases were reported (OCC Minute Books).

The National Pattern

The two schemes briefly outlined above give some indication of the national pattern in operation on the outbreak of war in 1939. They had to some extent lived up to their promise of 'being amenable to local variation' by being part of local government. 'No two maternity schemes are precisely similar . . . the best are, in general, those that take greatest cognisance of local conditions and difficulties.' (The *Medical Officer* 1936.) Rural areas had experienced particular practical difficulties in mounting their schemes, while urban areas had often found they needed to plan for larger numbers of hospital deliveries than their county counterparts. At their best—and Tottenham was one of the best—they could provide a flexible, co-ordinated maternity service which, under the public health department of the local authority, provided mothers with care throughout the neonatal period. As more local authorities had their own public hospitals, this co-ordination of service had an even better chance of success. But there were flaws in the scheme. The major one was financial; these schemes were not free to the consumer, and there were particular difficulties for the rural mother. The Ministry wanted schemes to be as cheap as possible, and was pleased wherever possible, to incorporate the voluntary nursing associations to attain this end. This laid mothers in Oxfordshire and elsewhere open to large financial burdens and to social prejudice. But it was expected practice. Ministry grants could usually be smaller for voluntary organizations. In 1937 the Chief Medical Officer at the Ministry of Health wrote: 'In the majority of cases, little difficulty was experienced by the Authorities in effecting co-operation with the voluntary organisations that employed or were willing to employ midwives in their area.' No figures were given for England; but Wales, usually known for its dearth of voluntary health bodies at the time, had fourteen of its eighteen maternity schemes operating with voluntary assistance in 1937 (Annual Report of the Chief Medical Officer at the Ministry of Health 1937).

The disruption to housing caused by the war was bound to increase the number of hospital births, and the wartime emergency hospital service had many more maternity beds planned. This situation need not have obtained after the end of the war. It was not until the 1960s and 1970s that an almost 100 per cent hospital delivery rate became a reality in Britain, and as late as the 1950s there were arguments in the DHSS to reduce hospital births (Webster 1988). There are several possible reasons for the running-down of a maternity service based on domiciliary midwifery backed up by specialist services where necessary. In his history of the National Health Service, Charles Webster (1988) has argued that hospital services organized under the consultants were very much strengthened under the National Health Service, at the expense of local authority public health services. With this balance of power, the co-ordination and co-operation that Dame Janet Campbell dreamt of in the 1920s would have been much harder to realize than under the maternity service of the 1930s. Public pressure for hospital maternity services has grown (see Lewis, Chapter 1), thus increasing the demand for hospital beds. Obstetric knowledge and methods have changed, classifying far more categories of pregnancy as unsafe (see Schwarz, Chapter 3), and including more hospital-based treatments. The National Blood Transfusion Service, the use of sulphonamides and later of penicillin (Loudon 1987), and the development of neonatal paediatrics have all been hospital-based developments in Britain, and have no doubt played their part in recent trends of birthplace. There is undoubtedly a lot more research to be done on the obstetric work of both general practitioners and hospital consultants in the 1930s.

The construction of a virtually 100 per cent hospital delivery system for childbirth in Britain was not a foregone conclusion in the 1930s. If anything, at that time the locally based, midwife-dominated scheme described above seemed launched on its way. The scheme had its critics, amongst obstetricians, general practitioners, and amongst lay groups; the first two felt that they, not the public health departments, should run the services, and the last felt that the only route to safe maternity lay in free services and material help for mothers. But even the critics recognized it for what it was—a national maternity service which we are in danger of forgetting ever existed.

References

Barnett House, 1938, 1940, *Social Services in the Oxford Region*, 2 vols. (London, Oxford University Press).

Bradbury, J., 1987, 'The Implementation of the 1929 Local Government Act and Central–Local Health Relations', a paper given at Queen Mary College, London, in April 1987.

Campbell, J. M., 1927, *The Protection of Motherhood* (Reports on Public Health and Medical Subjects, 48 (London, HMSO).

Fairbairn, J. S., 1926, *Obstetrics* (Oxford Medical Handbooks; London, Oxford University Press).

Harringay Local Record Office, 1919–39, Annual Reports of the Medical Officer of Health for Tottenham.

—— 1919–39, Minute Books of the Maternal and Child Welfare Committee, Tottenham.

—— 1917–39, *Tottenham Weekly Herald*.

Lewis, J., 1980, *The Politics of Motherhood* (London, Croom Helm).

Llewellyn Smith, Sir H. (ed.), 1932, *The New Survey of London Life and Labour*, iii (London, P. S. King & Son).

Loudon, I., 1986, 'Obstetric Care, Social Class and Maternal Mortality', *British Medical Journal*, 2, pp. 606–8.

—— 1987, 'Puerperal Fever: The Streptococcus and the Sulphonamides, 1911–1945', *British Medical Journal*, 2, pp. 485–90.

—— 1988, 'Maternal Mortality 1880–1950: Some Regional and International Comparisons', *Social History of Medicine*, 1, pp. 183–228.

Ministry of Health, 1938, Annual Report of the Chief Medical Officer of Health, 1937.

Oxford, 1931, County of Oxford Census for 1931, part 1 (London, HMSO).

Oxfordshire County Record Office, 1919–39, Annual Reports of the Medical Officer of Health.

—— 1919–39, Oxfordshire County Council, Public Health Committee Minute Books.

—— 1919–39, Oxfordshire Nursing Federation, Executive Committee Minute Books.

Radcliffe Infirmary, 1924, Annual Report for the Radcliffe Infirmary, Oxford.

Webster, C., 1988, *The Health Services Since the War*, i. *Problems of Health Care: The National Health Service before 1957* (London, HMSO).

Wellcome Unit for the History of Medicine, Public Health Records Collection, Midwifery, PH/6S/1.

The Engineering of Childbirth: A New Obstetric Programme as Reflected in British Obstetric Textbooks, 1960–1980

Eckart W. Schwarz

MATERNITY-CARE provisions have changed significantly over the last decades. Today, almost all expectant mothers will have their babies delivered in hospital. There has been a profound redistribution of manpower and responsibilities within the obstetric services. Both midwives and general practitioners have ceased to play an important independent role; instead, consultant obstetricians have taken over the ultimate responsibility for childbirth. Furthermore, interventionist obstetric techniques were employed far more frequently, particularly during the 1960s and 1970s. The use of various conventional surgical techniques like Caesarean sections, episiotomies, and instrumental deliveries reached unprecedented peaks, and a whole array of novel technologies such as intrapartum maternal and fetal monitoring devices were widely introduced into obstetric practice (Macfarlane and Mugford 1984). (See also Oakley and Richards, Chapter 10.)

The origins of these developments, and therefore of today's hospital-based, consultant-run, and technology-oriented system of maternity-care provisions, can be traced back far further than the last three or four decades. The consultant obstetricians' claim for the responsibility of handling childbirth dates from at least 1929 when the College of Obstetricians and Gynaecologists was founded, but possibly earlier. At first sight, the mushrooming of obstetric technologies during recent years seems to be explicable either in terms of the incorporation of growing scientific knowledge into clinical practice, or in terms of the consultant obstetricians' traditional orientation towards intervention. It could therefore be argued that the change of maternity-care provisions over the last decades represents the final and full implementation of policies and trends which had already been established long before. Thus, obstetricians have recently extended the scope of their influence simply by expanding further into previously staked-out territory. However, matters were not quite as straightforward. Consultant obstetricians have redefined the contents and methods of the obstetric programme, thereby enlarging the realm of their professional concern beyond the traditional and already demarcated confines. The obstetric profession, in fact, has altered the entire perspective on its role in childbirth. This change has been described by historians and social scientists from various angles (Cartwright 1979; Oakley 1984; Arney 1982).

This chapter will trace the development of a new obstetric programme in Britain by looking at obstetric textbooks of the period in question. The years 1960 and 1980 have been chosen as somewhat flexible perimeters, since it was between those years that many textbooks—albeit not all—changed in significant ways. The emphasis will be on those textbooks which underwent the most substantial alterations, irrespective of whether the texts were designed for medical students, qualified doctors, or (pupil) midwives. Undoubtedly, the policies advocated in such books do not necessarily represent the everyday practice of obstetricians or midwives. However, many authors claim that they have changed their books in the light of new developments in obstetric practice, and it is therefore likely that such changes occurred some time before their acknowledgement in textbooks. Hence, rather than representing the reality of obstetric practice at the time of publication, the main value of textbooks as a historiographic tool lies in the fact that they 'fly the flag of our [the obstetricians'] philosophy' (Donald 1964), i.e., that they reveal the profession's outlook on childbirth. It is not only the contents of a textbook which show this *philosophy*, language and semantics are equally important determinants: 'Whatever the nature of somatic phenomena—of physiological processes or disease entities—they enter human experience only as they

are made meaningful. Illness realities are therefore fundamentally semantic' (Good and Good 1981). The juxtaposition of
successive editions of obstetric textbooks reveals significant
changes in content and semantics, indicating that the outlook
of obstetricians on their role in childbirth underwent a
dramatic transformation.

The Transformation of Midwifery into Scientific Obstetrics

The first chapter of the 1961 edition of *Midwifery by Ten
Teachers* (Roques, Beatti, and Wrigley 1961:1) begins as
follows: 'Of all the jobs undertaken by the medical profession
midwifery is the most rewarding. Its aim is normality and if
normality is achieved there is a glow of satisfaction on all
those who have assisted the woman in her supreme fulfilment.'
Eleven years later (Clayton, Fraser, and Lewis 1972:1) the
book opens like this: 'Many doctors find great satisfaction in
the practice of obstetrics. The doctor forms a personal
relationship with his pregnant patient which is unique in
medicine.' The word *assist* implies that the person who is
assisted must be engaged in some sort of activity of his or her
own. Hence, the *woman* actively giving birth in 1961 has
slipped into the role of a person who is passively enduring the
activity of someone else: the word *patient* is derived from
patiens, the present participle of the Latin verb *pati*, which
means *to endure, to tolerate, to suffer*. Correspondingly, what used
to be a *supreme fulfilment* has turned into the qualifying
adjective *pregnant*. Also, the *job* [of] *midwifery* became the
practice of obstetrics. The title of the whole book had already
changed from *Midwifery by Ten Teachers* into *Obstetrics by Ten
Teachers* in 1966, and throughout this book and in other
obstetric literature the terms *midwifery* and *accoucheur* were
replaced by *obstetrics* and *obstetricians*. This terminological
realignment in itself mirrors the alteration in the nature of the
relationship between the mother and the birth attendant. In
the introduction to the 1981 edition of her *Textbook for
Midwives*, Myles explains the meaning of those terms (p. 10):
'The word "midwife" is derived from the Anglo-Saxon word

"mid" = together with, and "wif" = a woman. Literally it means a helping woman. The word "obstetrics" includes midwifery: the Latin derivation being "ob" = before and "sto" = to stand.' This change of names also reflects the redistribution of intraprofessional responsibilities. The very term *midwifery* implies that it is the domain of female midwives to attend childbirth, whereas this task is to be attributed to (predominantly) male obstetricians if the word *obstetrics* is employed. Moreover, the renaming of midwifery is paralleled by a broadening of the content and boundaries of this professional activity. Myles again (p. 10): 'From usage the word "obstetrics" has assumed a wider connotation than midwifery: being associated with the scientific and more advanced concepts of human reproduction.' The notion that obstetrics is dealing with *human reproduction*, and is dealing with it in a *scientific* way rather than solely with helping women in childbirth and labour, epitomizes the transformation of midwifery into scientific obstetrics. This change of outlook and approach altered the entire *raison d'être* of the obstetric profession; the status quo ante will therefore be looked at first.

Until the 1950s, obstetricians appeared to have been mesmerized by the mystery that surrounded childbirth. As Oakley (1984) has pointed out, there were no means to visualize the fetus *in utero* (ultrasonography was introduced into obstetric practice only by the end of the 1950s), and knowledge about uterine functioning was equally scanty. Some obstetricians, however, did not seem to be too concerned about this state of affairs, and emphasized that the aim of obstetrics was not scientific investigation but to get on with the job. In the preface to the first (1955) and second (1959) editions of *Practical Obstetric Problems* (p. ix), Ian Donald says that he 'gladly accepted' his publisher's request for a concise book as an excuse to 'omit the inevitable dreary irrelevance of such matters as ovulation, menstruation, conception, infertility, diagnosis of pregnancy and the early development of the ovum . . . Having got rid of this burden, I found myself free to get down to the real business of midwifery.' Whilst midwives and general practitioners traditionally dealt with normal pregnancy and labour, the *real business* for consultant obstetricians consisted mainly of the recognition and treatment of abnormalities. At that time, the working definition of abnormality was largely based on the occurrence of problems related to the mechanics of labour, and thereby to the anatomical configuration of the maternal pelvis (*the passage*), the size and presentation of the fetus (*the passenger*), and the expulsive forces (*the powers*). Such a mechanistic conceptualization implied that all the endeavours of the obstetrician became relevant only in the second stage of labour, when the fetus has physically to negotiate the birth canal. The therapeutic practices in which the obstetrician had traditionally been trained reflect this orientation: operative and surgical techniques enabled him either to overcome mechanical problems once they had occurred, for example, by carrying out an instrumental delivery, or to avoid mechanics of the second stage altogether, by performing an elective Caesarean section. The genuine difficulty was not the operative manœuvre itself, but the decision about when to abandon the policy of watchful expectancy. Even in the 1969 edition of the *Combined Textbook of Obstetrics and Gynaecology* (Baird 1969: 404) it is still acknowledged that 'the outcome of every first labour is rather uncertain since there is no reliable method of knowing beforehand which will be easy and which difficult, although it is now possible to give statistical probabilities in groups of cases with certain characteristics'.

The prospective anticipation of abnormalities, and hence making a decision about a certain mother in labour, rested upon the obstetrician's clinical experience, which he gained as a result of the outcome of many other labours. The consultant obstetrician had to use his clinical judgement to decide whether and when a labour was to be regarded as abnormal, which usually entailed the necessity to intervene. During the 1950s and 1960s an increasing number of women came into hospital for delivery, and obstetricians widened the 'abnormal bracket' at the expense of what the American obstetrician Friedman (1978) has called the 'vast, ill-defined gray zone between the obviously normal and the clearly abnormal case'. This increased 'detection' of abnormality resulted in steadily rising rates of operative intervention. However, instead of finally declaring all women in genuine need of operative delivery—which would have implied that such a thing as

normal childbirth did not exist—many obstetricians shifted
the focus of their attention. Already in 1950 Sir Dugald Baird
stated in the preface to the *Combined Textbook of Obstetrics and
Gynaecology* (p. v):

The increased scope and safety of surgery, due to antiseptic and
aseptic techniques, has led to great advances both in obstetrics and
gynaecology, but the pendulum has swung too far and there is a
tendency for obstetricians and gynaecologists to become essentially
operators. . . . It is unlikely that many striking advances remain to
be made in the surgical aspects of obstetrics and gynaecology, and
the main emphasis is now increasingly on the preventive and
physiological approach.

Obstetricians were able to adopt this new approach by
tackling the problem of abnormality. It was no longer to be
defined as a circumscribed pathological entity or process, but
it came to be defined as a gradational deviation from the
physiological norm. With respect to fetal deaths, Dugald
Baird (1950:v) writes: 'It has become apparent that many
foetal deaths are associated with forms of "physiological
failure" rather than with definite pathological processes.' The
new physiological angle of enquiry was designed to establish
the normal; it did not require clinical observation to produce a
static depiction of a disease reality, but called for exact
scientific determination of the dynamics of normal functioning.
Both clinical research and laboratory investigation of 'the
physiology of human and mammalian reproduction . . .
developed extensively in the period from 1950' (Walker,
MacGillivray, and Macnaughton 1976). For instance, Reynolds
postulated mechanisms for the process of labour, and Caldeyro-
Barcia and Csapo studied the physiology of uterine activity.
Friedman defined the cervical dilatation–time function, and
described patterns of fetal descent. Du Vigneaud's work on
the posterior pituitary hormone oxytocin made it possible to
produce a synthetic analogue of that hormone, and more
recently Karim has studied the role of prostaglandins in
childbirth.

By 1980 it was possible to write (Dewhurst 1980:ix): 'None
of us [obstetricians] needs to be reminded that a thorough
understanding of the principles of basic science applied to the

process of human reproduction is the only sound foundation for clinical practice in obstetrics.' The advent of an entirely new genre of obstetric textbook reflects this novel attitude. During the 1960s and 1970s, books on the scientific basis of obstetrics appeared on the market for the first time (e.g. Macdonald 1971), and the language of nearly all existing textbooks changed. A style of scientific objectivity was adopted: childbirth, pregnancy, and labour were referred to as *human reproduction*; mothers became *parturients* or *pregnant patients*; and the anecdotal elements of many books were abandoned. Also, the Royal College of Obstetricians and Gynaecologists introduced a primary examination in basic sciences in September 1970.

The scientific approach has affected all areas of obstetric practice, and has resulted in the obstetric profession rewriting its entire job-description. For instance, obstetricians 'discovered' a new patient, the fetus, who had hitherto been hidden by barriers which could now be overcome (Chamberlain 1975:48): 'Anatomical—can be overcome by indirect testing; physiological—need understanding of interaction of fetal and maternal physiology; psychological—need explanation to both mother and . . . staff to overcome inborn resistance to investigating the unborn.' The growth of fetal medicine, and the inclusion of material on intra-uterine fetal welfare into virtually all textbooks, reflects that development. The most striking example, however, is the change of policies on the management of labour, which is a direct result of research work undertaken by Friedman in the United States. During the 1950s Friedman tried to establish objective criteria by which labour and its variants could be described as an ongoing dynamic process, and showed that cervical dilatation and fetal descent are the only useful parameters for doing so. Plotting these parameters against time for a large study population, he obtained distribution data which were subjected to statistical analysis. As a result, Friedman extrapolated an 'ideal labor pattern' (Friedman 1978). The *Friedman curve* of the normal average progress during labour was soon introduced into British clinical practice in the form of the so-called partogram, and enabled obstetricians to define abnormality as a dynamic aberration from the ideal pattern of labour. The following juxtapostion of two editions of *Midwifery by Ten Teachers* will give an idea of how dramatically Friedman's work and the ensuing change of outlook have altered the policies and practices of the management of labour. In 1955 Roques *et al.* (p. 123) advised the accoucheur that he 'should go as soon as he is sent for . . . His presence may be unnecessary for some hours, but it is not safe to count on this. If he goes at once he might find a malpresentation, presentation or prolapse of the cord, a pre-eclamptic state or . . . a contracted pelvis . . .'. Hence, the obstetrician's task for the first stage of labour (the 'non-mechanical' stage of cervical dilatation and effacement) consisted of the exclusion of discrete detectable abnormalities. He is then advised about such matters as asepsis, the lying-in room, and the bed. The care advocated is purely supportive, reflecting the policy of watchful expectancy. In 1980, by contrast, Clayton, Lewis, and Pinker state: 'rarely the patient will not have had any antenatal supervision', and her records can be 'reviewed' for abnormal features. During the first stage:

once labour has been established . . . all events are noted on a partogram—a most useful graphical record of the course of labour. Routine observations of the mother's pulse rate and blood pressure, with an assessment of the strength of the uterine contractions are entered on it. Records of the findings at successive vaginal examination are plotted on a graph, showing the dilatation of the cervix in centimetres against the time in hours. The curve obtained is compared with an average normal curve for primigravidae or multigravidae as may be appropriate. If the patient's progress is normal her curve will correspond with the normal curve . . . If for any reason labour is not progressing normally . . . the patient's partogram will be 'to the right' of the normal curve . . . augmentation of the uterine action by administration of an oxytocic infusion is to be considered (pp. 116–19).

The Engineering of Childbirth

The traditional dichotomy of normal childbirth versus childbirth with distinct abnormalities was absorbed into the new concept of abnormality as representing a dynamic departure from normal physiological functioning. Having established what Arney has called 'the optimal birthing trajectory' (Arney and Bergen 1984), obstetricians were able prospectively to assess the course of labour. Any deviation from the ideal norm led to direct action on the obstetrician's part, bringing the mother back, as it were, on to the path of virtuous parturition. Obstetricians no longer viewed themselves as dreaded heroes, rushing in with their surgical armamentarium when things went wrong. Chamberlain (1975:vii) looks back: 'In the last thirty years it [obstetrics] has become more than just a rescue service, salvaging babies from awkward situations in the pelvis. Obstetrics has pushed therapy back from the curative into the preventative field . . .'. Instead of being mechanics responsible for the mending of faults, they became engineers in charge of the smooth running of 'all systems' so that faults did not even occur. The obstetric engineer has to master and control normal physiology in order to prevent the abnormal from happening. The absorption of abnormality into this concept of normality is clearly reflected in the obstetric literature. For instance, the 1972 edition (Clayton, Fraser, and Lewis) of *Obstetrics by Ten Teachers* introduced the partogram as a useful means to detect early deviation from the norm, in the chapter titled 'Abnormal Uterine Action'. By 1980, however, Clayton, Lewis, and Pinker had incorporated the partogram under the heading 'Management of Normal Labour'. The chapter on 'Prolonged Labour' in Ian Donald's 1969 edition of *Practical Obstetric Problems* disappeared entirely from the 1979 edition, and its content reappeared in the chapter called 'Management of Labour'. Similar rearrangements took place in the *Combined Textbook of Obstetrics and Gynaecology*, *Mayes' Midwifery*, *Scientific Basis of Obstetrics and Gynaecology*, and even in *Munro Kerr's Operative Obstetrics*. Rather than advocating those operative techniques which gave their name to the title of the book, recent editions have done away with the traditional juxtaposition of *eutocia* (normal labour) and *dystocia* (difficult labour), and stress the preventative approach. The new emphasis on managing physiology, however, does not imply that all childbirth is to be regarded as essentially normal, nor, as Arney claims, that the idea that childbirth is potentially pathological has disappeared in the 'monitoring period' (Arney 1982). On the contrary. The 1980 edition of *Obstetrics by Ten Teachers* (Clayton, Lewis, and Pinker) tells the reader that 'no labour is certainly normal until the third stage is safely concluded', and the 1986 edition of *Undergraduate Obstetrics and Gynaecology* (Hull, Joyce, and Turner: 247) explains that 'labour is a physiological process which if left to its own devices is associated with maternal and fetal mortality and morbidity. Like all physiological processes it has its limitations and pathology supervenes at times.'

In order to prevent such pathological deviations occurring, obstetricians sought to extend the scope of their professional attention to *all* women: *all* births require to be engineered. O'Driscoll pioneered a policy of managing labour at the National Maternity Hospital in Dublin which he called the *active* management of labour (O'Driscoll and Meagher 1980:3):

> it soon became clear that the person ultimately responsible must return to the delivery unit in person and assume direct control, not only in theory but also in practice, for the welfare of all. Whereas previously the consultant obstetrician had been involved directly with a small number of abnormal women . . . he must now become involved with the much larger number of normal women who had hitherto been overlooked at this level, because they suffered from no organic disease. . . . the consultant, rather than remain off-stage, as it were, waiting for a summons to perform an emergency operation, as a belated attempt to retrieve a situation which could have been anticipated at an early stage, must seek to prevent such emergencies arising in women who were normal when they first entered hospital in labour.

The word *active*, as O'Driscoll points out, refers to the obstetrician and to the nature of his involvement (p. 3). The implications of this new concept were vast indeed. Many elements of O'Driscoll's *active management* policy were adopted in Britain, resulting in the introduction of new technologies of monitoring and controlling labour. Surveillance techniques like tocography, fetal heart-tracing, and biochemical analysis of fetal blood samples became increasingly popular, and induction and/or acceleration of labour was employed as a means of continually assessing the mother's potential deviation from the scientifically established norm. The technologies themselves were not introduced on the basis of rigorous scientific studies. Cartwright (1979), for instance, has shown that induction policies were not related to maternal characteristics or fetal risk factors, but to institutional attributes like the size and type of the hospital. Cochrane (1979) pointed out that 'obstetricians started to introduce a whole series of expensive innovations into the routines of pre- and postnatal care and delivery, without any rigorous evaluation'.

However, it appears that obstetricians were not primarily interested in scientific evaluation of these techniques. Rather, novel technologies represented the tools with which the obstetrician could implement the programme of childbirth engineering. Conversely, using those tools might also help to further the programme: one American monograph on induction of labour argues that 'the aims of obstetrics can be augmented materially by the proper utilization of induction of labour' (Fields, Greene, and Smith 1965), and it seems likely that this applied equally to England. Using those techniques, of course, also entailed a dramatic change in the nature and atmosphere of childbirth. Whereas in 1960 the Central Health Services Council (1961) still demanded that 'hospital confinement should achieve as nearly as possible the atmosphere of home confinement', a House of Commons committee recommended in 1980 that 'the labour ward should be regarded as an intensive care area in which staffing and equipment are optimal' (Social Services Committee 1980). Obstetricians, however, do not regard this change as necessarily detrimental to mothers' experience of childbirth. One declared aim of O'Driscoll's active management policy, for instance, was to reduce the rate of operative intervention (a goal which he actually achieved), and in the 1980 edition of *Obstetrics by Ten Teachers* (Clayton, Lewis, and Pinker: 114) it is stated that 'there is no reason why modern methods of monitoring during labour should be psychologically harmful or lead to interference with normal labour; indeed there is some evidence that they can sometimes prevent unnecessary intervention. If their purpose is explained to the patient they are also reassuring to her.'

The active management (or engineering) of childbirth by consultant obstetricians has also led to a redistribution of intraprofessional responsibilities. In her 1981 *Textbook for*

Midwives Myles says (p. 2): 'The basic role of the British midwife . . . [as] a "delivery woman" who practised independently . . . has been superseded. . . . It would now be considered a retrograde step for a midwife to take sole charge of an expectant mother, thereby depriving her of the scientific expert care only the obstetric team can provide.' One of the tasks assigned to the midwife in her new role as subcontractor to the engineering programme is to explain and to make mothers feel at ease with novel technologies: 'The midwife in a supportive role provides professional companionship and demonstrates a "caring" attitude as an integral part of good obstetric practice.' (Myles 1981:3.) This development is clearly reflected in the standard textbooks for midwives, which started to include material on psychology, sociology, the family, etc.

The programme of childbirth engineering, therefore, goes far beyond the active management of labour alone. The preface to the 1985 edition of the *Scientific Basis of Obstetrics and Gynaecology* (Macdonald 1985) makes the point: 'The narrow view of obstetrics must be widened to that of human reproduction, encompassing such disciplines as genetics, physiology, embryology, psychology and sociology.' It is all-embracing, and 'preparation for childbirth begins when the mother herself is born' (Walker *et al.* 1976). Only the expert, the consultant obstetrician, can safely and efficiently achieve what Baird had already demanded in 1950—'the attainment of efficient physiological reproduction'. This programme is not meant to alienate mothers from the experience of childbirth, but the reverse. Since childbirth engineering tries to optimize natural processes, it ultimately ensures that 'mothers can look on pregnancy and labour as an enjoyable experience' (Walker *et al.* 1976). Whether mothers share that view is a different question altogether!

References

Arney, W. R., 1982, *Power and the Profession of Obstetrics* (Chicago, University of Chicago Press).
—— and Bergen, B. J., 1984, *Medicine and the Management of Living* (Chicago, University of Chicago Press).
Baird, D., 1950, 1969, *Combined Textbook of Obstetrics and Gynaecology*, 5th and 8th edns. (Edinburgh, E. and S. Livingstone).
Cartwright, A., 1979, *The Dignity of Labour?* (London, Tavistock).
Central Health Services Council, 1961, *Annual Report for 1960* (London, HMSO).
Chamberlain, G., 1975, *Musgrove's Lecture Notes on Obstetrics*, 3rd edn. (Oxford, Blackwell).
Clayton, S. G., Fraser, D. and Lewis, T. L. T. (eds.), 1972, *Obstetrics by Ten Teachers*, 12th edn. (London, Edward Arnold).
—— Lewis, T. L. T. and Pinker, G. (eds.), 1980, *Obstetrics by Ten Teachers*, 13th edn. (London, Edward Arnold).
Cochrane, A. L. 1979, 1931–1971: A Critical Review with Particular Reference to the Medical Profession', in *Medicines for the Year 2000* (London, Office of Health Economics).
Dewhurst, J., 1980, Foreword to Hytten, F. E. and Chamberlain, G. (eds.), *Clinical Physiology in Obstetrics* (Oxford, Blackwell).
Donald, I., 1959, 1964, *Practical Obstetric Problems*, 2nd and 3rd edns. (London, Lloyd-Luke).
Fields, H., Greene, J. W. and Smith, K. 1965, *Induction of Labour* (New York, Macmillan).
Friedman, E. A., 1978, *Labor: Clinical Evaluation and Management* (New York, Appleton Century Crofts).
Good, B. J. and Good, M. V., 1981, 'The Semantics of Medical Discourse', in Mendelsohn, E. and Elkana, Y. (eds.), *Sciences and Cultures* (Sociology of Sciences, 5; Reidel, Dordrecht).
Hull, M. G. R., Joyce, D. N., and Turner, G., 1986, *Undergraduate Obstetrics and Gynaecology* (Bristol, John Wright).
Macdonald, R. R., (ed.), 1971, 1985, *Scientific Basis of Obstetrics and Gynaecology*, 1st and 3rd edns. (Edinburgh, Churchill Livingstone).
Macfarlane, A. and Mugford, M., 1984, *Birth Counts* (London, HMSO).
Myles, M., 1981, *Textbook for Midwives with Modern Concepts of Obstetric and Neonatal Care* (Edinburgh, Churchill Livingstone).
Oakley, A., 1984, *The Captured Womb* (Oxford, Blackwell).
O'Driscoll, K. and Meagher, D., 1980, *Active Management of Labour* (London, W. B. Saunders).

Roques, E. W., Beatti, J., and Wrigley, J. (eds.), 1955, 1961, *Midwifery by Ten Teachers*, 9th and 10th edns. (London, Edward Arnold).

Social Services Committee of the House of Commons, 1980, *Perinatal and Neonatal Mortality*, second report, 1979–80 (London, HMSO).

Walker, J., MacGillivray, I., and Macnaughton, M. C. (eds.), 1976, *Combined Textbok of Obstetrics and Gynaecology* (Edinburgh, Churchill Livingstone).

4

Maintaining the Independence of the Midwifery Profession: A Continuing Struggle

Sarah Robinson

THE history of midwifery in Britain is, in many ways, one of a profession struggling to develop and maintain its independence and to safeguard the unique contribution which its members make to the care of childbearing women. Midwives are qualified to provide care throughout pregnancy, labour, and the puerperium on their own responsibility, to recognize those signs of abnormality which require referral to medical staff, and to provide women with advice, information, and emotional support, from the early stages of pregnancy to the end of the post-natal period. Policies for the health services have at times facilitated the fulfilment of this role. At other times, and particularly in recent decades, health-care policies have hindered and obstructed the full use of midwifery skills and knowledge.

Within the confines of a single chapter it is not possible to provide an exhaustive history of the profession; various sources are available, however, which outline the main developments in differing degrees of detail (Donnison 1977; Cowell and Wainwright 1981; Bent 1982; Robinson *et al.* 1983; Towler and Brammall 1986). The approach of this chapter is to focus on three main themes which have characterized the development of midwifery in the twentieth century: changes in the structure and organization of the maternity services, in

I wish to thank the following: Josephine Golden and Susan Bradley, co-authors of 'A Study of the Role and Responsibilities of the Midwife' (Robinson *et al.*, 1983), from which this chapter is drawn; the Department of Health and Social Security for funding the study; and Carolyn Dereky and Bea Ogilvie for secretarial assistance.

particular those which have affected provision of continuity of care by midwives and women's access to midwives; the division of responsibility between midwives and medical staff for the care of childbearing women; and the extent to which midwives have been able to exert control over their own profession through representation on those committees, organizations, and management structures which determine policies in the maternity services and control midwives' practice and education. Some of these themes had their roots in the midwife's struggle for professional recognition at the end of the last century, and so this chapter begins with that period.

Gaining Professional Recognition

Midwifery attained legal recognition as a profession with the passing of the first Midwives' Act in 1902, which made provision for the training and registration of midwives. Prior to this Act, few formal training opportunities had been available to those wishing to practise as midwives; and there were no restrictions on attendance on women in childbirth. Opportunities for formal instruction comprised courses provided by the London Obstetrical Society and some of the lying-in hospitals, but for most practitioners, apprenticeship to another midwife was the usual means of attaining midwifery skills and knowledge (Bailey 1976; Donnison 1977).

Concern over this lack of training facilities and the high levels of infant and maternal mortality motivated a small group of women to found a society aimed at increasing the competence of midwives and improving their status (Donnison 1977; Cowell and Wainwright 1981). Known first as the Matrons' Aid Society, it was later renamed the Midwives' Institute. The Institute's members, most of whom were midwives who held the London Obstetrical Society certificate, set out to achieve their aims by organizing lectures and meetings for midwives, and by campaigning for parliamentary legislation for the state registration of midwives. State registration was seen as the most effective means of regulating midwives' practice, providing them with training, and enhancing their status. Between 1890 and 1900 eight bills were introduced into Parliament to this end, but they were all lost. This was due primarily to opposition from some sections of the medical profession and to lack of parliamentary interest (Donnison 1977; Cowell and Wainwright 1981; Towler and Bramall 1986).

One of the main features of the campaign was the diversity of view among midwives, doctors, and nurses as to whether registration was desirable, and if so who should control the examining and legislative machinery (Donnison 1977; Cowell and Wainwright 1981). Many of the leading medical figures of the day supported the registration and training of midwives, which would mean that qualified personnel would be available to attend the poor in childbirth. This support, however, was usually on the understanding that the proposed Central Midwives' Board, which was to be responsible for the practice and examination of midwives, would be under the control of the General Medical Council. On the other hand, some sections of the medical profession were opposed to any scheme to register midwives; in particular some general practitioners who feared that registered midwives would compete with them for maternity cases, thus depriving them of a source of income. Donnison's study (1977) provides a fascinating and detailed account of the views that were expressed and the campaigns that were waged by various sectors of the medical profession as they pursued their differing objectives in relation to the registration of midwives.

The reader is also referred to Donnison (1977) for an account of the equally complex relationship between midwifery and nursing which developed over the issue of state registration for midwives. Some nurses, including Florence Nightingale, supported registration for the midwife; others, and in particular Mrs Bedford-Fenwick, opposed it. In 1887 Mrs Bedford-Fenwick had founded the British Nurses' Association to campaign for state registration of nurses, and had originally invited the Midwives' Institute to join forces with her to press for registration for both groups. However, the Institute took the view that midwives, unlike nurses, were independent practitioners in their own right and that their registration was therefore more urgent and should be dealt with separately. Having failed to make an ally of the Midwives' Institute, Mrs

Bedford-Fenwick subsequently branded midwives as 'an anachronism and an historical curiosity', maintaining that they should be replaced 'by the better educated and more efficient "obstetric nurse"' working under medical supervision (Donnison 1977).

Registration proposals were also opposed by some midwives; the Manchester Midwives' Society, for example, maintained that the midwife's status and training would not be improved by a system controlled by the medical profession, and that no registration at all was preferable to registration under medical domination (Donnison 1977). Members of the Midwives' Institute were not entirely satisfied with some of the proposals either, but supported the various bills on the grounds that their main concern was to secure legislation which would protect women from unqualified practitioners calling themselves midwives.

The ninth bill for the registration of midwives, introduced in 1902, differed from its predecessors in that the Central Midwives' Board was to be directly responsible to the Privy Council and not to the General Medical Council. According to Donnison (1977), this change was partly due to the influence of some Home Office officials who regarded the complete control of midwifery by the medical profession as undesirable. The ninth bill had the support of several leading members of the medical profession, but it was opposed by the General Medical Council primarily on the grounds of insufficient medical control of the registration and examination machinery. But by this time the case for the registration of midwives enjoyed widespread public and parliamentary support, as it was seen as an important component of the drive to improve maternal and child health. These were now receiving increasing attention as a result of national concern over both the condition and numbers of the population; the Boer War had revealed that many army recruits were in poor physical health, the birth-rate was falling, and infant and maternal mortality figures remained high (Lewis 1980; Oakley 1984).

The ninth midwives' bill was consequently passed to become the first Midwives' Act of 1902. In contrast to most legislation concerned with the recognition of professions, however, the Act was not designed to protect legitimate practitioners from competition by those who were unqualified. Rather, its central concern was the protection of the public against unqualified practitioners. As Bent (1982) comments, this was reflected in the composition of the Central Midwives' Board; the Act did not stipulate that a midwife had to be included in its membership.

From Independent Practice to Salaried Employment

Under the provisons of the Act, women were entitled to register with the Board until March 1905 if they held a certificate approved by the Board, or if they could produce evidence that they had been in practice for at least a year and 'bore a good character'; this latter group were known as 'bona fide' midwives. After 1905 the title of 'midwife' was protected, in that women could only call themselves midwives if they were already registered with the Board, or if they had passed the Board's examination after taking an approved three-month training course. The proportion of trained midwives steadily increased from 30 per cent in 1905 to 74 per cent by 1915 (Central Midwives' Board 1916).

In the years immediately following the Act, the majority of midwives continued to work as independent practitioners, earning their living from fees paid to them by the women they attended. A small proportion of midwives were salaried employees, however; some were employed by voluntary organizations which ran their own domiciliary service, others by nursing organizations which provided midwifery services as well as nursing services in sparsely populated rural areas where independent practice was not viable, and a third group worked in institutions such as voluntary maternity hospitals, teaching hospitals, poor-law infirmaries, and local authority maternity homes.

The services of a trained midwife could not, of course, become immediately available to all women throughout the country, as numbers were insufficient (see Peretz, Chapter 2). By the late 1920s, 20 per cent of the rural population of

Sarah Robinson

England and Wales were still without trained midwives (Ministry of Health 1929). In many rural areas, care in childbirth was provided by village nurse-midwives (Baly 1987; Peretz, forthcoming). However, women continued to be attended in childbirth by the unqualified 'handywoman', despite the provisions of the 1902 Act forbidding such people to practise after 1910. Even where trained midwives were available, the handywoman was sometimes preferred as she was cheaper and willing to help with housework and child care (Donnison 1977).

State involvement in maternity care gathered momentum from the early years of the century onwards. Despite their success in obtaining state registration for midwives, members of the Midwives' Institute were concerned that the interests and views of the profession would be ignored by those responsible for formulating law and policy in maternity care, and that this would be exacerbated by the lack of female suffrage. As Cowell and Wainwright have documented (1981), these fears were not without foundation.

From the outset midwives were denied officially recognized control over their own profession, in that there was no requirement under the 1902 Act for the Central Midwives' Board to include a midwife in its membership; three of the original members were in fact midwives, but they were representing other organizations and not the Midwives' Institute. From 1920 onwards it was mandatory to have midwife-members on the Board, but they were always statutorily precluded from comprising a majority of the membership. No midwife was included in the membership of a committee set up by the Ministry of Health to consider the working of the 1902 Act, and Institute members had to lobby strongly to ensure that the word 'midwife' was inserted into the National Insurance Bill of 1911, that it made provision for childbearing women to decide whether they were attended by a midwife or a medical practitioner, and that they should have free choice in the selection of either (Cowell and Wainwright 1981).

From 1915 onwards the Local Government Board encouraged the growth of salaried and subsidized midwifery services and the establishment of ante-natal clinics in existing maternity centres (Lewis 1980). The Maternal and Child Welfare Act of 1918 gave further impetus to both these developments, but provision was not mandatory and the growth of municipal maternity services throughout the country was uneven.

Members of the Midwives' Institute were particularly concerned that local government circulars on schemes to improve maternal and child health did not place any particular weight on the possible influence of the midwife (Cowell and Wainwright 1981). This was despite the significant progress that had been made with regard to midwifery training. The Institute had provided lectures and discussions, in London and elsewhere, for both trained and 'bona fide' midwives (Wood 1963). In 1916 training was lengthened to four months for nurses and to six months for those without nursing qualifications, and the extended syllabus included lectures on ante-natal care. In the early years following the 1902 Act, midwifery practice had, as before, been primarily concerned with care during labour and the puerperium, but now the view was gaining ground that ante-natal care was a key factor in maternal and child welfare (Lewis 1980; Oakley 1984), and the midwifery profession's leaders were anxious for this to be reflected in their education and practice.

Midwives' concerns that their contribution to maternal and child health might be ignored were not lessened in the 1920s and 1930s. Although still regarded as unacceptably high, the infant mortality rate had dropped by the early 1920s, but the maternal mortality rate remained static, with 3,000 women dying in childbirth every year. The Ministry of Health launched a major investigation into the problem (Campbell 1923, 1924, and 1927; Ministry of Health 1930 and 1937), and it concluded that the routine provision of ante-natal care was one of the key factors in reducing maternal mortality and morbidity levels. The need for midwives, doctors, and the public to be aware of its value was stressed, and a huge expansion in the number of local authority ante-natal clinics was recommended, making ante-natal supervision available for women whose midwives or doctors were unable to provide it.

Views expressed by the Institute in the 1920s demonstrate that although it was anxious for the profession to become more involved in the expanding field of ante-natal care, it was concerned about the overtly medical orientation of contemporary ministry reports, and the fact that they did not place sufficient emphasis on the contribution which midwives might make to reducing the mortality and morbidity figures (Lewis 1980). The ministry reports exhorted midwives to make more frequent visits to pregnant women, and if they identified any complicating factors necessitating medical advice, to refer them to the clinics which were under the overall direction of a full-time salaried Medical Officer of Health (Campbell 1924 and 1927). It was also recommended that these clinics should be linked to maternity homes or hospitals in which beds were available for women requiring ante-natal observation, those with abnormal and complicated conditions, and those whose home circumstances were unsatisfactory. There was therefore a sense in which the new ante-natal clinics posed a threat for independent midwives; if they referred their patients to a clinic for advice, there was a possibility that institutional confinement might be recommended and the midwife might lose her fee.

During the 1920s, 50–60 per cent of women were attended in childbirth solely by a midwife, and so the provision of sufficient numbers of well-trained midwives was regarded as of paramount importance in the battle against maternal mortality (Campbell 1923). A high level of training would, it was hoped, attract well-educated women into midwifery who in turn would raise the standards and status of the profession. Campbell's 1923 report recommended an increase in the length of training to allow time to cover the midwife's demanding and increasing responsibilities. This proposal was in accord with the views of the Midwives' Institute and the Central Midwives' Board, and in 1926 the training was lengthened to one year for non-nurses and to six months for nurses, who by this time were undertaking midwifery training in increasing numbers. Attention was also drawn to the need for post-certificate courses and courses for midwifery teachers (Campbell 1923, 1924; Ministry of Health 1929).

The difficulty experienced by independent midwives in making an adequate living was also seen as a deterrent to attracting well-educated women into the profession. Independent practice had always been subject to financial problems. The 1902 Act, for example, had made no provision for the payment of doctors called out by midwives in emergencies. In cases where the woman was unable to meet this cost, the midwife often did so herself. This situation continued until 1918, when the second Midwives' Act required the local authority to pay the fee, although they were empowered to recover it from the woman (Donnison 1977).

The precarious financial situation of the independent midwife was compounded in the 1920s by a number of factors. The range of duties that the midwife was expected to undertake for each childbearing woman was extended, but this was not reflected in extra remuneration, and data provided by the Midwives' Institute showed that many of them took on more cases than they could really cope with in order to make an adequate living (Ministry of Health 1929). In some areas, certified midwives found themselves in competition with unqualified handywomen who still continued to deliver women despite many attempts to prevent this practice. A departmental committee was therefore set up to review the whole question of the training, supply, and subsequent employment of midwives (Ministry of Health 1929).

The committee outlined plans for a national system of maternity care in which the services of a midwife and general practitioner, plus an obstetric specialist if required, were provided through national insurance schemes and administered by local authorities (see Peretz, Chapter 2). They maintained that the first basic requirement of such a system was the full services of a qualified midwife throughout pregnancy, labour, and the puerperium, but they were also of the opinion that medical supervision of pregnancy and the puerperium was desirable. They thus cast doubt on the midwife's ability to provide this care on her own responsibility, a view which has persisted in some quarters until the present day.

The committee recommended improved conditions for midwives, but the lack of importance accorded to the views of midwives themselves was evidenced in the committee's membership, only one of whom was a midwife. Of particular concern to midwives was the committee's proposal that responsibility for approving and inspecting training institutions and teachers, and formulating the curriculum, should be transferred from the Central Midwives' Board to the Ministry of Health. Strong opposition to these proposals was voiced by the Board, by midwives, by the medical profession, and by two members of the committee who wrote a minority report. The latter maintained that these changes were inconsistent with improving the status of the midwife and making the profession attractive to well-educated women, commenting that: 'It is the general rule for all professions—medical, legal and others—that they retain in their own hands the decision as to what is the proper training for and entry into them.' (Ministry of Health 1929.)

In the event, all the committee's proposals were shelved as a result of the economic depression of the early 1930s. By this time working conditions had worsened for independent midwives, who by now represented just under half of the 15,000 in practice (Donnison 1977). The birth-rate was falling and the institutional confinement rate was rapidly rising—to 15 per cent in 1927, 24 per cent by 1932, and 36 per cent by 1937 (figures for England and Wales quoted in Walker 1954); however, these figures did conceal wide regional variations. The trend towards institutional confinement was due primarily to two factors: first, the Local Government Act of 1929 placed hundreds of poor-law hospitals under municipal control, which removed the stigma of giving birth in a poor-law hospital; second, many of the leading obstetricians of the day were advocating hospital delivery on the grounds of greater safety for women and their babies.

The development of a nation-wide, salaried, domiciliary service was proposed as a means of improving the working conditions of midwives. This in turn, it was argued, would attract well-educated entrants to the profession, and enable it to make the maximum contribution to improving the maternity services and reducing the maternal mortality rate, which still stood at 3,000 deaths per annum. The Midwives' Institute was in favour of a salaried service, but anxious that the right of midwives to practise independently should be preserved (Cowell and Wainwright 1981). Provision for a salaried service was brought about with the passing of the 1936

Midwives' Act; the service was to be under the control of local supervising authorities, who could either employ salaried midwives themselves or arrange for their employment by welfare or voluntary organizations. The Act also provided for local authority midwives to be engaged as maternity nurses in cases where a general practitioner was in charge of the delivery; this was in order to make it unnecessary to employ unqualified handywomen, who were banned by the Act from attending women in childbirth in any capacity (Donnison 1977).

Period of Professional Consolidation: 1936–1960

The years between the Midwives' Act of 1936 and the introduction of the National Health Service in 1948 have been described as the heyday of the domiciliary midwife and the small maternity home (Barnett 1979). As before, midwives provided ante-partum, intrapartum, and post-partum care, but they participated much more than before in the work of the municipal ante-natal clinics, which, like the salaried midwifery service, were under the control of the local authorities (Wood 1963). After considerable debate and lobbying, midwives were allowed to administer certain types of analgesia to women delivered at home, from whom there was an increasing demand for pain-relief in labour (Lewis 1980; Beinart, Chapter 6). This period also saw a continued increase in the proportion of women delivered in an institution, a trend given further impetus by the war, with pregnant women being evacuated from areas likely to be bombed, and delivered in hospitals or maternity homes (Walker 1954; Bent 1982). By 1946 the institutional confinement rate had reached 54 per cent, and, correspondingly, the proportion of midwives in institutional as opposed to domiciliary employment also rose, reaching 31 per cent by 1944.

In both environments, midwives continued to be responsible for the care of the majority of women who experienced a normal pregnancy, labour, and puerperium. But by 1947 a working party set up by the Ministry to enquire into the current shortage of midwives had sounded a warning note on

an issue which was increasingly to dominate the profession—
the erosion of the role of the midwife by medical involvement
in normal maternity care (Ministry of Health *et al.* 1949).
Concerns in this respect were heightened by discussions about
the proposed National Health Service, and by the views of the
two groups of doctors involved in maternity care: general
practitioners on the one hand and obstetricians on the other.

By the end of the war only about one in three general
practitioners was involved in maternity work. Following the
National Insurance Act of 1911 which had guaranteed them
remuneration for other work, many general practitioners had
tended to leave maternity work to midwives. In the negotiations
leading up to the implementation of the National Health
Service, however, general practitioners maintained that they
should all be entitled to provide maternity care under the new
service. This demand was agreed by the government, although,
as Honigsbaum (1979) records, it was in the face of opposition
by some health officials and obstetricians, who wanted general
practitioners to be selected for maternity work on the basis of
postgraduate qualifications and experience.

The other group of medical staff—consultant obstetricians
—gradually increased their role and influence in the maternity
services, particularly towards the end of the 1920s. By this
time they were represented in some strength on the Ministry
of Health committees investigating maternal mortality. From
the early 1930s onwards they advocated an increase in
institutional confinement and maternity schemes based on
large sixty- to seventy-bedded hospitals. A policy statement
published in 1944 (Royal College of Obstetricians and
Gynaecologists) argued for a 70 per cent institutional confinement rate, with the maternity services in each area focused on
a large hospital under the overall leadership of a consultant
obstetrician. While the document recognized the excellent
results achieved by midwives, the following passages indicate
how the obstetricians sought to curtail independent clinical
judgements by midwives: 'Midwives should not be regarded
as competent to undertake unaided the antenatal care of the
expectant mother, but should always work in collaboration
with the general practitioner or the obstetrician.' 'Midwives
and health visitors would be taught the management of

breastfeeding from the paediatrician, who would direct its detail in the maternity ward.'

The College of Midwives (the name accorded to the Midwives' Institute in 1941 following the award of its own charter) expressed concern that the 1944 government white paper on the proposed National Health Service contained 'no clear-cut account of the midwives' part in the service' (Cowell and Wainwright 1981). In particular, they were concerned that their role in ante-natal care and delivery might be supplanted by the general practitioner, as women would be able to book the services of a doctor without payment of a fee, a concern that was also shared by the Central Midwives' Board (Central Midwives' Board 1949). The issue of ante-natal care in particular was the focus of comments by the 1947 working party on the potential dangers facing midwifery as a result of the provisions of the National Health Service:

Our attention was drawn to the many complaints from both Medical Officers of Health and midwives that general practitioners giving maternity care under Part II of the National Health Service Act are tending to take over the whole of antenatal care as well as relegating midwives to the status of maternity nurses. In some cases, midwives are not seeing patients until they go to deliver them. Furthermore, pupils are getting no opportunity to see antenatal care. (Ministry of Health *et al.* 1949.)

The working party's concerns about the role of the midwife under the provisions of the National Health Service were part of their wider concern about the interrelationship of the roles of midwifery and medical staff. They considered that the midwife's three main strengths—'time to spend with her patients, great experience and skill in the management of normal pregnancy and an attitude focused on its normality as a physiological process, not on its potential abnormality as an illness—had been overshadowed by the campaign to reduce maternal mortality which has rightly focused both public and medical attention on potential abnormalities'. They argued, however, that such abnormalities were rare in comparison with uneventful confinements, and that 'it is time the pendulum swung back to a greater emphasis on the normality of childbirth, a swing which should bring the midwife back into her rightful place'. They emphasized how important it was for medical and midwifery staff to work together: 'the doctor must accept the midwife as his fellow practitioner and not relegate her to the status of his hand-maiden, and the midwife must be willing to summon the doctor whenever his skill was required'.

Throughout the 1950s the midwife remained the most senior person present at approximately three-quarters of all deliveries (Central Midwives' Board 1963). The nature of their clinical work in the ante-partum and intrapartum periods changed little, but post-partum care was characterized by a move away from carrying out detailed procedures for 'lying-in' women, and towards early ambulation and independence in self-care and infant care.

Under the provisions of the 1946 National Health Service Act, maternity care was provided by all three branches of the new service: the hospital services, the domiciliary services, and the general-practitioner services. According to Audrey Wood, the General Secretary of the Royal College of Midwives from 1952 to 1970, midwives and general practitioners worked together well in the years following the introduction of the new health service, despite the midwives' initial misgivings (Wood 1963). Although many women did book a general practitioner for confinement, doctors were in fact present at delivery in only 26 per cent of the cases for which they were booked (Central Midwives' Board 1957), and so the domiciliary midwife continued to take responsibility for the majority of home confinements.

Changes did occur, however, in the provision of ante-natal care. The proportion of general practitioners providing ante-natal care rose rapidly to approximately three-quarters by the end of the 1950s (Ministry of Health 1959). They gradually took over the provision of community ante-natal care from the local ante-natal clinics, and the Cranbrook Committee recommended that the general-practitioner obstetrician should in fact replace the local Medical Officer of Health (Ministry of Health 1959). Midwives continued to provide ante-natal care in women's own homes, at local authority clinics, and increasingly at general practitioners' surgeries. Their relationship with childbearing women had been changed in a fundamental way, however. Increasingly, women went to the general practitioner rather than to the domiciliary midwife for confirmation of pregnancy, as they could now book the former for confinement without payment of a fee (Bent 1982), and this meant that for the majority of women the doctor became the first point of contact with the maternity services, not the midwife as hitherto.

Hospital midwives, like their community colleagues, still enjoyed a fair measure of clinical independence. In hospital clinics they worked alongside medical staff in providing antenatal care for women booked for hospital delivery, but in many hospitals they also held their own clinics at which women were examined by a midwife and only seen by a doctor if the midwife detected a complication which she thought necessitated medical advice. In most maternity hospitals, each ward had several labour and delivery rooms as well as its own post-natal beds. As the majority of women stayed in hospital for at least ten days after delivery, hospital midwives, like their counterparts in the community, were able to provide women with continuity of care throughout pregnancy, labour, and the puerperium.

Decades of Constraint: the 1960s and 1970s

In the 1960s and 1970s, however, a number of interrelated changes in the organization of the maternity services led to the fragmentation of care between an increasing number of health professionals, and to the restriction of opportunities for midwives to provide continuity of care. These two decades also saw the gradual diminution of the midwife's independence in assessing and monitoring the course of pregnancy, labour, and the puerperium as medical staff became increasingly involved in normal maternity care.

Turning first to organizational changes, the Cranbrook Committee (which was set up to look at the problems of the maternity services under the tripartite Health Service) recommended provision for 70 per cent of confinements to take place in hospital (Ministry of Health 1959). Eleven years later, by which time the institutional confinement rate was over 80 per cent, the Peel Committee recommended a further increase to 100 per cent, as, in its view, hospital delivery afforded greater safety for mother and baby (Department of Health and Social Security 1970). Both committees sought to centralize services under the control of consultant obstetricians, recommending that general-practitioner maternity beds should be situated within, or very close to, consultant units, and that a consultant should have overall responsibility for these beds; the Peel Committee also advocated that all women, wherever they were delivered, should be seen by a consultant obstetrician at least once or twice during pregnancy.

As noted, it had been policy in the 1950s for women delivered in hospital to remain there for ten days post-partum. The Cranbrook Committee said that their recommendations for an increase in the institutional confinement rate and provision for 20 per cent of hospital beds to be reserved for ante-natal admissions could either be met by increasing the number of beds or by discharging women to the care of community staff prior to the tenth day. The latter option was vigorously opposed by the Royal College of Midwives in its evidence to the committee, on the grounds that it would disrupt continuity of midwifery care in the puerperium (Ministry of Health 1959). Although the committee accepted this view, it proved not to be feasible with the rise in both the birth-rate and the institutional confinement rate, and early-discharge schemes were introduced. The Royal College of Midwives expressed the view that they should be regarded as a 'temporary emergency measure' (Royal College of Midwives 1964), but events proved otherwise; by 1970 discharges before ten days represented 51 per cent of total births, and by 1979 the figure was 91 per cent (Central Midwives' Board 1979 and 1980).

Ante-natal care also became fragmented between hospital and community staff. In the 1960s it had been the policy of most hospitals to provide ante-natal care for those women booked for hospital delivery, but as the birth-rate and the institutional confinement rate rose, this became increasingly impractical. Consequently, many areas moved to a policy of sharing ante-natal care with community staff. These changes in the provision of ante- and post-natal supervision fragmented the continuity of care by midwives. Moreover, the work of hospital midwives became subject to increasing specialization. This was partly due to changes occasioned by the Ministry of Health's ten-year hospital plan of 1962, which saw the replacement of independent maternity hospitals by maternity units in district general hospitals. In the former, there were usually several labour and delivery rooms, each attached to their own post-natal wards, and so the midwife who delivered a woman was likely to be involved in her subsequent post-natal care. The new units, however, tended to have one central delivery suite, staffed by one group of midwives who then handed over the care of newly delivered women to the staff of the post-natal wards. So, whereas in 1968 approximately one-quarter of midwives were, at any one time, working solely on one aspect of care (Department of Health and Social Security 1970), by 1979 this proportion had risen to 64 per cent (Robinson *et al.* 1983). Some community midwives were able to provide continuity of care through domino deliveries; under these schemes the midwife provided ante-natal care, delivered the woman in hospital, and then continued her subsequent post-natal care at home. Although these schemes were welcomed by the Royal College of Midwives, they have never constituted more than a very small proportion of deliveries.

Changes in policies for the maternity services not only led to a loss of opportunity for midwives to provide continuity of care, but also to a curtailing of their freedom to exercise their clinical judgement. The Cranbrook Committee had commented that 'a midwife should be given every opportunity to participate in the care of her patients to the fullest extent to which her skill and experience entitle her. Nothing should be done to lessen the importance of the midwife.' (Ministry of Health 1959.) In contradiction to this statement, however, the committee also recommended that both doctors and midwives should be present at ante-natal examinations and at deliveries, and that doctors rather than midwives should be responsible for ensuring the necessary co-ordination for the provision of adequate care. This would lessen the degree of responsibility which midwives had previously enjoyed, and it was this

sentiment rather than the former one which characterized
events in the 1960s and 1970s.

In the first instance, the incidence of obstetric interventions,
which had begun to rise in the 1960s, climbed sharply in the
1970s (Butler and Bonham 1963; Chalmers and Richards
1977; Chamberlain *et al.* 1978; Government Statistical Service
1980). This meant an increase in the proportion of labours in
which medical staff participated and which were not managed
entirely by midwives. At the same time an increasing number
of units developed policies for the 'active management' of
labour which staff were required to follow; these included, for
example, the frequency of vaginal examinations, when to
rupture membranes, and the length of time to be allowed for
the second stage of labour. Medical staff became increasingly
involved in the ante-natal care of women with normal
pregnancies, and many midwives' clinics were closed down.
This was partly due to the delegation of care to community
staff, and to the view that hospital visits should be for the
purpose of assessment by the obstetrician. Childbirth became
characterized by the philosophy that 'labour is only normal in
retrospect' (Percival 1970): a philosophy which overshadowed
the role of the midwife in caring for women who experienced a
normal pregnancy, labour, and puerperium, and a trend
identified some two decades earlier by the 1947 working party
on midwives.

Midwives became increasingly concerned about the erosion
of their role by the medicalization of childbirth. In their
evidence to the Royal Commission on the National Health
Service, the Royal College of Midwives said: 'the midwife is
trained and capable of giving prenatal care on her own
responsibility, but in some hospital prenatal clinics and family
group practices the total prenatal care is given by medical
staff' (Royal College of Midwives 1977). Brain (1979)
expressed her concern that 'midwives in some clinics are only
used as receptionists or chaperones and to test urine and
weigh women', while in similar vein Barnett (1979) commented:
'many midwifery skills have been ignored or abandoned in the
need to give sophisticated care in the electronic age'. In her
view, 'although midwives regarded doctors as their partners,
the reverse was not always true'.

No information existed, however, on the overall extent to which the midwife's role was being eroded, and whether this varied in different practice settings. A national survey of midwives, obstetricians, general practitioners, and health visitors was undertaken by the present author and colleagues, with funding from the Department of Health and Social Security (Robinson *et al.*, 1983; Robinson 1985*b* and *c*), in order to provide this information. The survey found that although midwives were responsible for much of the care provided for childbearing women, many were not able to exercise their clinical judgement in decision-making about the management of that care. In the ante-natal period, less than 5 per cent of hospital midwives and less than a third of community midwives took responsibility for assessing the course of pregnancy; the majority worked in clinics in which either medical staff examined women or did so after the midwife had already examined them. A substantial majority of midwives worked in labour wards in which certain decisions that are basic to the management of labour were either made by medical staff or determined by unit policy: for example, 41 per cent of midwives with regard to the timing of vaginal examinations and 37 per cent with regard to rupturing membranes. Although midwives are qualified to assess the condition of post-natal women, and make daily examinations to do so, over 80 per cent of those who took part in the survey worked in units in which medical staff also made these examinations and made the decision as to when women and their babies were fit to go home.

This medical take-over of decision-making in the management of normal pregnancy, labour, and post-natal care limits opportunities for students to develop confidence in their skills and decision-making, and limits opportunities for qualified midwives to maintain such confidence. Moreover, unit policies, whether formulated by medical staff alone or by medical staff in consultation with senior midwives, require midwives to follow a predetermined course of action whether or not they regard it as appropriate in particular cases. Many of these policies are of unproven efficacy (Chalmers 1978), yet they restrict the development and maintenance of clinical judgement with consequent loss of skill in the profession.

The survey also demonstrated that midwives working in general-practitioner units, separate from consultant units, were much less likely to have had their responsibilities for decision-making eroded than midwives in consultant units, particularly those situated in teaching hospitals (Robinson *et al.* 1983; Robinson 1985*c*). Data from the study showed that fragmentation of care and shortage of staff also prevented midwives from making their full contribution to the care of childbearing women (Robinson 1985*a*).

Although these two decades ended with the midwifery profession much concerned about the extent to which its members were being allowed to use their skills and knowledge in the care of childbearing women, other, more positive, developments had none the less occurred in relation to midwifery education and management. The two-part training was replaced by a single-period course; this in turn was lengthened when it was found that it was not long enough to cover the syllabus in sufficient detail and to develop confidence in clinical skills (Central Midwives' Board 1977; Stewart 1981). Changes in the curriculum reflected developments in obstetric technology and the increasing emphasis now being placed on health education, parentcraft, and emotional support for women and their families. Post-basic opportunities for midwives increased with the introduction of the Advanced Diploma in Midwifery, the extension of the Midwife Teacher's Diploma to one year full-time, and the availability of specialist courses such as care of the new-born, family planning, and parentcraft.

In the early 1960s both the professional and the statutory bodies for midwifery expressed concern that the lack of high-level administrative posts for midwives, and their consequent poor promotion prospects, were a deterrent to retaining 'leaders' in the profession (Royal College of Midwives 1964; Central Midwives' Board 1964). Both nursing and midwifery management were restructured, however (Ministry of Health and Scottish Home and Health Department 1966; Department of Health and Social Security *et al.* 1969), and with the introduction of a management system that went right up to Principal Nursing Officer, midwives gained more direct control over the day-to-day running of their affairs. The

problem of co-ordinating the midwifery services provided by
the three branches of the Health Service was remedied by the
1974 Health Service reorganization, which resulted in the
hospital and community midwifery services of each area being
brought together into a single midwifery division under the
leadership of a midwife.

Moves to Restore Professional Independence

The end of the 1970s was in many ways a turning-point for the
profession, with the recognition that certain trends in the
health services over the past two decades had undermined
various aspects of their contribution to maternity care. The
1980s have witnessed a response to this situation, with many
midwives involved in setting up schemes which make full use
of their knowledge and skills. They have re-established
midwives' clinics (e.g. Flint 1982; Morrin 1982; Stuart and
Judge 1984), and delivery suites in which the intrapartum
care of low-risk women is provided by midwives alone (e.g.
Towler 1981; Rider 1983). They have also set up schemes to
help particular groups of women: these include midwifery
support during pregnancy for high-risk women (Davies and
Evans 1986; Elbourne *et al.* 1989); ante-natal day wards for
women who are unable to stay in hospital (Penny 1986);
support schemes for parents of pre-term babies (Goodley
1986; Hughes 1986) and those who have experienced a
perinatal or neonatal death (Gilligan 1980; Mulkerrins and
Gunn 1985; Collins 1986).

   More ambitiously, the midwives have addressed the issue of
how they might once again be able to provide continuity of
care for women, from early pregnancy to the end of the post-
natal period (Flint 1979; Thomson 1980; Cameron 1985;
Walker 1985; Curran 1986; Association of Radical Midwives
1986; Flint and Poulengeris 1987; Royal College of Midwives
1987). Continuity of ,this kind is advocated on two grounds:
first, women are more likely to feel confident about their
pregnancy and be able to discuss their concerns if they get to
know a few people well, rather than being confronted with
new faces at each ante-natal visit and others during labour

and the post-natal period; second, midwives will be more likely to detect abnormalities and problems if they get to know a woman and her clinical history well over a period of time. Recognizing, however, that it is no longer practicable to return to a system in which one midwife provides sole care for individual women, midwives have suggested instead the establishment of small teams of midwives, each caring for a group of women, and schemes of this kind have now been introduced in some areas (Curran 1986; Flint and Poulengeris 1987).

Of no less concern to midwives was women's lack of direct access to midwifery care now that the general practitioner has become the first point of contact with the maternity services. A number of committees suggested the establishment of local ante-natal clinics, staffed by midwives and health visitors, which women could attend without necessarily seeing a general practitioner first (Social Services Committee 1980; Maternity Services Advisory Committee 1982; Royal College of Midwives and Health Visitors' Association 1982), and a number have now been set up. As well as initiating patterns of care which use their skills to full effect, midwives have also sought to extend the knowledge-base of their profession through research. This was a development which began with a few studies in the 1970s and then gathered momentum in the 1980s; a wide range of subjects, relevant to practice, education, and management, have now been investigated (Flint 1985; Thomson and Robinson 1985).

Despite these developments, the underuse of midwifery skills continues to be a cause for concern. Subsequent research (e.g. DHSS 1984; Garcia *et al.* 1985) has shown that midwives' responsibilities for clinical assessment and decision-making concerning the management of care continue to be restricted in much the same way as the earlier study by Robinson and her colleagues (Robinson *et al.* 1983) demonstrated. The statutory bodies for midwifery in the United Kingdom felt that the situation warranted the issuing of a booklet outlining the level of responsibility for which the midwife is qualified and which she should be allowed to take (Central Midwives' Board for Scotland *et al.* 1983), and the subject is regularly debated at the profession's annual conference. Recommendations made by the Maternity Services Advisory Committee (1982, 1984, 1985) have been criticized as continuing to restrict midwives from exercising their clinical judgement in intrapartum (Flint 1984; Kilvington 1985) and post-partum care (Henderson 1985; Rider 1985).

One of the main problems for midwifery has been the increasing tendency to see maternity care in terms of the role of the consultant on the one hand and the general practitioner on the other. Shared ante-natal care, for example, has assigned the supervision of low-risk women to the general practitioner, with intermittent assessment by the obstetrician (i.e., two groups of medical staff). Both may decide to delegate responsibility for this care to midwives or to undertake it themselves, but it is the midwife and not the doctor who has been specifically trained to provide care for this group of women. It has also been suggested that general practitioners should have an increased role in the delivery of low-risk women (Royal College of Obstetricians and Gynaecologists and Royal College of General Practitioners 1981); but if schemes to this effect are implemented, they will constitute the same duplication of professional skills and resources as can be seen in ante-natal care.

However, the profession's concerns during the 1980s are not exclusively focused on the effective deployment of midwifery skills and knowledge, but also on the extent to which it controls the management and education of its members. The Nurses', Midwives', and Health Visitors' Act had been passed in 1979 and had made provision for a new statutory framework for the three professions. This comprises a Central Council and four National Boards for Nursing, Midwifery, and Health Visiting, and was implemented in 1983. The Central Council has a standing midwifery committee, whose membership comprises a majority of midwives, and although the Council is responsible for midwifery rules, the Act states that they have to be framed in accordance with the recommendations of the committee. The National Boards also have midwifery committees which advise them on all relevant matters. Opinion in the midwifery profession was divided over the desirability of the new framework, the proposals for which had emanated from the 1972 report of the Committee on

Nursing (Briggs 1972). The Royal College of Midwives supported the proposals, primarily on the grounds that they would enable midwives to be responsible for governing their own profession, which had not been the case with the Central Midwives' Board. The Board itself opposed the proposals; they maintained that control of the profession would be fragmented and weakened between the Central Council, the National Boards, and their midwifery committees. Many individual members of the profession thought that opting for the new framework would mean exchanging control by the medical profession for control by nurses. This view found forceful expression through the Association of Radical Midwives, a pressure group founded in the 1970s in response to the erosion of the midwife's role.[1]

Concern about the extent to which the profession was controlled by its own members was also generated by further changes in Health Service management, particularly those following in the wake of the Griffiths Report (DHSS 1984). In particular, the integrated midwifery units established under the 1974 reorganization came under threat: in some districts, hospital and community midwifery services were separated and then incorporated within other units of management; in others, midwives were placed in a position of accountability to nursing rather than midwifery managers.[2] Intensive campaigns were waged by midwives in some districts to prevent these changes, and in some cases they met with success.

Some aspects of the new proposals for the education of nurses, midwives, and health visitors (UKCC 1986) were also the cause of considerable alarm to the profession. In the view of the Royal College of Midwives, the new proposals failed to recognize the legal status of the midwife as an independent practitioner, and were couched in terms which saw midwifery very much as a nursing specialism (Royal College of Midwives 1986). At the time of writing, various educational alternatives for midwifery are under consideration, one of

---

[1] The various arguments for and against the proposals can be found in letters and statements in the *Midwives' Chronicle* for April and Dec. 1978.

[2] See reports on RCM conferences in *Nursing Mirror*, 21 July 1982; *Nursing Times*, 25 July 1984, 24 July 1985; letters to the *Midwives' Chronicle*, June 1984.

which is an increase in direct-entry training (Radford and Thompson 1988).

Issues for the Future

As this chapter has sought to demonstrate, midwives have faced continual challenges to the development and maintenance of their professional independence. In looking to the future, the main issues facing the profession appear to be fourfold: the interrelationship of its responsibilities with medical staff; adequate staffing levels; control over those bodies responsible for midwifery education and practice; and independent management structures.

Turning first to the interrelationship of the midwife's responsibilities with those of medical staff: restrictions of the former in favour of the latter have occurred despite any evidence that this has any advantages in terms of perinatal and neonatal outcome, and women's satisfaction with childbirth. Although the effectiveness of midwifery versus medical care has in fact rarely been evaluated, reviews of those prospective and retrospective studies which have sought to make this comparison have concluded that medical care affords no advantage in terms of perinatal and neonatal outcome, and that midwifery care has benefits in terms of providing advice and emotional support (Thomson 1986; Robinson, 1989). Not only do midwives need to have this evidence marshalled, but they also need to campaign for the implementation and evaluation of many more schemes which do use their skills fully. Only in this way will women be able to enjoy the benefits of midwifery care in the future.

Staffing levels have been of concern from the mid-1940s until the present day (Ministry of Health 1949; Central Midwives' Board 1957; Ministry of Health 1959; Royal College of Midwives 1964; Robinson 1980; Royal College of Midwives 1988), and strategies to improve recruitment and retention of staff are currently the focus of much attention. Midwives have had greater control over the training curriculum since the Central Council and National Boards replaced the

Central Midwives' Board, but the extent to which the profession feels that this change of statutory framework has been entirely beneficial has yet to be evaluated. At the time of writing, management structures in the Health Service, and their effect on the provision of an integrated midwifery service, are still a cause for concern. All in all, the profession faces as many challenges in the future as it did when the first Midwives' Act was passed in 1902.

References

Association of Radical Midwives, 1986, *The Vision: Proposals for the Future of the Maternity Services* (Ormskirk, Association of Radical Midwives).

Bailey, R. D., 1976, 'A Short History of Midwifery', in *A Textbook for Midwives*, 9th edn. (London, Tindall).

Baly, M. E., 1987, *A History of the Queen's Nursing Institute: 100 Years 1887–1987*. (London and Sydney, Croom Helm).

Barnett, Z., 1979, 'The Changing Pattern of Maternity Care and the Future Role of the Midwife', *Midwives' Chronicle and Nursing Notes*, 92/1102, pp. 381–4.

Bent, E. A., 1982, 'The Growth and Development of Midwifery', in Allan, P. and Jolley, M. (eds.), *Nursing Midwifery and Health Visiting since 1900* (London, Faber and Faber).

Brain, M., 1979, 'Observations by a Midwife', in *Report of a Day Conference on the Reduction of Perinatal Mortality and Morbidity* (Children's Committee and Department of Health and Social Security; London, HMSO).

Briggs, A., 1972, *Report of the Committee on Nursing* (Cmnd 5115; London, HMSO).

Butler, N. R. and Bonham, D. G., 1963, *Perinatal Mortality* (Edinburgh, Churchill Livingstone).

Cameron, J., 1985, 'Midwifery in the Real World', *Nursing Mirror* 161/16, pp. 42–4.

Campbell, J. M., 1923, *The Training of Midwives* (Ministry of Health Reports on Public Health and Medical Subjects, 21; London, HMSO)

—— 1924, *Maternal Mortality* (Ministry of Health Reports on Public Health and Medical Subjects, 25; London, HMSO).

—— 1927, *The Protection of Motherhood* (Ministry of Health Reports on Public Health and Medical Subjects, 48; London, HMSO).

Central Midwives' Board, Annual Reports for 1916, 1949, 1957, 1963, 1964, 1979, 1980.

—— 1977, Letter to Midwifery Training Schools and Regional and Area Nursing Officers regarding the decision to extend the 12-month training to 18 months.

Central Midwives' Board for Scotland, Northern Ireland Council for Nurses and Midwives, An Bord Altranais, Central Midwives' Board 1983, *The Role of the Midwife* (Suffolk, Hymns Ancient and Modern Ltd.).

Chalmers, I., 1978, 'Implications of the Current Debate on Obstetric Practice', in Kitzinger, S. and Davis, J. (eds.), *The Place of Birth* (Oxford, Oxford University Press).

—— and Richards, M., 1977, 'Intervention and Causal Inference in Obstetric Practice', in Chard, T. and Richards, M. (eds.), *Benefits and Hazards of the New Obstetrics* (London and Philadelphia, Spastics International Medical Publications).

Chamberlain, G., Phillipp, E., Howlett, B., and Master, K., 1978, *British Births 1970*, ii. *Obstetric Care* (London, Heinemann).

Collins, M., 1986, 'Care for Families following Still-Birth and First Week Deaths', *Midwives Chronicle*, 99/1176, Supplement pp. xiii–xv.

Cowell, B. and Wainwright, D., 1981, *Behind the Blue Door: The History of the Royal College of Midwives, 1881–1981* (London, Tindall).

Curran, V., 1986, 'Taking Midwifery off the Conveyor Belt', *Nursing Times*, 20 Aug. 1986, pp. 42–3.

Davies, J. and Evans, F., 1986, 'Evaluating an Inner City Community Care Project', in Robinson, S. and Thomson, A. (eds.), *Research and the Midwife Conference Proceedings 1986* (University of London, King's College).

Department of Health and Social Security, 1970, *Report of the Sub-Committee on Domiciliary and Maternity Bed Needs* (London, HMSO).

—— 1984, *Study of Hospital Based Midwives: A Report by Central Management Services* (London, DHSS).

—— 1984, *Health Service Management: Implementation of the NHS Management Inquiry Report* (HC (84) 13; London, DHSS).

——, Scottish Home and Health Department, and Welsh Office, 1969, *Report of the Working Party on Management Structure in the Local Authority Nursing Services* (London, Edinburgh, and Cardiff, HMSO).

Donnison, J., 1977, *Midwives and Medical Men: A History of Interprofessional Rivalries and Women's Rights* (London, Heinemann).

Elbourne, D., Oakley, A., and Chalmers, I., 1989, 'Social and Psychological Support During Pregnancy', in Chalmers I., Enkin, M., and Keirse, M. (eds.), *Effective Care in Pregnancy and Childbirth* (Oxford, Oxford University Press).

Flint, C., 1979, 'A Continuing Labour of Love', *Nursing Mirror*, 15 Nov. 1979, pp. 16–18.

—— 1982, 'Antenatal Clinics', *Nursing Mirror*, 24 Nov., 1, 8, 15, and 22 Dec. 1982, and 5, 12, 19, and 28 Jan. 1983.

—— 1984, 'A Mother's Birthright', *Nursing Times*, 22 Feb. 1984, pp. 18–19.

—— 1985, 'Three Steps Forward', *Nursing Times*, 11 Sept. 1985, p. 23.

—— and Poulengeris, P., 1987, *The 'Know your Midwife' Report*

(Published by C. Flint, 49 Peckarmans Wood, Sydenham Hill, London SE26).

Garcia, J., Garforth, S., and Ayers, S., 1985, 'Midwives Confined? Labour Ward Policies and Routines', in Thomson, A., and Robinson, S. (eds.), *Research and the Midwife Conference Proceedings 1985* (University of London, King's College).

Gilligan, M., 1980, 'The Midwife's Contribution to Counselling Parents who have Suffered a Perinatal Death', in Robinson, S. (ed.), *Research and the Midwife Conference Proceedings 1979 and 1980* (University of London, Chelsea College).

Goodley, S., 1986, 'Family Care and the Pre-Term Baby', *Midwives' Chronicle*, 99/1176, Supplement pp. viii–x.

Government Statistical Service, 1980, *1973–76 Hospital In-Patient Enquiry: Maternity Tables* (MB4, no. 8; London, HMSO).

Henderson, C., 1985, 'Response to the Third MSAC Report', *Midwives' Chronicle*, 98/1169, p. 162.

Honigsbaum, F., 1979, *The Division in British Medicine* (London, Kogan Page).

Hughes, P., 1986, 'Neonatal Community Liaison Visiting', *Midwives' Chronicle*, 99/1176, Supplement pp. xi–xii.

Kilvington, J., 1985, 'Response to the Third MSAC Report', *Midwives' Chronicle*, 98/1169, p. 162.

Lewis, J., 1980, *The Politics of Motherhood* (London, Croom Helm, and Montreal, McGill-Queen's University Press).

Maternity Services Advisory Committee, 1982, *Maternity Care in Action*, i. *Antenatal Care* (London, HMSO).

—— 1984, *Maternity Care in Action*, ii. *Care during Childbirth* (London, HMSO).

—— 1985, *Maternity Care in Action*, iii. *Care of the Mother and Baby* (London, HMSO).

Ministry of Health, 1929, *Report of the Departmental Committee on the Training and Employment of Midwives* (London, HMSO).

—— 1930, *Interim Report of the Departmental Committee on Maternal Mortality and Morbidity* (London, HMSO).

—— 1937, *Report on an Investigation into Maternal Mortality* (London, HMSO).

—— 1959, *Report of the Maternity Services Committee* (London, HMSO).

—— 1962, *A Hospital Plan for England and Wales* (Cmnd. 1604; London, HMSO).

—— and Scottish Home and Health Department, *Report of the Committee on Senior Nursing Staff Structure* (London, HMSO, 1966).

—— Department of Health for Scotland, Ministry of Labour and National Service, 1949, *Report of the Working Party on Midwives* (London, HMSO).

Morrin, H., 1982, 'Are we in Danger of Extinction?', *Midwives' Chronicle*, 95/1128, p. 17.

Mulkerrins, M. and Gunn, P., 1985, 'The Visiting Midwives' Participation in a Confidential Enquiry into Perinatal Death Conducted by the North West Thames Regional Health Authority', in Thomson, A. and Robinson, S. (eds.), *Research and the Midwife Conference Proceedings 1985* (University of London, King's College).

Oakley, A., 1984, *The Captured Womb* (Oxford, Blackwell).

Penny, Y., 1986, 'Modern Prenatal Management: Pattern of Care for the Future', *Midwives' Chronicle*, 99/1126, Supplement pp. ii–iii.

Percival, R. C., 1970, 'Management of Normal Labour', *The Practitioner*, 1221/204 (Mar. 1970).

Peretz, L., forthcoming, 'Regional Variation in Maternal and Child Welfare between the Wars: Merthyr Tydfil, Oxfordshire and Tottenham', in Swan, P. (ed.), *Essays in Regional History* (Hull, Hutton Press).

Radford, N. and Thomson, A., 1988, *Direct Entry: A Preparation for Practice* (University of Surrey).

Rider, A., 1983, 'Report on Dettol Sword Award', *Midwives Chronicle*, 96/1444, p. 165.

—— 1985, 'Midwifery after Birth', *Nursing Times*, 7 Aug. 1985, pp. 27–8.

Robinson, S., 1980, 'Are there Enough Midwives?', *Nursing Times*, 24 Apr. 1980, pp. 726–30.

—— 1985a, 'Caring for Childbearing Women: Some Factors Restricting the Midwife's Contribution', *Nursing Times*, 81/2, pp. 28–31.

—— 1985b, 'Midwives, Obstetricians and General Practitioners: The Need for Role Clarification', *Midwifery*, 1/2, pp. 102–13.

—— 1985c, 'Responsibilities of Midwives and Medical Staff: Findings from a National Survey', *Midwives' Chronicle*, 98/1166, pp. 52–3.

—— 1989, 'The Role of the Midwife: Opportunities and Constraints', in Chalmers, I., Enkin, M., and Keirse, M., (eds.), *Effective Care in Pregnancy and Childbirth* (Oxford, Oxford University Press).

—— Golden, J., and Bradley, S., 1983, *A Study of the Role and Responsibilities of the Midwife* (NERU Report, 1; University of London, King's College).

Royal College of Midwives, 1964, *Statement of Policy on the Maternity Services* (London, Royal College of Midwives).

—— 1977, *Evidence to the Royal Commission on the National Health Service* (London, Royal College of Midwives).

—— 1986, *Comments by the Royal College of Midwives on UKCC Project 2000: A New Preparation for Practice* (London, Royal College of Midwives).

—— 1980, *Comments by the Royal College of Midwives on UKCC Project 2000: A New Preparation for Practice* (London, Royal College of Midwives).

—— 1987, *The Role and Education of the Future Midwife in the United Kingdom* (London, Royal College of Midwives).

—— 1988, 'Evidence to the Review Body for Nursing Staff, Midwives, Health Visitors and Professions Allied to Medicine for 1988', *Midwives' Chronicle*, 101/1200.

—— and Health Visitors' Association, 1982, Statement on Antenatal Care.

Royal College of Obstetricians and Gynaecologists, 1944, Report on a National Maternity Service.

—— and Royal College of General Practitioners, 1981, Report on Training for Obstetrics and Gynaecology for General Practitioners.

Social Services Committee, House of Commons, 1980, *Report on Perinatal and Neonatal Mortality* (London, HMSO).

Stewart, A., 1981, 'The Present State of Midwifery Training', *Midwife, Health Visitor and Community Nurse*, 17/7, pp. 270–2.

Stuart, B. and Judge, E., 1984, 'The Return of the Midwife?', *Midwives' Chronicle*, 97/1152, pp. 8–9.

Thompson, J. B., 1986, 'Safety and Effectiveness of Nurse-Midwifery Care: Research Review in Nurse-Midwifery in America', in Rooks, H. P. and Haas, J. E. (eds.), *A Report of the American College of Nurse Midwives' Foundation* (Washington).

Thomson, A., 1980, 'Planned or Unplanned? Are Midwives Ready for the 1980s?', *Midwives' Chronicle*, 93/1106, pp. 68–72.

—— and Robinson, S., 1985, 'Dissemination of Midwifery research: How this has been facilitated in the UK', *Midwifery*, 1/1, pp. 52–3.

Towler, J., 1981, 'Out of the ordinary: Park Hospital Maternity Unit', *Nursing Mirror*, 152/11.

—— and Bramall, J., 1986, *The Midwife in History and Society* (London, Sydney, Dover and New Hampshire, Croom Helm).

United Kingdom Central Council for Nursing, Midwifery and Health Visiting, 1986, *Project 2000: A New Preparation for Practice* (London, UKCC).

Walker, A. L., 1954, 'Midwife Services', in Munro Kerr, J. M., Johnstone, R. W., and Philipps, M. H. (eds.), *Historical Review of British Obstetrics and Gynaecology 1800–1950* (Edinburgh and London, Livingstone).

Walker, J., 1985, 'Meeting Midwives Midway', *Nursing Times*, 81/43, pp. 48–50.

Wood, A., 1963, 'The Development of the Midwifery Service in Great Britain', *International Journal of Nursing Studies*, 1, pp. 51–8.

5

Strategies of the Early Childbirth Movement: A Case-Study of the National Childbirth Trust

Jenny Kitzinger

THE National Childbirth Trust (NCT) was set up in 1956 under the name of the *Natural* Childbirth Association (NCA) (Williams 1968). Prunella Briance, the founder, formed the organization to promote the ideas of one particular British doctor—Grantly Dick Read (Briance 1965)—and started by placing an advertisement in *The Times* inviting people to attend a meeting about his work. About a hundred people turned up to that first event, and a small, London-based group of women continued to meet monthly over the next two years. They co-ordinated publicity about Dick Read's teachings, regularly showed his film *Childbirth without Fear*, and tried to collate a list of doctors prepared to help women have natural childbirth. Their aim was to encourage women to approach labour free from ignorance and fear.

At first the group was financed by donations and hand-to-mouth fund-raising such as selling milk-bottle tops and hiring out baby-walking pens (*Newsletter* 4 (Summer 1958)). But by 1959 it had office premises, had set up an official committee, and had obtained charitable status (thereby becoming a 'Trust' rather than an 'Association'). It also began to shift away from Dick Read's philosophy towards Lamaze's theory of prepared childbirth. Area organizers co-ordinated a dozen local branches around the country. There was a total

I would like to thank everyone who spoke to me about the early days of the NCT, and also the staff at NCT headquarters for their patience in allowing me to sift through the Trust's archives. Thank you also to the Contemporary Medical Archives Centre at the Wellcome Institute for the History of Medicine.

membership of about 500 and an income of just under £1,000, most of which was spent on hiring halls, and printing and postage costs. By this point the Trust was producing its own information sheets and leaflets about breathing and relaxation, trying to educate both pregnant women and professionals about a 'natural' or 'prepared' approach to birth.

In the 1960s, with the rise of consumer and anti-establishment action in many areas of British life, and an increasing concern for the individual's right to control her or his own health, the organization was able to grow and expand. The NCT had by now dropped the word 'Natural' from its title and was called by the name it has today, The National Childbirth Trust (NCT). By 1968 its income had risen to about £12,000 per year, most of which came from membership subscriptions and fees paid to NCT teachers for ante-natal classes. Many NCT members, especially those already qualified in midwifery and physiotherapy, were by this time trained in ante-natal teaching and formed a private ante-natal teaching structure independent from the National Health Service. The teachers did not make money out of their work, however; they claimed expenses and donated the fees to the Trust. The Trust had also begun to promote breast-feeding, and had launched its own magazine, *New Generation.*

By 1986 the national membership had risen to 40,000, and with the help of a grant from the Department of Health and Social Security (DHSS), the Trust now employs sixteen salaried staff. There are 320 branches all over Britain, from the Shetlands to the Channel Islands, and there are many different subgroups within the Trust, ranging from the Teacher's Panel to the Postnatal Support Committee (which was formally established in 1979).

My research, conducted in 1986, drew on the Trust's papers and correspondence as well as on discussions with some of the women involved in the founding group. My aim was not so much to evaluate the different approaches to childbirth, as to look at the ways in which these had been adapted and promoted by one particular childbirth organization, albeit by far the largest in Britain. In this chapter I intend briefly to introduce the two theories that have had most influence on the

NCT: those of Dick Read and Lamaze. After looking closely at the strategies of the early NCT, I will explore the ways in which these strategies influenced the NCT's portrayal of both professionals and women in labour. I will conclude with a brief discussion of the NCT's current development.

Origins of the National Childbirth Trust

Dick Read argued that childbirth was not meant to be painful, but that the pain experienced by 'civilized' women was a consequence of their fear. If this fear could be replaced with knowledge and understanding, then, he argued, most healthy women could have pain-free, and drug-free, labours. Ever since his first books were published in the 1930s (Dick Read 1933), individual women all over the world had tried out his approach and thousands wrote to thank him for the birth experience that he had made possible for them. However, Dick Read's ideas were not popular among his obstetric or midwifery colleagues, and they were largely neglected in this country until the establishment of the NCT (Noyles Thomas 1957).

For the first year the Association was run by women with a high degree of commitment to, and belief in, Dick Read's principles. One of their visions was to set up a Dick Read College to train health professionals in his methods. In such a college, Briance (1956) wrote: 'this work can be given to the world in its perfect form, none of the present-day half measures will do masquerading under the name of natural childbirth' (*Newsletter* 1 (Sept. 1956)).

However, Briance's views of the NCT's objectives were very different from those of the committee that eventually became responsible for running the NCT. Unconvinced that Dick Read offered the only correct method of natural childbirth, the committee preferred to develop another approach. While Briance was away in America the constitution was changed to exclude all mention of Dick Read, and by 1960 the Trust was deeply committed to Lamaze's theory of 'prepared' childbirth (Minutes of the AGM 20 Nov. 1958; Committee minutes 22 Sept. 1960). Lamaze's teaching was based on Pavlov's work on conditioning—the theory presupposed that birth was inherently painful, but that women could be trained, with the help of breathing techniques, to distract themselves from the pain. It was a method easily learned and taught and more adaptive to the rising rate of hospital delivery than Dick Read's philosophy.

This shifting allegiance led to bitter conflict between some members of the committee and officials of the NCT. Dick Read, who was the honorary president, saw the adoption of Lamaze as a betrayal. Both the Lamaze technique, and the Russian method of so-called 'natural' childbirth from which it originated, were, he argued, 'materialistic and mechanistic . . . the miracle of reproduction is distorted [by these techniques] to become a means of demonstrating the absence of God and the Omnipotence of the Communist leaders' (quoted in Briance 1963). Briance was no happier with the turn of events. She wrote to the Charity Commission suggesting that the NCT's funds ought to be returned because the money was no longer being used for the purposes for which it had been collected, and she asked the NCT to stop using the emblem that until then had represented their work (Briance 1986a).

The developments within the NCT that resulted in this transfer of loyalties from Dick Read to Lamaze were mirrored in other childbirth organizations during this time. Several medical sociologists have written about the relative merits of these competing theories of childbirth. Some, such as Lumley and Astbury (1980) argue that Dick Read's theory mystifies childbirth and blames women for their own pain. Others, such as Katz Rothman (1982), describe Lamaze as a 'cooption' of natural childbirth. Here, however, I want to look at the developments within the movement not just in terms of the qualities of the various 'natural' or 'prepared' childbirth theories, but also in terms of the strategies adopted by the childbirth organizations (in this case by the NCT) to try to promote natural childbirth generally. Childbirth activists were not just passive relayers of theory, but were active consumers and interpreters of both the Dick Read and Lamaze approach to labour. The NCT chose to emphasize some aspects of the original theories over others as part of a wider strategy.

The Socio-Medical Context

To understand the strategies adopted by the NCA, it is necessary to understand the social context in which it developed. The NCA originated as a middle-class organization based in the South of England. Although about a third of births took place at home, childbirth was, for many people, shrouded in ignorance and secrecy. Labour was seen as something to be got over for the sake of the end-product—the baby. It had no value as an experience in itself, indeed, it was best forgotten as quickly as possible. The whole event was often portrayed as an undignified, if not disgusting, ordeal that should be kept private from the world at large. Public discussion of childbirth was taboo.

Childbirth: A Private, Undignified, and Disgusting Spectacle

It was in 1957 (just after the NCA had been formally inaugurated) that a scene of a woman actually giving birth was first shown on television. This screening was preceded by a warning to the public, but, in spite of this, there were still some shocked reactions. 'Revolting, beyond the pale', 'tasteless', declared the *Daily Sketch* (5 Feb. 1957): 'They showed us a baby being born in all its stark and primitive detail.'

This type of attitude persisted well into the mid-1960s. When a photograph of a woman giving birth was printed in the *Sun* on 4 February 1965, readers wrote in expressing various degrees of disgust. One woman said: 'My reactions were shock and anger that such a picture should be flaunted in a daily newspaper for all and sundry to see.' Another added: 'Such a picture should be published in a journal for the training of doctors and midwives and not for people to gloat over'; while a third woman concluded her letter with the demand to know 'How many men were put off their breakfast?' Such reactions were not exclusive to readers of the *Sun*; when *Nova*, a glossy and 'socially aware' women's magazine, printed a similar photo, readers wrote in describing it as 'distasteful', 'vulgar', 'gruesome', and 'disgusting', (*Nova* Dec. 1965).

Childbirth was seen as primitive, animalistic (*Sunday Pictorial* 11 Nov. 1956), and, by association with other natural functions such as defecation and sex, degrading. 'Nice' middle-class women sought medical attendance to sanitize the event; medical control and interventions were part of the ritual purification and segregation of a rather sordid biological function. The Association's discussions of childbirth and its invitation to women's male partners to view slide-shows about labour exposed it to accusations of obscenity and 'exhibitionism' (*Sunday Express* 6 Jan. 1957), not to mention the threat of legal action by a man who claimed that the slides had made him impotent (Rankin 1986*b*). The Association's birth films were tainted with the stigma of pornography, and some people would not admit to having seen one because they were perceived as 'dirty' (Micklethwait 1986). Given this context, it is perhaps not surprising that, as an early NCT teacher told me (Micklethwait 1986): 'You were discreet, you kept quiet about what you were doing in the NCT.'

The concept of childbirth as private, if not shameful, acted as a powerful sanction against public–political discussion. Medical and midwifery journals were the only fit place for the portrayal of childbirth, and doctors' and midwives' views were the only ones which counted as legitimate. The professionals were thus able to maintain a monopoly over the definition—and, therefore, the management—of childbirth.

The medical monopoly had, ironically, been reinforced by women's demands for proper medical consideration for female maladies, and criticisms of the continued high maternal mortality rates (see Lewis, Chapter 1). For years women had been struggling to have the pain and dangers of childbirth recognized, and campaigning for the labouring woman's right to a hospital bed and effective pain-relief. The NCA's stand for a woman's right *not* to have pain-relieving drugs was viewed with suspicion. The introduction, during the first half of the twentieth century, of effective pain-relief in childbirth was represented as the triumph of rationality over religious bigotry (Claye 1939), and during the 1940s and 1950s doctors and midwives were roundly criticized for their failure to allow women sufficient pain-relieving drugs. They were accused of having a 'callous attitude to distress', and taking 'an almost sadistic joy in withholding sedatives from mothers in labour' (*British Medical Journal* [*BMJ*] 12 May 1945). 'A lazy acceptance of the curse of Eve' was said to 'blind them to the sufferings of women in labour' (*BMJ* 9 June 1945). Professional and lay people alike condemned the lack of proper training and resources for the relief of women's pain: 'How are we going to explain away this indifference and neglect of the suffering of their young wives to our returning soldiers, sailors and airmen?' (Letter to the *BMJ* 7 Apr. 1945.) The Health Service was urged to ensure that every woman could have access to drugs in childbirth, as this was seen as the only way to halt the falling birth-rate in post-war Britain (*BMJ* 26 May 1945). In contrast to the NCA, one of the early demands of the Society for the Prevention of Cruelty to Pregnant Women, soon to be renamed the Association for Improvements in the Maternity Services (AIMS), was a national epidural service. AIMS donated a gas-and-air machine to one hospital.

The NCA faced an awesome challenge. To mount *any* kind of lay campaign about childbirth they had to challenge the taboo and bring childbirth back into the public–political arena. To promote 'natural' (or 'prepared') childbirth they had to try to undermine the powerful association of birth with unbearable pain, and rid it of its negative animalistic connotations. Contrary to the contemporary framing of the debate, they had to assert that an anti-drugs stand did not necessarily entail a pro-pain and old-fashioned anti-woman complacency. Dick Read himself had been reported to the General Medical Council for advocating 'cruelty to women' (Noyles Thomas 1957: 113). In addition, women and their medical attendants had to be encouraged to value being 'awake and aware' for birth, and they had to be convinced that childbirth could be an experience *in itself*, not just a means to an end. The NCA was faced with no less a task than the reconstruction of the meaning of birth.

Strategies: Packaging the Message and Choosing the Audience

The NCA had little direct access to conventional power, but it tried to establish itself as an organization with influence by drawing on the commitment and hard work of its supporters, and by trying to associate natural childbirth with more orthodox values. Under the direct guidance of Dick Read and Briance, the NCA initially associated innovative theories of natural birth with such values as improving the race, reinforcing motherhood and family life, and re-establishing the Empire. Both Briance and Dick Read made direct appeals to Britain as 'the mother country' to lead the world by adopting a more enlightened approach to birth (*Newsletter* 2 (Mar. 1957)). The NCA, like many other reform movements of the time, also explicitly promised that their campaign had eugenic implications. As Briance wrote (*Newsletter* 2 (Mar. 1957)): 'Babies born this way are better babies . . . and we urgently need in Britain a race of good quality men and women.' The Association exploited the post-war concern with the quantity and quality of the British population. It promoted motherhood as woman's ultimate duty and fulfilment, and promised that natural birth contributed towards family harmony and therefore reinforced the foundations of society.

Popes and Ladies

At the same time the NCA associated natural birth with good old-fashioned religious morality. Dick Read himself saw childbirth and motherhood as spiritually uplifting experiences, and drew on the Bible to back up his case. The early NCA literature reflected this emphasis and declared that the Pope had given his approval to Dick Read's approach (Publicity leaflet *c.*1958). The group also tried to cloak natural childbirth in the respectability of high society (a tactic that was to persist into the late 1960s). Several titled ladies were involved as committee members or patrons; a glance at the 1967–8 annual report, for instance, shows that there was only one untitled vice-president—the others were either baronesses, viscountesses, dames, ladies, bishops, knights, or lords (Annual Report in *New Generation* July 1968). The gentry were encouraged to discuss their own experiences and thus make it an acceptable or even fashionable thing to do. When Viscountess Enfield opened the group's new premises in 1964, one disapproving journalist said that she 'treated her audience to a blow by blow account' of her own labour (*Daily Mail* 5 Dec. 1964), and the organization even managed to involve Princess Grace. This 'gentrification of natural childbirth' was pursued in the hope, presumably, that what Queen Victoria could do for chloroform, several ladies and one princess could do for drug-free childbirth.

By the 1960s, however, the NCA (now the NCT) was beginning to formulate the major strategy that was to dominate it for the next decade. This was *not* the attempt to associate natural childbirth with old imperial or eugenic values, or to court the patronage of high society or popes. Instead the Trust focused its attention on wooing doctors and midwives. The 1960s saw its concerted attempt to obtain the blessing of health professionals. It is this central strategy, occupying perhaps the most formative period of the Trust's history, that I will concentrate on for the rest of this chapter.

Wooing the Professionals

During the early years the NCA had not been known for its tact towards the medical profession. Papers from the 1950s accuse doctors of damaging babies by unnecessary interventions, and call explicitly for a radical change of approach to childbirth (Briance 1956; *Newsletter* 2 (Mar. 1957)). However, once the committee had established itself, things began to change and the NCT adopted a more conciliatory approach. As a founder-member wrote: 'The realisation of the importance of working with (and therefore gaining the trust of) midwives, physiotherapists and doctors was one of the most important turning points in our history.' (Williams, 1968.) By 1961 the Trust had appointed an obstetrician as its chairperson, and he affirmed this position in his AGM address: 'The aim must be to secure the active interest of professionals in the Trust's ideals. Any step which antagonises them . . . will be a step backwards.' He went on to remind members who may have chafed under such restrictions that 'the Trust is a young and fast-growing body and, just as with an exuberantly growing plant, a little judicious pruning back may sometimes be advisable' (Perchard 1961). The NCT was consciously trying to change its image and to persuade 'many who had been offended and alarmed by our early didactic approach to re-assess the "new us"' (Williams 1968).

It was because of the medical scorn that had been poured on the word 'Natural' in their original title that in 1961 the NCT changed its name to the *National Childbirth Trust* (Minutes of the Area Organizers' meeting 3 May 1960; Briance 1986*b*). However, this still left many—doctors and lay people alike—unconvinced: 'It takes more than knocking the word "natural" out of the title to clear out the cranks inevitably attracted by the word—and a pregnant crank is an awesome thing.' (*Observer Weekend* review 5 Dec. 1965.)

Surrounded by people ready to label them fanatics, extremists, and 'cranky old girls with queer ideas' (Enfield 1964), the NCT committees were, not surprisingly, very protective of the Trust's image. They tried to preserve it from association with anything too extreme or threatening. Looking through the papers in the NCT archives, it is fascinating to see the way in which the same information would be drafted and redrafted as committee members debated which refinement would be most acceptable to health professionals, or at least would incite the least antagonism.

An early draft of a card which the NCT designed for women to take into hospital provides a space for the woman's name, followed by the words 'has prepared herself for, and is hoping to achieve, a natural birth. We know she can rely on your help and co-operation'. Some Trust members were completely opposed to these cards on the grounds that they would alienate hospital staff, but eventually an acceptable wording was achieved. The final version has been altered to 'has been preparing for a natural birth. We hope you will give her the help and encouragement she will need'. The NCT no longer presumes to 'know' that the staff will help, nor do they ask staff to 'co-operate' with patients. Instead the emphasis is on the woman's dependence on the staff's help, the tone is softer— more of an appeal than a demand—and even the typeface, which had originally been in block capitals, has been changed to less aggressive lower case lettering.

Lay Teachers

The Teacher

Perhaps the most challenging area of the NCT's work was the establishment of a lay teaching network. The original ante-natal teachers were all health professionals, and the involvement of lay teachers was intended to be a stop-gap measure until such time as professional ante-natal teachers within the NHS had been trained (Williams 1968). However, the profession failed to respond to the invitation to train in natural childbirth, and lay teachers soon became a leading feature of the NCT (Williams 1968). This alternative lay teaching structure could have presented a major threat to the professionals, and the Trust was twice investigated by the Ethical Committee of the British Medical Association ('though each time we were given encouragement to keep on going—quietly' (Rankin 1986a)).

It was precisely because some professionals found the establishment of a lay teaching network so threatening—it challenged their monopoly over the official definition of birth—that it involved some of the most delicate negotiations and detailed image-management. The Trust was very careful to present its teachers in ways which would mollify the opposition. Firstly, the organization accepted doctors' rights to control 'their' patients' access to NCT classes, and teachers had to obtain the written permission of every woman's doctor before they could offer any ante-natal instruction (*Newsletter* 10 (July 1962)). Secondly, the NCT emphasized that lay teachers were filling a gap in the National Health Service, acting as 'unpaid medical ancillaries', and not competing with the professional staff at all (Memorandum to BMA Working Group *c.*1966). Thirdly, the Trust explicitly paid homage to the status of the professionals, and lay teachers were correspondingly devalued. Although the Trust quickly realized the benefit of having non-professional teachers (Annual Report in *New Generation* July 1968), their role was carefully played down at first—they were 'just mothers', women who would chat to a pregnant woman over a friendly cup of tea,

Conduct of antenatal classes

For those running "authentic Dick Read classes" the following instructions are issued by Mrs. Dick Read who is running the model class for our association. They must be carried out if the mention of this method is made.

1. The dignity of the conduct of classes must be maintained. Teachers should be neither familiar nor in any way bossy. Quiet companionship is the keynote.

2. In this teaching the classes have always been run strictly on the harem fashion, no men have a place there. If there are interested doctors they should be invited to attend after the relaxation and exercises but only on invitation in order to answer questions, or at the lectures for labour. The reason for this rule is that there are many women who, in the presence of a man, find themselves unable to maintain a natural state of relaxation and then the atmosphere of the class loses its benefit. Also for religious reasons women dislike being seen partly dressed by strange men whether they are medically qualified or not.

3. There should be no smoking during class because we must maintain an air of efficiency and scrupulous cleanliness—we are teaching women hygiene and how to breathe well and smoking is not in keeping with healthy pregnancy also it is obnoxious to some people especially when they are pregnant.

4. Teachers of this method should bear in mind that there should always be great respect for the placenta and also remember that childbirth is considered a Divine thing deserving nothing but greatest seriousness. Bantering and talking are deplored during class. Remember that the women are rehearsing for labour and that whispered conversations, chattering and laughter are not conducive to a state of physical and mental relaxation.

5. You who are teaching this method are in the position of diplomats in it, for people from other countries will, directly you consider that your class and atmosphere is right, be sent on a tour of instruction. Therefore it is extremely important that high standards are maintained because remember just because this method is not recognised by those in control in England does not mean that other countries have not the greatest respect for it. Therefore until our college is founded the burden of demonstration will fall on you.

6. Teachers should always see that the class room is in impeccable condition and that their clothes are neat and attractive for our aim is to teach women that pregnancy is a time of added beauty and attraction.

FIG. 5.1 Notice to NCT Area Organizers, 1957.

lending the ear that the busy professional had no time
to provide (*New Generation* editorial, July 1968; Williams
1968).[1]

It is significant that these women were sometimes referred
to as 'hostesses' rather than as teachers (Mansfield 1977), but
none the less they were very carefully screened. They were
encouraged to represent the NCT in a clean and respectable
home, and they were not allowed to use the Trust as a vehicle
for spreading other unorthodox views (e.g. about religion, the
family, CND, or vegetarianism). Figure 5.1 reproduces a
notice that was sent out to Area Organizers in 1957 about the
conduct of classes. The Trust was particularly wary of the
discrediting power of the 'old wives' tale' label. The teachers
presented themselves as committed to eradicating 'mis-
conceptions' about childbirth, and allied themselves with
those who characterized such tales as ignorant, distorted, and
exaggerated horror stories. From the very beginning, of
course, the Trust had been rooted in a virulently anti-old-
wives'-tales philosophy. Dick Read saw the 'exaggerated
stories of suffering' passed from woman to woman as the chief
cause of labour pain, and wished to see severe sanctions
enforced against women who 'gossiped' about birth: 'In many
tribes there is an excellent rule which I wish we could enforce
amongst European women . . . If the childbirth is difficult and
it is known that some unauthorized woman has mentioned
childbirth to the mother then the offender is subject to severe
punishment, even to being thrown out of the Kraal to wander
in the jungle amongst the beasts.' (Quoted in *Parents* July
1954.)

Such hostility to women's 'unauthorized' birth stories was
shared by most doctors and midwives of the time and is still in
evidence today, as is shown by the reference in a well-known
childbirth handbook to 'wicked women with their malicious,

---

[1] It was in this context of veneration for professionalism that one leading NCT
spokeswoman was discovered falsely to have laid claim to midwifery credentials.
Although unqualified, she was not only a NCT teacher-trainer but had also written a
book claiming to be a midwife. The exposé almost led to the downfall of the NCT, as
it confirmed all their enemies' accusations that Trust teachers were a bunch of
quacks. Fortunately, by this time (the late 1960s) the NCT had begun to applaud lay
teachers in their own right, and was able to survive the storm (*Bulletin for Trust
Helpers*, 13 July 1968).

lying tongues' (Bourne 1975: 27). The NCT, however, managed to escape most such accusations, and it is noteworthy that the spate of newspaper headlines about old wives' tales in the mid-1960s all referred to pro-NCT articles (e.g. *Cambridge News* 21 Mar. 1965; *Chester Chronicle* 18 Apr. 1965). Many childbirth activists today would reject such an approach to their work, seeing the caricature of old wives' tales as a punitive label used to silence and control women's versions of reality. The early NCT chose to ally itself with the forces of 'truth', 'education', and 'science', publicly joining in the condemnation of women's unsupervised 'gossip' about birth. However, regardless of its public image, the NCT was in fact encouraging women to speak out about their experiences of childbirth, and, in the process, was legitimizing and politicizing another area of women's lives.

The Image of the Doctor

The NCT of the 1960s also tried to defuse antagonism by committing its lay teachers to respecting the status of the professionals. The Trust reinforced the idea that, basically, the 'doctor knows best' and that the professionals should be ultimately responsible for, and in control over, any particular labour. There was at this point no discussion of the midwife's role as distinct from the doctor's. It was doctors who were the main focus of the Trust's campaign. Far from explicitly challenging medical power (power over women as midwives or as women in labour), the NCT appealed to doctors' paternalism, asking them to be more indulgent of women at a time of particular vulnerability. The Trust made great play of the idea that pregnant women were hypersensitive, and doctors were encouraged to have 'especial regard to the susceptibilities of the minds of pregnant and parturient women' (Resolution to the National Council of Women, recorded in NCT Committee Minutes 2 Mar. 1960). Thus, the NCT's campaign for the more humane treatment of women drew on and reinforced mainstream values of male chivalry, doctors' paternalism, and female weakness.

Reinforcing the Image of the Feminine Woman and the Ideal Patient

The image of the ideal woman implicit in much of the NCT committee's statements in the 1960s draws on a very conventional image of femininity. NCT teachers were supposed to encourage women to exercise charm and 'feminine appeal', to act, like the organization as a whole, with tact and subtlety. The NCT also explicitly promoted a very conventional image of 'patienthood'. NCT teachers were told actively to reinforce women's faith in, and compliance with, the professionals (Perchard 1962). During training weekends, teachers were reminded that they should encourage women to 'obey' staff (*New Generation* Oct. 1968), and that 'we should do nothing to sap a woman's confidence in the place where she is to be delivered nor encourage her to discuss the use of drugs with her doctor when she would soon be out of her depth' (*New Generation* Apr. 1968).

The NCT even promised that its classes, far from encouraging distrust, as many doctors and midwives feared, would in fact produce a better-quality patient—more compliant, less hysterical. The NCT argued that the 'prepared' woman would know what was happening and so would not fight it; she would accept rather than be terrified by what the staff were doing to her. The *Newsletters* of the 1960s proudly report staff praise for the obedience of NCT patients, and birth accounts often end with a note about·how the nurses were impressed with the woman's self-control and were pleased with her co-operation (*Newsletter* 10 (July 1962); Enfield 1964; *New Generation* July 1968). Writing in 1965, Jill Tweedie commented on this approach at the time: 'Mrs 1965', she wrote, 'is, in fact, the victim of as false an image of childbirth as was her great grandmother . . . She is expected to breathe in a certain way or let her doctor down. She must be quiet and decorous or the nurses might become nervous. She has to jolly her husband along . . .' (Tweedie 1965).

Politics and Practice: The Concepts Developed by the NCT

The Trust's commitment to wooing the professionals clearly confined the way in which it could portray doctors and midwives, and meant that it had to reinforce a very compliant and feminine image of the pregnant and labouring woman. The strategies adopted in the 1960s also severely restricted the development of 'alternative theoretical approaches to the childbirth issue. These constraints can be highlighted by a closer look at three concepts which are central to the modern childbirth movement: control, choice, and communication.

Control

Dick Read's theory promoted the idea that a woman should *submit* to her uterus and surrender to nature (*Parents* Aug. 1956). The early Trust literature encouraged passivity. As the NCT transferred its loyalties to Lamaze, however, the imagery changed to one of victory over the body rather than surrender to it. According to the Lamaze theory: 'A trained woman has been conditioned to help her labour with controlled activity. This is not a method where the woman . . . passively submits to labour. In this method she learns to control her body.' (Bing and Ramel 1961: 12.) During the Lamaze-dominated era the NCT wished women to develop their self-control: 'Her ability to follow the directions of her midwife and doctor and to maintain control of her own reactions to the sensations of childbirth can enable a mother to give birth with great joy.' (Proctor 1968.) In both, the issue of control is located internally to the woman; the concern is about a woman's control over her own body rather than her control over what other people are doing to it. Whether the NCT was telling women to release control or to take charge, there was little evidence of any concept of the kind of control promoted by many childbirth activists today. Dick Read's idea about the release of conscious control over the body relied on the simultaneous surrender of the woman to her professional attendants: a woman's performance depended upon her having sufficient trust in her midwife and doctor to hand over control to them (*Newsletter* 2 (Summer 1958)). Lamaze's theory offered even less room for the development of the principles of external control. His ante-natal training promised to train the patient to 'react in a precise and orderly manner to uterine stimuli' (Bing and Ramel 1961: 12). In other words, it was supposed to produce well-behaved patients. As Enkins (1986: 155) has commented about the Lamaze theory in America: 'A woman who maintained a fixed if somewhat glazed, cheerful expression and continued her breathing patterns regularly, was said to be "in control" as she was carted from one room to another strapped flat on her back with her legs in the air.'

With the benefit of hindsight, one can see aspects of both men's work that could have been developed into the emphasis on external control that is seen as so important today (in particular, Dick Read's stress on a woman's right to dignity in labour, and on childbirth as a momentous event in itself). However, the NCT did not feel it could risk such an interpretation. The organization had promised to uphold the status of the professionals, and it could not threaten this by promoting ideas about a woman's right to control the staff.

Choice

In the beginning the NCT promoted a particular way of giving birth, it was not *pro*-choice for its own sake (Briance 1986*a*). Indeed, this was one of the reasons for curtailing relations with the newly founded Association for Improvements in the Maternity Services in 1960: '[AIMS promotes the idea that] women should be free to choose whatever way they want to have their babies . . . in the circumstances the committee feels we would not wish to be officially associated with them' (Minutes of Area Organizers' meeting 3 May 1960). However, by the late 1960s and early 1970s the NCT started to express its ideas in terms of a woman's right to choose. Choice has increasingly become a popular and acceptable banner for a wide range of contemporary campaigns, but perhaps this means that it lacks any political meaning and is susceptible to manipulation. Gwen Rankin,

commenting on the rise in the hospitalization and medicalization of birth since the 1950s, suggests:

As ante-natal teachers we have not been blameless . . . We have lost
faith in our original aim of believing in and promoting natural birth
. . . We are very fearful of the risks that commitment may bring; the
failure and recrimination, the opposition of so many—and so
powerful—the dubious morality of promoting ideals on to other
people who don't share, or haven't reached our standpoint. (Rankin
1982.)

The increase in the rhetoric of 'choice' in NCT literature
should be seen in the context of contemporary debates about
the limits of 'choice' as a political concept (Richards 1981)
and about whether the modern NCT really *does* promote
choice (Toynbee 1986). However, the NCT of the 1980s
explicitly espouses the 'right to choose' in a way it never did in
the beginning. In its early years the Trust shared the medical
view that most women did not know what was best for them,
but today a woman's right to make her own decisions is
central to the Trust's campaigns.

Communication

It was a logical consequence of the Trust's 'non-threatening'
stance that it should present the inhumanity of the obstetric
services as the unfortunate side-product of misunderstandings
rather than the consequence of any conflict of interest or
power-imbalance. The Trust worked from the premiss that
the staff would give women what they wanted if only they
knew what this was. The solution was thus seen in terms of
improving communication. From the staff's point of view, this
meant that the answer could lie in making eye-contact with
patients, polishing up their bedside manner, and improving
their 'human relations within obstetrics' (a title originally
used by Norman Morris in 1960 and then picked up and used
for a formal paper by the Ministry of Health) (Morris 1960;
Central Health Services Council 1961). From the individual
woman's point of view, the solution lay in persuading the
doctor or midwife to listen to her with all the charm and tact
she could muster. This focus on the personal relationship
between the woman and her doctor or midwife was, perhaps,

inevitable given that teachers were faced with the practicalities of trying to help individuals to have happy birth experiences. It was also probably a feature of the middle-class bias of the organization. The NCT was trying to be 'nice' and 'respectable' and consistently failed to look at the problem in terms of inequality, whether of class, race, or gender. The communication model, then, suited the organization because it offered a gentle and personal path to reform. However, it was also a model that could easily be turned to the medical profession's advantage. The focus on communication meant that women's resistance to medical control could be explained away either in terms of their inability to understand or in terms of the profession's failure to explain things properly. As a member of AIMS commented: 'They can swallow that one alright—"the poor little woman doesn't understand". What they can't swallow is her saying, "yes doctor I understand completely and, no thank you, I don't want it".' Beech 1986. The 'breakdown of communication' approach obscures the political dimensions of the struggle and it allows the medical profession to negate women's resistance.

To sum up: the NCT of the 1960s presented its focus on the medical profession as both unproblematic and inevitable. However, with the benefit of hindsight one can see that this emphasis on co-operation with the medical profession, whether or not it was *necessary*, was certainly not without compromise. This dominant strategy meant that the NCT drew on, and therefore reinforced, doctors' perceptions of childbirth even while, in other ways, it might have empowered women and challenged the status quo.

The NCT Today and in the Future

Some of the themes described in this paper are still evident in the NCT today. The Trust still relies heavily on the 'communication' model. This model has been adapted to include assertiveness as well as 'charm', but it can still individualize the problem (perhaps inevitably so, given the Trust's commitment to the individual women it teaches). The Trust still courts the respect of the professionals and can still be accused of being white, middle-class dominated, and having too gentle an approach to protest. However, the Trust now champions choice and control in childbirth, and has developed the confidence to challenge the wisdom of many medical treatments. It now sponsors its own research and has campaigned against, for instance, slick and misleading advertising by companies selling epidurals.

It was the increasingly interventionist nature of obstetrics in the 1970s that had the most dramatic effect on the Trust's relationship with the medical profession. With the rise in a whole range of interventions, particularly inductions, the NCT began publicly to challenge the golden rule of 'doctor knows best'. The double-edged influence of the NCT teachers was clearly illustrated during this time. The rank-and-file members of the NCT were keener to enter the induction debate than many of the teachers who had a more directly dependent relationship with obstetricians. The press outrage against induction had been going for some time before the NCT officially went public on the issue. NCT teachers have always represented both an inhibiting and a radicalizing force within the organization.

New dynamics (and conflicts) have also been introduced into the Trust. The rise of feminism, for instance, has increased tensions between members who uphold childbirth as a traditional family event and those who focus on women's control over their own bodies. This split is also about different attitudes to the role of male power in the medical profession. When preparing a press release about the Wendy Savage case in 1986, the NCT Council was divided over whether or not to refer to obstetrics as 'male-dominated'. The phrase was eventually excluded.

It is perhaps those feminist insights combined with the new activism among midwives themselves that has helped to change the NCT's relationship with midwives. Most of the early NCT papers failed to discriminate between doctors and midwives, and in spite of the fact that midwives were responsible for the vast majority of deliveries, little direct reference was made to them as practitioners in their own right. On the one hand, midwives (like all the health professionals) were courted by the NCT, and, on the other hand, they were perceived as heartless, insensitive enemies of the cause. During the 1950s and 1960s midwives were subject to many condescending and sexist accusations by doctors sympathetic to the NCT. In particular, 'post-menopausal spinster' midwives were accused of having 'unresolved conflicts about sex' and frustrated, 'mixed-up emotions' which led to a 'punitive' attitude towards women having babies (Morris 1960). However, the NCT has gradually achieved a more constructive relationship with midwives, recognizing their potential as the guardians of natural childbirth, and their own struggle against medical imperialism. The NCT headquarters in London were used to host the first meetings of the Association of Radical Midwives.

Changes in the political, professional, and obstetric environment have thus introduced new dynamics into the NCT—or revitalized old ones. Other changes have resulted from the Trust's development of new areas of work. The growth of the Breastfeeding Promotion Group has helped the organization to develop a concern for the Third World, and to take a stand against the aggressive promotion of powdered milk. There are now over 500 breast-feeding counsellors working within the Trust. The establishment of post-natal support has also been important:

The advent of . . . Postnatal Support has made a qualitative change to the way we work and our whole philosophy. In the postnatal groups we meet women who first come to NCT after, and not before they have their babies. They discuss their experiences and often share their anger at what's happened to them. In this way they are gaining power and wanting to take control of their future birthing experiences and when they come to NCT classes for their second babies, they know very much what they want. They are often the people who are changing our relationship with the medical world. (Corbishley 1987.)

The NCT has helped to change women's expectation and understandings of pregnancy and labour. Childbirth has undoubtedly been placed firmly in the political arena. In the last few years childbirth activists have adopted traditional political modes of protest as they have taken to the streets, first about the active birth issue and then in support of Wendy

Savage (Savage 1986). Women's versions of childbirth are being reclaimed (and changed), and lay movements may now take on further challenges with new impetus and support.

The NCT has a chequered history, involving constant tension between ,challenge and compromise, radicalism and reform. It is easy to look back and see how the organization in part fell for the medical mystique in the early 1960s (a medical mystique that it eventually helped to expose), and it is perhaps too easy to criticize the compromises which were judged to be necessary survival strategies by the activists at the time, without paying sufficient attention to the forces which shaped those decisions. The NCT did vital political groundwork, by setting up as a lay movement in the first place and fighting to reconstruct the meaning of birth. The Trust is also a central part of the contemporary childbirth movement in Britain. It has grown from a small group of enthusiastic women who funded their activities out of their own pockets to a national organization partly funded by the DHSS. The danger is, of course, that the NCT could be becoming institutionalized and professionalized. Too much investment in the status quo, and dependence on the DHSS could prevent its growth in any very challenging direction. However, many professionals still resent the Trust's existence, and a large proportion of the members see the NCT's independence and lay status as its most vital asset and will guard against its erosion. There is also debate about the middle-class bias of failing to give teachers adequate status or financial recogition. It is ironic that the Trust's independence, far from being actively sought, was originally determined by the medical profession's hostility, and that this hostility still plays a part in preserving that independence. As one founder-member who has participated in many of the changes in the NCT over the years concluded: 'Our strength is in being a lay movement. We *had* to find strength in being a lay movement. Our strength came from the downright antagonism from doctors.' (Rankin 1986*b*).

References

Barndon, D., 1987, 'How much Influence?', *New Generation*, Mar. 1987, pp. 8–9.

Beech, B., 1986, Interview with author.

Bing, E. and Ramel, M., 1961, *A Practical Training Course for the Psychoprophylactic Method of Painless Childbirth* (New York, Bantam).

Bourne, G., 1975, *Pregnancy* (London, Pan Books).

Briance, P., 1956, 'The Natural Childbirth Association of Great Britain.' Introduction to *Newsletter*.

—— 1957, 'Natural Childbirth: Childbirth without Fear' (NCT archives).

—— 1963, 'Read v. Psychoprophylaxis', *Newsletter*, Mar. 1963.

—— 1965, 'The Origins of the NCT' (NCT archives).

—— 1986a, Interview with author.

—— 1986b, Letter to editor of *New Generation*, 23 June 1986.

Central Health Services Council, 1961, *Human Relations in Obstetrics* (London, HMSO).

Claye, A., 1939, *The Evolution of Obstetric Analgesia* (Oxford, Oxford University Press).

Corbishley, H., 1986, 'How much Influence?' *New Generation*, Sept. 1986, p. 16.

—— 1987, Letter to author, 3 June 1987.

Dick Read, G., 1933, *Natural Childbirth* (London, Heinemann).

Enfield, V., 1964, Address at the official opening of the NCT headquarters, Dec. 1964.

Enkins, P. (ed.), 1986, *The American Way of Birth* (Philadelphia, Temple University Press).

Griffin, M., 1987, 'The Ghost in the Delivery Room: Could it be you?', *New Generation*, Mar. 1987, pp. 20–1.

Katz Rothman, B., 1981, 'Awake and Aware or False Consciousness?' in Romalis, S. (ed.), *Childbirth: Alternatives to Medical Control* (Austin, University of Texas).

—— 1982, *In Labour: Women and Power in the Birth Place* (London, Junction Books).

—— 1986, 'The Social Construction of Birth', in Enkins, P. (ed.), *The American Way of Birth*, q. v.

Lumley, J. and Astbury, J., 1980, *Birth Rites, Birth Rights: Childbirth Alternatives for Australian Parents* (Victoria, Australia, Sphere Books).

Mansfield, R., 1977, 'Look Back', *New Generation*, May 1977, pp. 7–8.

Micklethwait, P., 1986, Interview with author.

—— 1987, Letter to author, 5 July 1987.

Morris, N., 1960, 'Human Relations in Obstetric Practice', the *Lancet*, 1, pp. 913–15.

Newson, J. and Newson, E., 1963, *Infant Care in an Urban Community* (London, Allen and Unwin).

Noyles Thomas, A., 1957, *Doctor Courageous* (London, Heinemann).

Perchard, D., 1962, AGM Address for 1961, *Newsletter*, 10 (July 1962), 1.

Proctor, A., 1968, 'How our Trust Works', *New Generation*, Apr. 1968, p. 4.

Rankin, G., 1982, 'Birth Revolution: Fact or Fiction?' *New Generation*, Dec. 1982, p. 3.

—— 1986a, 'The Birth of the NCT', *New Generation*, June 1986, pp. 4–5.

—— 1986b, Interview with author.

Richards, M. P. M., 1981, 'Whose Choice in Childbirth?' *Proceedings of the NCT Silver Jubilee Conference* (London, National Childbirth Trust).

Savage, W., 1986, *A Savage Enquiry: Who Controls Childbirth?* (London, Virago).

Thorn, H., 1986, 'Soapbox: Guilt, Failure and the NCT', *New Generation*, Dec. 1986, pp. 20–1.

Toynbee, P., 1986, 'Behind the Lines', the *Guardian*, 12 May 1986.

Tweedie, J., 1965, Article in *Weekend Telegraph*, 23 Apr. 1965.

Wertz, R. and Wertz, D., 1977, *Lying In: A History of Childbirth in America* (New York, Free Press).

Whitford, J. 1987, 'Teachers' Reply', *New Generation*, Mar. 1987, p. 29.

Williams, L., 1968, 'The Early Years', *New Generation*, Oct. 1968, pp. 2–3.

6

Obstetric Analgesia and the Control of Childbirth in Twentieth-Century Britain

Jennifer Beinart

THIS chapter is about the *history* of obstetric analgesia, not current practice; but, as with many issues, the past has shaped the present, and understanding the past can help in making policies for the future. The chapter begins by suggesting that, despite the drawbacks associated with the various drugs used for obstetric analgesia, they have been much in demand by women. Like the debate on the place of birth (see Campbell and Macfarlane, Chapter 12), discussion about obstetric analgesia has tended to be dominated by the professionals, whose main criterion has been safety. Another important area in modern studies of obstetric analgesia is effectiveness. Mothers are also concerned with these issues, but it will be argued that the main focus of their attention in the past has often been the lack of availability of pain-relief in labour.

The chapter then offers a brief history of the use of different types of analgesia, relating these to social class, place of birth, and the interests of professional groups. Looking at initiatives in the past enables us to see how safety and effectiveness were frequently neglected, though often with the best of intentions. However, it would not further our understanding of our current problems simply to look at advances in technique and to say, for instance, that at least epidurals are a lot safer than chloroform. The underlying issue which this chapter attempts to explore is the link between obstetric analgesia and control over labour. Studying the past can help to illuminate the double-sided nature of this relationship. Pain-relief may enable a woman to remain in control of the process and to give birth the way she wants to, or it may remove her control and place her in the hands of others. She may want to be numbed to the pain of labour, or rendered unconscious; or she may want to feel everything including the pain. But now, as in the past, these choices are never made in a vacuum. They are affected by the place of birth, the availability of different kinds of attendants, and current views on drugs and techniques. While this chapter does not pretend to deal with these questions fully, it will try to show the complexity of the issues involved.

A last word of introduction is needed, on terminology. The discussion in this chapter has deliberately been limited to obstetric *analgesia*, that is, pain-relief for normal labour pains. Obstetric *anaesthesia*, that is pain-relief for painful interventions or operative procedures (often, but not necessarily, general anaesthesia), is obviously very closely linked to obstetric analgesia, and there is some overlap. However, anaesthesia is a huge field in its own right, and raises further issues which cannot be considered here. But there is one conceptual difference which is relevant: whereas it has been accepted by the medical profession and the public since the nineteenth century that *anaesthesia* is desirable for most operations, there has always been a debate over the desirability of *analgesia* in normal labour. This debate continues today, and the issue of control is at its centre.

Resistance to the Curse of Eve

> In sorrow shalt thou bring forth . . .
>
> Genesis, 3:16

Pain-relief has been one area in which women have consistently called for medical intervention in childbirth, from the mid-nineteenth century right up to the present. For those who could afford to pay for a doctor to attend them, the physician's ability to use chloroform was a strong attraction; it appears that it was the desire of the mothers, as much as the pioneering spirit of the early chloroformists, that brought this particular innovation to prominence so rapidly. With further new techniques, the voices of campaigning women were raised in support of increasing the availability of analgesia, in terms

that have changed little over the past seventy years. Hanna
Rion, an advocate of 'twilight sleep', wrote at the time of the
First World War: 'The only way in which the general
adoption of the method by the entire medical profession can
be brought about is by the mothers themselves. Let every
mother take up the fight for herself and her fellow-mothers . . .
there is no longer any necessity for them to suffer the "pains of
maternity".' (Rion 1915: 24.)

That call proved premature. Twilight sleep had a dubious
safety record, and was limited mainly to women who could
afford clinic fees. In the inter-war period there was an
influential campaign, led by society women like Lady Baldwin,
to find some means of analgesia that could safely be given by a
midwife. With gas and air (nitrous oxide and air) they seemed
to have found the answer, and Lady Baldwin announced in a
letter to *The Times* that the co-operation of the Central
Midwives' Board should 'finally dispel the illusion that no safe
means exists for providing relief during childbirth to those
mothers who cannot afford the services of a doctor. It is now a
mere matter of organization to ensure that no woman is forced
to suffer on account of poverty.' (Baldwin 1936.) This again
was over-optimistic. Ten years later, on the eve of the
introduction of the National Health Service, it was observed
that the provision of analgesia varied very much from one area
to another, and that it was particularly inadequate for home
births (Royal College of Obstetricians and Gynaecologists
and Population Investigation Committee [RCOG/PIC] 1948).

By the 1980s, the provision of pain-relief for all women in
labour still remains an unrealized dream, and also an area of
heated controversy. Attempting to launch a campaign to
increase the availability of epidurals, Maureen Treadwell
claimed that she would like to see all women free to choose
either a natural birth or an epidural. However, her position
has been portrayed by some as diametrically opposed to that
of the campaigners for natural childbirth. A newspaper article
by Polly Toynbee, an influential woman journalist, depicts the
advocates of natural childbirth as lentil-eating earth mothers,
with Maureen Treadwell as the voice of the silent majority of
mothers who would prefer epidurals (Toynbee 1986). The
Association for Improvements in the Maternity Services,

launched in 1960, pressed in the 1970s for epidurals to be made more widely available, but later came to have serious reservations about them. It now places greater emphasis on the supportive role of midwives in enabling women to labour in their own way.

Some historians have focused on the viewpoint of professionals in attempting to explain changes in obstetric analgesia during the twentieth century. Shorter, for example, argues that modifications in analgesia followed the shift in concern among obstetricians—from the mother to the fetus—when maternal mortality had been brought under control in the mid-twentieth century (Shorter 1982). Although there would seem to be some logic to this, it does not appear to fit the facts, for this country at least. Here, a form of analgesia which was very safe but which was not totally effective for the mother (nitrous oxide) was displaced by a drug which gave the mother a greater degree of relief from pain but produced longer-lasting effects in the baby (pethidine)—at a time when concern for the fetus was supposed to be growing. An American historian of anaesthesia credits the invention of the Apgar score (an assessment of new-born babies' functions) with subsequent advances in obstetric anaesthesia, without acknowledging the concern that was felt by mothers and midwives as well as by doctors when confronted with drugged babies, from the days of twilight sleep on (Poppers 1985).

Chloroform and Twilight Sleep: Oblivion for the Well-off

In one of the most helpful and important contributions to the literature on the history of obstetric analgesia, Judith Leavitt discussed the campaign to introduce the use of twilight sleep into the United States in the first decade of this century (Leavitt 1980). This form of pain-relief, pioneered in Germany, used scopolamine and morphine to produce a state of semiconsciousness in which the woman appeared to feel pain but retained no memory of it. The importance of Leavitt's paper is its demonstration that, contrary to first appearances, the advocacy of twilight sleep did not equate with submission to the expertise of the medical profession. Although the women choosing this method were relinquishing control over the birth to their medical attendants, they were retaining overall control in that they themselves had made the positive choice to give birth without pain. Those women who supported the use of twilight sleep, mainly middle- and upper-class women of the East Coast, described by Leavitt as feminists, formed an alliance with obstetricians against general practitioners and midwives who opposed it. This opposition was based on the latters' fear of losing control over the process of childbirth as more women opted for the clinic- or hospital-based, painless, twilight sleep birth. The new method meant, in effect, greater specialization among doctors, and closer medical supervision of labour, and this was what the most progressive (and wealthy) women chose. Their campaign suffered a severe set-back, however, with the death of one of its leading lights in a New York hospital in 1915 whilst undergoing a twilight sleep delivery.

In this country the method appears to have been taken up to a limited extent by obstetricians, and in some places it was used in a modified form up to the Second World War. An obstetrician in Leeds, A. M. Claye, gave scopolamine alone, but still found the restlessness of some of the women in labour a problem: 'To obviate this, leg-holders, by which the knees are secured, have been advocated, and the wrists and elbows may be bound with bandages . . . Some observers state that the patients are amenable to gentle restraint: my experience has not confirmed this in every case.' (Claye 1939: 67.) According to Claye, although the uterine and accessory muscles acted efficiently with this form of pain-relief, it was associated with an increase in the rate of forceps usage to 15 per cent, mainly because the mother's restlessness often necessitated prolonged general anaesthesia. At the very least, chloroform *à la reine* was recommended for the second stage. As so often happens, one intervention tended to lead to another.

Up to the Second World War, however, the predominant form of obstetric analgesia continued to be chloroform, most often administered by a general practitioner at a home delivery. Although hospital deliveries were increasing, they only accounted for 25 per cent of births by 1937. Women who gave birth in hospital were possibly more likely to receive analgesia than those who gave birth at home, depending on the policy of the hospital. In private nursing homes, where the clients were middle-class women, often attended by their own doctor, chloroform was frequently used. But the majority of births, domiciliary or hospital, were attended by a midwife rather than a doctor, and midwives were not permitted to administer chloroform. Thus the prevailing pattern of obstetric analgesia in Britain throughout the inter-war period was one of non-use.

Nitrous Oxide: Analgesia for the Masses?

Although it is clear that access to obstetric analgesia was class-differentiated, the evidence on the attitudes to pain-relief of women from different social backgrounds is less clear. Jane Lewis suggests in Chapter 1 that fear of pain in childbirth was a serious concern for women from all social classes, but that it was a campaigning issue chiefly for middle-class women, while working-class women were pressing for improvements in midwifery and medical care. One of the best-known sources on actual experiences of childbirth, *Maternity*, published in 1915 (also quoted by Lewis), is a collection of working-class mothers' accounts of childbirth gathered together by the Women's Co-operative Guild as part of a campaign for a maternity allowance. Many letters refer to the hardships imposed by the low wages of the women's husbands, and to the sufferings endured during pregnancy and after the birth, which might have been averted with proper medical attention, better food, and rest. But in all the terrible catalogue of suffering—for these are often very harrowing accounts—the pains of childbirth are scarcely mentioned. They seem to be the one thing that is regarded as sufficiently 'natural' to be accepted, and therefore not worth writing about. One woman says: 'any special information other than the ordinary childbirth pains I cannot give'. Another, in a long account of a normal delivery, speaks of how the nurse 'looked at me in my agony, and said: "Oh, not likely to come off yet, ma"', and sent the mother off to boil up her rubber gloves. Apart from that, there are almost no references to the pain of labour. There are also very few references to the use of pain-relief, and those that do occur are to the anaesthetic rather than the analgesic use of chloroform. This is evident from the context: from the coupling of 'instruments and chloroform', the mention of having been near death's door, or the statement that two doctors were needed to chloroform the woman. In only one case is there a reference to what appears to be an opiate, and then it is given to the delicate husband so that he will not be disturbed if his wife cries out in labour (Women's Co-operative Guild 1915).

There does appear to have been some change in these attitudes during the inter-war period. In her study of working-class women based mainly on interviews, Elizabeth Roberts states that women's attitudes to their own health changed gradually, and that this included their expectations in relation to childbirth: 'The fatalism, the shame, the stoicism, and the traditionalism are all still very apparent, but a growing number of women from all levels of the working class began to expect more professional help, whether in the form of a doctor or a qualified midwife; they began to expect analgesics, and a hospital bed "in case something should go wrong".' (Roberts 1984: 108–9.) With the increasing regulation of the midwifery service, the expectation of attendance by a qualified midwife was likely to be fulfilled; the provision of pain-relief, however, remained more problematic.

Progressive doctors, like some women's organizations, favoured the widening of access to hospitals to all mothers, or at least to all first-time mothers, and regarded the benefits of modern scientific medicine as a boon which should not be restricted to wealthy women. On the issue of safety, however, there was a debate over whether, from the point of view of maternal mortality, home or hospital was the safer location for births, and both sides mentioned the use of anaesthetics— one, as a factor in the higher maternal mortality rate of better-off women, the other, as one of the great attractions of hospital deliveries for less well-off women (Palmer 1986: 104–10). The meaning of the term 'anaesthetics' could vary, but usually it would have implied chloroform or another agent used as an analgesic. Figures for anaesthetic-related deaths before the Second World War must be regarded with caution; it would be misleading to quote a figure for maternal deaths due to anaesthesia or analgesia. However, it can be said with some confidence that this cause of death was insignificant compared with the major causes of maternal mortality, puerperal fever and haemorrhage.

It has recently been argued that the reverse class differential in the maternal mortality rate, giving the professional classes a worse rate than the labouring classes, can probably best be explained by the greater medical attention received by the better-off women. Since most of them were attended by general practitioners, who were more likely to intervene in a normal labour than midwives were, the chances of iatrogenic complications were greater than they were for poorer women, whose midwife attendants generally allowed the labour to take its own course (Loudon 1986). This applies chiefly to home or nursing-home births; however, it is worth noting that the demands which were seen at the time as being progressive, and these included greater medical attention, were not necessarily those which ensured greatest safety for the majority of mothers. On the other hand, the increased use of anaesthetics by doctors attending middle- or upper-class women was not the major culprit that some observers thought at the time; the doctors' hands employed in frequent vaginal examinations were a greater hazard.

Improving the provision of hospital maternity beds was perhaps seen as one way of increasing access to obstetric analgesia. An alternative solution, pursued by an active group of upper-class women, was to extend the provision of analgesia in both home and hospital deliveries by finding a method that could be used by midwives. The National Birthday Trust Fund had been established in 1928 as a result of concern over the high maternal mortality rate. It raised substantial amounts of money for the improvement of maternity services, appealing to the middle classes to make donations as tributes to the sufferings undergone by their own mothers. Soon after its establishment, the Fund began to seek a means of extending the provision of analgesia. It sponsored the experimental use of chloroform capsules, to enable midwives to give a controlled dose of chloroform, and it also financed the development of a nitrous-oxide-and-air apparatus for obstetric use, by Dr R. J. Minnitt, a general practitioner and part-time obstetrician at Liverpool Maternity Hospital. The Fund succeeded in securing the co-operation of the British (later Royal) College of Obstetricians and Gynaecologists, which undertook a study involving thirty-six hospitals in what they called 'a controlled trial' of five methods of analgesia likely to be suitable for use by midwives. Three of these methods employed chloroform, one used paraldehyde given rectally, and one used gas and air given by the Minnitt apparatus. (Other types of gas-and-air apparatus were available, but they were mainly designed for anaesthetic use.) Nearly 10,000 cases were recorded; an analysis of the results, published in 1936, indicated that nitrous oxide was safer than chloroform (British College of Obstetricians and Gynaecologists 1936).

Accordingly, the Central Midwives' Board issued regulations on the use of analgesics by midwives: those acting without a doctor should not use chloroform at all, but they could use the Minnitt apparatus if another midwife, nurse, or pupil midwife were present. A certificate of proficiency must be obtained by any midwife intending to use the Minnitt apparatus. The National Birthday Trust Fund began distributing gas-and-air machines, free or at a discount price, mainly to hospitals, but their work was limited by the shortage of analgesia training for midwives (NBTF Archives, Minutes of Analgesia Sub-Committee 1937–9). Diana Palmer has shown how slow local authorities were to take advantage of their powers to provide midwives with training: by 1939, only 29 out of 188 authorities had done so (Palmer 1986: 268). Commenting on the situation in 1946, a journalist wrote that 'over 100 authorities do not possess any means whatever for bringing relief to the average mother', contrasting this with provisions under the London County Council and a few other 'good' authorities which had made efforts to train midwives in analgesia and to provide machines (Morgan 1946).

One of the most interesting aspects of this story, in the light of Leavitt's study of twilight sleep in America discussed earlier, is the alliance between upper-class women, obstetricians, and midwives interested in providing obstetric analgesia for more women. There was opposition from some quarters in the medical profession, especially from general practitioners whose obstetric practice relied partly on their ability to provide analgesia. The support of midwives is easily explained, as their status would be enhanced if they could perform one of the functions previously reserved for doctors. But there is more of a query over the co-operation of obstetricians. Part of the answer may be that they themselves could not realistically provide analgesia for every labouring woman, and that they were keen that some provision should be made. It should also be noted that the 1936 trials were conducted in hospitals, and although the aim was ostensibly to establish a method of analgesia which could be used by unsupervised midwives, the obstetricians were ensuring that their interests were fully represented. They were, in effect, taking another step towards squeezing out the general-practitioner obstetrician. The post-war expansion of maternity hospital beds did indeed give more women access to pain-relief—but that could have been achieved through better provision of analgesia in the domiciliary midwifery services. The move to hospital, of course, greatly increased the power of obstetricians, relegated midwives to a definitely secondary position, and led to the virtual obliteration of general-practitioner domiciliary obstetrics by the 1970s.

Post-War Developments and the Current Situation

A 'time capsule' overview of the provision of maternity services in this country on the eve of the introduction of the NHS is provided by the report, *Maternity in Great Britain* (RCOG/PIC 1948), which has a section on the relief of pain in childbirth. The survey on which the report was based had been conducted in 1946, when gas and air was regarded as the method to be propagated. In hospital deliveries, just over a third of mothers received gas and air, and just over a half had some form of analgesia. In domiciliary confinements, only one-fifth of mothers had analgesia, and of these, two-thirds were given chloroform by a general practitioner. In all, over 60 per cent of women delivered their babies without analgesia. When asked to comment on many aspects of the services, the

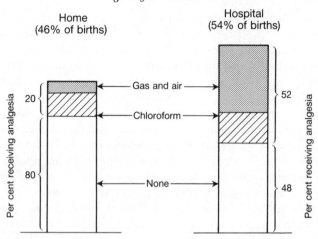

FIG. 6.1 Proportion of women receiving obstetric analgesia in home and hospital deliveries, and major types of analgesia given, 1946.

main complaint of mothers was the 'lack of analgesia' (RCOG/PIC 1948: 86). The findings of this survey in relation to analgesia are roughly summarized in Figure 6. 1.

Further surveys of the maternity services showed a fall in the percentage receiving no analgesia to 21 per cent in 1958 and 3 per cent in 1970 (NBTF/RCOG 1975: 29; and 1978: 192). The use of gas and air, and then gas and oxygen (very similar from the point of view of the recipient), rose to over 50 per cent. Chloroform went out and trilene came in. Pethidine was very widely used, often in conjunction with another method. A noticeable characteristic of the practice of obstetric analgesia was the use of more than one kind of analgesic; this was not new, but it had become very pronounced by 1970.

The great rise in epidurals, a form of regional analgesia, post-dated the 1970 survey, but then their use escalated rapidly, for conditions were ripe: hospital births had risen to 85 per cent of the total by 1970; there was a suitable analgesic agent available (narcaine, now largely supplanted by longer-lasting drugs such as bupivacaine); and there was a much larger body of trained anaesthetists, although not enough to provide a universal epidural service. Throughout the 1970s and into the 1980s the debate has continued about the advantages of epidurals for mothers and babies. There is less discussion about their effectiveness, which is considered superior to many other forms of analgesia, than about their side-effects. In particular, evidence points to a slowing-down of labour, and to an increase in the rate of forceps deliveries (Avard and Nimrod 1985). In both these respects, an epidural may actually decrease a mother's control over her labour. Given the shortage of anaesthetists, it is possible that a woman might be denied an epidural or asked to undergo an induced labour in order to ensure the presence of an anaesthetist. Alternatively, other medical personnel can be trained to give epidurals; here the debate enters the realm of interprofessional rivalries. Also it is worth reiterating the obvious: that epidurals entail hospital delivery; they fit with the view of labour as a potentially pathological process, requiring intervention.

An apparently alternative view has been offered since the Second World War by the natural childbirth movement. In Chapter 5 Jenny Kitzinger argues that the early natural childirth movement sought to woo the professionals, bowing to the medical mystique rather than challenging it. This has some parallels with the interpretation of American versions of natural childbirth offered by Margarete Sandelowski (Sandelowski 1984). There were major differences between the United States and Britain, however, both in the place of birth and the availability of midwives. By the 1950s most American women gave birth in hospitals, and midwives had virtually disappeared. In Britain the switch to hospital births was much slower, and in the late 1950s about a third of deliveries still took place at home. Midwives fought successfully for their role to continue even after the move to hospital deliveries became absolute. Thus the question of which professionals to woo was still open—midwives, general practitioners, or obstetricians? Kitzinger suggests that the early natural childbirth campaigners did not distinguish clearly between these groups, but sought to avoid alienating obstetricians in particular. The latter, however, consolidating their power base throughout this period, began to introduce as a norm many interventions which ran directly contrary to the philosophy of natural childbirth, including inductions and

heavier use of analgesics. In resisting these, the NCT
radicalized itself and its public. But it had failed to oppose
perhaps the biggest intervention: carting all parturient women
off to hospital.

It was not to be expected that the natural childbirth
movement would oppose the increase in hospital deliveries.
After all, this had been part of the programme for improvements in maternity services advocated by the more progressive
women's organizations for years (see Lewis, Chapter 1).
Moreover, both of the original gurus followed by the natural
childbirth movement, Grantly Dick Read and Fernand
Lamaze, taught their techniques in the context of a nursing
home or clinic, not in women's own homes. Judging by Dick
Read's writings over many years, he is unlikely to have
approved of the approach of Lilian Bethune, one of many
women who reported their experiences to him. After reading
his book, she and a friend 'arranged to be confined at home
with a wise old midwife, and both . . . gave birth peacefully
and joyfully without a doctor present' (Dick Read archives,
Bethune to Dick Read 30 Aug. 1947). The tendency of the
natural childbirth movement to uphold the central role of the
doctor derived directly from Dick Read and Lamaze as well as
from previous campaigns on maternity. Only in establishing
their network of lay teachers did the natural childbirth lobby
perhaps challenge the status quo. The incorporation of some
of their ideas into hospital preparation classes can be seen as a
very limited success in spreading the movement's message
wider than its essentially fringe middle-class base.

This chapter began by arguing that there has been a constant
demand from women for pain-relief in childbirth, but that the
issues surrounding analgesia are quite complicated. In the
early part of this century, upper-class women campaigned for
twilight sleep, supported by obstetricians. However, it turned
out to be unsafe for both mothers and babies. Meanwhile,
middle-class women often booked general practitioners to
attend them because they wanted chloroform, while most
working-class women were delivered by midwives and had no
pain-relief. For poorer women, it is suggested, the sorrows of
maternity were so manifold, spanning the years of child-

rearing as well as the problems of childbirth, that actual labour pains paled into relative insignificance. During the inter-war years, hospital deliveries were increasing but were still a minority. Upper-class women began to campaign for pain-relief in labour to be made available to the majority of mothers, and a form of nitrous oxide analgesia was developed which could be used by midwives in domiciliary as well as hospital deliveries. The extension of this service was very slow and limited, despite the efforts of a voluntary body offering cut-price machines to midwives and hospitals. It was clearly not regarded as a priority by the various public and private bodies providing maternity care. After the war, the picture altered considerably. While the coming of the National Health Service did not mean full integration of the services, it did remove the notion that good pain-relief was a privilege to be bought by the wealthy. A far wider range of drugs and techniques became available, ranging from pethidine which a midwife could administer by injection, to epidural analgesia which should ideally be administered by a skilled anaesthetist.

In the field of obstetric analgesia, as in other areas of maternity policy, one must resist the temptation to see historical change as a continuity of 'progressive' or more correct approaches. What was progressive in one context can be the reverse in another. With a matter as subjective as the experience of pain in childbirth, it is doubtful whether there could ever be one standard answer for all women. The same woman may have different degrees of pain in different labours. Pain perception is partly conditioned by cultural expectations. What is particularly striking, after looking at the history of obstetric analgesia, is the continued inadequacy of the maternity services in this area. Although the move to deliver almost all women in hospital has been accompanied by a rise in the provision of analgesia, the type of analgesia offered varies enormously, and choice by the mother can be severely limited.

Are women more in control of childbirth the less they feel? The twilight sleep women felt that surrendering consciousness and handing over the entire process of birth to a highly skilled doctor was the ideal. Advocates of epidurals now believe they have the best of both worlds—freedom from pain without loss of consciousness—but natural childbirth supporters regard sensation as helpful in gaining control over birth. How important is the place of birth for the balance of control? In the hospital, which is the medical domain, it may be very difficult, even impossible, to escape from seeing pain as pathological. In either hospital or home deliveries, midwives may be able to offer something that doctors and drugs cannot provide—helping women to keep on top of the process of labour instead of being submerged by it.

References

Avard, D. M. and Nimrod, C. M., 1985, 'Risks and Benefits of Obstetric Epidural Analgesia: A Review'. *Birth*, 12/4, pp. 215–25.

Baldwin, L., 1936, Letter to the editor, *The Times*, 23 Oct. 1936.

British College of Obstetricians and Gynaecologists, 1936, *Investigation into the Use of Analgesics Suitable for Administration by Midwives* (London, BCOG).

Claye, A. M., 1939, *The Evolution of Obstetric Analgesia* (Oxford, Oxford University Press).

Dick Read, G., Archives (Wellcome Institute, London).

Leavitt, J. W., 1980, 'Birthing and Anesthesia: The Debate over Twilight Sleep', *Signs*, 6, pp. 147–64.

Loudon, I., 1986, 'Deaths in Childbed from the Eighteenth Century to 1935', *Medical History*, 30, pp. 1–41.

Morgan, L., 1946, 'Why Deny Women Painless Childbirth?', *News Chronicle*, 26 Nov. 1946.

National Birthday Trust Fund, Archives (Wellcome Institute, London).

——and Royal College of Obstetricians and Gynaecologists, 1975 and 1978, *British Births 1970*, 2 vols. (London, Heinemann).

Palmer, D., 1986, 'Women, Health and Politics, 1919–1939: Professional and Lay Involvement in the Women's Health Campaign', Ph.D. thesis (University of Warwick).

Poppers, P. J., 1985, 'The History and Development of Obstetric Anesthesia', in J. Rupreht, M. J. van Lieburg, J. A. Lee, and W. Erdmann (eds.), *Anaesthesia: Essays on its History* (Berlin and Heidelberg, Springer-Verlag).

Rion, H., 1915, *Painless Childbirth in Twilight Sleep* (London, Werner Laurie).

Roberts, E., 1984, *A Woman's Place: An Oral History of Working-Class Women 1890–1940* (Oxford, Blackwell).

Royal College of Obstetricians and Gynaecologists and Population Investigation Committee, 1948, *Maternity in Great Britain* (London, Oxford University Press).

Sandelowski, M., 1984, *Pain, Pleasure and American Childbirth: From the Twilight Sleep to the Read Method, 1914–1960* (Westport, Conn. and London, Greenwood Press).

Shorter, E., 1982, *A History of Women's Bodies* (New York, Basic Books; London, Allen Lane, 1983).

Toynbee, P., 1986, 'Natural Childbirth, a Child of the Sixties, Was and Is Largely a Nutty Fad from a Noisy Group of Lentil-Eating Earth Goddesses', the *Guardian*, 12 May 1986.

Women's Co-operative Guild, 1915, *Maternity: Letters from Working Women*, ed. Margaret Llewelyn Davies, 1st edn. (repr. London, Virago, 1978).

7

Learning about Birth: Parenthood and Sex Education in English Secondary Schools

Shirley Prendergast and Alan Prout

THE topics of birth and maternity occur in many contexts in our society and are diffused through a variety of social settings. No TV soap opera, for example, could exist for long without pregnancy and birth as part of its continuing narrative. Such series are often used to promote particular health messages, and sometimes deliberately set out to explore controversial aspects of the topic precisely because these give productions a dramatic tension around an event that is recognized as being of crucial importance in everyday life.

In this chapter we will discuss another setting in which pregnancy and birth also appear as a topic because of their prominence in relation to health and the life cycle: the school class-room and 'parenthood education'. We will suggest that the representation of birth and pregnancy in school is dominated by medical definitions, and that, although teenage boys and girls need and want to understand more, current approaches should be broadened and modified. In this discussion we will first describe the general situation in English schools, and then use the example of films about birth and the way they are used to exemplify and explore the issues in more detail.

Background

A research survey of English secondary schools (Grafton *et al.* 1983) showed that the topic of parenthood was dealt with mainly by two types of course: examined courses such as 'Child Development' (which lead to nationally recognized school-leaving qualifications), and non-examined courses under the heading of 'Personal and Social Development'.

The first of these, Child Development courses, tend to be rather didactic and concentrate on the transmission of knowledge about parenthood. In recent years they have moved away from a practical skills' base (archetypically 'bathing the baby') towards more knowledge-based courses focused on the needs of the developing fetus, baby, and young child, and how best their parents or care-givers can meet those needs. The content of such courses overlaps with that period of a woman's reproductive life that is of most intense interest and concern to the medical profession—pregnancy and birth, a concern that is echoed in the areas of study. For example, most examination-based syllabuses focus in detail on pregnancy, ante-natal care, birth, breast-feeding, as well as the growth and development of the fetus, baby, toddler, and young child, rather than on parenthood from the parents' perspective, or across the life cycle.

Personal and Social Development, on the other hand, tends to tackle parenthood in a rather different fashion, as part of the broad development of the individual schoolchild. Here the stress is not primarily on the transmission of knowledge but on pupils' skills of self-understanding, relating to others, developing self-confidence, and discussing values and attitudes (see e.g. Button 1974; Baldwin and Wells 1980; Hopson and Scally 1981). Despite this emphasis on what has become known as the 'affective curriculum' knowledge transmission still takes place even if presented in a wider personal context. Indeed, it could be argued that the 'affective' focus of this style of teaching has tended to leave such issues as what counts as appropriate knowledge undefined and taken for granted.

Despite their apparent differences, *both* forms of parenthood education draw upon a range of common resources which are used to shape and structure the teaching. These include school textbooks, popular child-care books (for example, *The St Michael Complete Book of Babycare* (Nash 1980), sold at Marks and Spencer's is widely used in schools), films about aspects of parenthood, and talks from a range of visitors, including health visitors, school nurses, and doctors. Such resources tend to be dominated by medical and biological, and to a lesser extent psychological, frameworks and approaches. These represent parenthood in a particular way which comes to be seen as the 'normal', the 'correct', and 'the proper way to do it', legitimized by its inclusion in the curriculum of schooling.

In a sense this is entirely comprehensible; for although parenthood and reproduction are 'natural' events, their expression and form are socially regulated—in this society as in any other. In our society this regulation is partly accomplished by making parenthood the province of professionals. As Graham and Oakley (1981) have suggested, in the area of reproduction the medical framework acts as a powerful ideological system. They comment, for example (p. 51) that: 'In talking about the different ways in which doctors and mothers view pregnancy, we are talking about a fundamental difference in their perspective . . . a qualitatively different way of looking at the nature, context and management of reproduction.'

A central effect of this in schools is to legitimize medically framed knowledge about parenthood and reproduction as 'proper' knowledge—specialist subjects in which professionals are the recognized experts. Women's collective and individual experience and understanding of pregnancy, birth, and the transition to motherhood tend to be discounted in favour of medical definitions. It is also clear, however, that alongside the mechanistic model of women as 'manipulable reproductive machines', the medical ideology of birth also makes major assumptions about gender, constituting what Oakley (1979) labels the 'feminine paradigm': women as naturally maternal, domesticated, family-oriented people. This approach to parenthood appears to have been more or less uncritically adopted in examined courses in school. This is most apparent in Child Development courses, but even the affective forms of teaching and learning, from which we might have hoped for a challenge to these ideas, appear to be immobilized by 'expert' frameworks. We suggest that this is because the affective curriculum does not examine the underlying issues about knowledge which are at stake: who defines what 'counts' as knowledge;

who speaks it; to whom is it spoken; what happens to other bodies of knowledge and experiences outside of its remit? In this sense, the medical framing of parenthood, and all that it entails, can enter into the school setting via resources related to health and reproduction, dominated by the 'medical expert' or the 'gynaecological consultant', as they are often termed in leaflets or films.

In this chapter, then, we will look at the processes whereby these 'expert' knowledges and frameworks enter the school curriculum in the teaching of parenthood. We will take birth as our example since most school courses include some teaching on it, frequently planning what is taught around the use of a film. Our discussion is based on material that was gathered during a larger study of parenthood education (Prendergast and Prout 1987) in which we followed groups of 14-year-old male and female pupils through these sorts of classes in five schools.[1] During the course of our fieldwork we frequently observed such films on birth being used as part of parenthood courses, of both the Child Development and Personal and Social Development type. We were able to interview the boys and girls after the films and discuss their reactions to them. Our discussion here centres on the most frequently used of such films, *The First Days of Life*,[2] although we observed other films being used and will make it clear when our discussion refers to these. We were later.able to review these films and analyse them in detail.

The study from which this material is drawn was a small-scale one and we do not know how widespread such reactions are, although our experience of secondary schools tells us that they are not untypical. However, we draw no general conclusions and offer our insights only so that others might take them to their own particular experience and settings. We start with a description of one particular occasion in school, at which we were present and which can act as an illustration of

[1] The research was funded by the Health Education Council (now Authority). The ideas discussed in this chapter are those of the authors and do not necessarily reflect those of the HEA.

[2] *The First Days of Life*, produced by Les Films du Levant, distributed by Boulton-Hawker Films Ltd. Details of other films mentioned in this chapter can be obtained from the Health Education Authority Resources Dept., 78 New Oxford Street, London WC1A 1AH.

the type of context in which films were shown; the pupils' later comments refer to this occasion.

Scenes from a Class on Birth

It was a Tuesday morning in an English comprehensive school. A local health visitor had been invited to run a short course on parenthood with a class of fourth-year pupils. Her first session was on contraception, and this week she intended to follow on with pregnancy and birth. Her plan was to show a birth film (*The First Days of Life*) and then to discuss it with the thirty or so boys and girls who were sitting on separate sides of the classroom.

The film started with scenes showing the face of a woman in labour, and opened up to show the delivery room with its white-coated doctors and nurses. A male (doctor's?) voice was urging the woman to 'Push, push'. The film cut to scenes of the woman playing with her small child in a park. A narrator (again male, for throughout the entire film the woman giving birth was never heard) intoned the importance of the 'first days of life', suggesting that every act of a parent can shape and influence a child's development.

So far the film had lasted a few minutes and still seemed to have the pupils' attention. The next section was lengthy (about ten minutes, or two-thirds of the film). It showed the process of conception and fetal development in some detail, and had a commentary which used a lot of bio-medical terminology. The scenes appeared to be filmed in the womb, and showed the stages of growth of the embryo, accompanied by science fiction music which emphasized the mystery of the process. The voice-over stressed the harm that can be done to the fetus as it develops. Throughout this stage of the film the pupils had become progressively more restless and uninterested. Eventually they began chattering and were told to be quiet by the health visitor who was taking the class.

When the film reached the point of complete fetal development it abruptly cut back to the opening scene in the delivery room. The camera moved from the woman's agonized face to show the head of the baby forcing its way out of her vagina.

There was blood as her perineum tore, and a passing shot of scissors. As this happened the girls in the classroom seemed tense, and many looked aside or groaned, especially when the head of the baby was seen to emerge. Some of the boys were laughing, either nervously or mockingly, and some, to the amusement of others, called out 'heave'. The film ended in slow motion as, with romantic music in the background, the doctor handed the new baby to the smiling but tearful parents. There was a general sense of shock and relief among many pupils, both boys and girls, as the film ended.

Teachers' and Pupils' Reactions to the Film

Even before they showed the films, several teachers registered with us their ambiguous and anxious feelings about using them in school. Whilst these were in part to do with contemporary political concern about sex education in school, and fears that some parents might object, they also went beyond these considerations. They seemed to involve a tension between the desire to present birth as 'normal' and 'natural' for adult (married?) women, and the recognition that there is something about the visual representation of the physical process of birth which is disturbing and even frightening. For example, one teacher said to us: 'It's beautiful, lyrical really. But it's too gory, there's a lot of blood.' Another said: 'I don't even like to look myself, though I've had children, so I don't know what *they* will make of it.' A third noted later to the class, using the fear as a warning: 'Yes, well, perhaps it's done some good, because there were gasps of horror . . . did it make you feel a little more responsible, boys, by the end?' These tensions may reflect a more widespread phenomenon. A playgroup leader (who was helping one of the schools with their parenthood education) said to us: 'If I'm honest having a baby was the most painful experience of my life. Of course you don't say that to the younger women, you don't want to put them off.'

Teachers tended to anticipate pupils' reactions to the film by stressing the outcome of the birth rather than the event itself. Before they showed the film they often reminded the class that, whatever it looked like, it was all made worth while by having a new baby. The girls, although sharing many of the teachers' ambiguous feelings about seeing it, were actually more interested in the birth process itself. For example, in our later discussions with them, several girls were anxious to establish whether the film had portrayed a *normal* birth: 'Was it a difficult birth? People were shocked. It put them off temporarily . . . because it looked so painful.' The moment when the baby's head emerged from the mother's body was identified as particularly difficult, and many girls confirmed our observation that they were unable to watch at this point. Several were struck by the violence of the contractions, one referring to it as 'like something being ripped through your body'. The amount of blood was also a shock to many. Several girls asked both us and their teacher why all babies could not be delivered by Caesarian section, and many said they would prefer this because 'you have anaesthetic'. Related to this was their perception that although the mother in the film had clearly been experiencing pain, the film and its commentary had not mentioned this. In particular, they commented on how the film seemed to ignore what the mother herself might be feeling: 'You are sitting there and trying to keep the breathing up and everything and you think "Is she in pain or isn't she?" . . . You can't see it from her point of view really, you can't say what she's feeling.'

This desire for more information about the mother's experience and more honesty about the pain was widely expressed, but almost wholly by girls. One thought that the film was dishonest: 'I think in this film [*The First Days of Life*] they were trying to disguise the fact that it hurt . . . The other film I saw at home on TV—they talked to the mothers before . . . and they said that they knew it was going to be painful, but not how painful, and when they had it they said it hurt like hell . . .'.

Among the boys these issues were more muted, and there seemed to be an easier and perhaps more glib acceptance that although birth was difficult and painful, it was nevertheless 'natural'. As one boy said: 'It's just what happens if you want a baby. It's like animals, you just give birth. It's a natural process.' The boys, unlike the girls, tended to emphasize the safe arrival of the child, and the joy and relief that was shown

at the end of the film. However, they did criticize the film for
not seeming to reflect contemporary practices in childbirth
('like natural childbirth and that sort of thing'), which they
knew about through TV programmes such as BBC *Horizon*
(*Nova* in the USA). Finally, some of the boys acknowledged
the girls' different reaction: 'I think a lot of people, at the end
of it, the actual birth, found it a bit difficult to take. Some of
the girls particularly.'

Filming a Birth: Whose Point of View?

It becomes possible to understand both teachers' apprehen-
sions and pupils' responses when we consider the ways in
which birth is presented on film. We would suggest that three
related features predominate:

(*a*) birth is presented from a medical point of view;
(*b*) issues of power and autonomy are presented in a highly
gendered fashion;
(*c*) the baby, both unborn and being born, is placed at the
centre of our attention.

(*a*) *Medicalization*

It is not at all clear what distinctions might be made between
films about birth made for ante-natal classes, and those made
for schools, or how film-makers have conceptualized, these
differences, if at all. The notes that accompany *The First Days
of Life* describe the aims of the film as being 'to teach adults,
particularly expectant mothers and fathers, and children aged
13 or over, about sex and human reproduction, with special
reference to the importance of events and care immediately
following conception to an individual's future mental [and]
physical development'. This school/ante-natal overlap is also
true for several other films about birth used in school—for
example, *Preparing for Sarah*, the *Having a Baby* series, *Giving
Birth*, and *Birth and Breastfeeding*. Likewise, *Facts for Life* and
Everyday Miracle—made for school use—are frequently shown
in the ante-natal setting. It seems fair to suggest that the
predominant obstetric concerns of the 1960s and 1970s—

regulating and controlling the timing of birth, and preparing women to accept as routine and normal a series of medical interventions —extend to almost all films on birth made in this period. For example, *Preparing for Sarah* shows hospital birth, pubic shaving, prone delivery position, induction, and episiotomy as procedures that are necessary for all women, about which they have no choice and to which they must submit under the authority of the doctor. The Granada television series for schools, *Facts for Life*, while not quite so medicalized, adopts a similar approach.

In some cases there are very obvious problems of time-lag; films may seem hopelessly out of date, and pupils are quick to spot old-fashioned clothing or furnishings, or the grossly paternalistic and unreal treatment of women by doctors, which makes them laugh. Other kinds of time-lag and 'out of dateness' may not be so obvious. For example, how could pupils know about alternative delivery positions, the changing debates about induction or analgesics, or the variety of practices related to general-practitioner deliveries, and there-fore be able to judge how *technically* dated a film was?

Likewise, the debates about hospital and home births are not properly explored and presented. In *Facts for Life*, for example, the home birth is shown so clinically that the midwife, apparently dressed in waterproof dungarees, wears a mask the whole time, even on the telephone to the doctor, and behaves as though she has not met the mother before. Hospital births are presented as highly medicalized, with a large number of masked and gowned attendants. In one school, a film about alternative birth (part of the *Facts for Life* series) was being shown to a group of 14-year-old girls. The consultant obstetrician, demonstrating a forceps delivery, noted that they 'protect the baby's head like a cage—a steel cage', by clamping the forceps round his fist. Neither he nor anybody else said what it might feel like for the mother to have a 'steel cage' inside her body, or how she would cope, but the girls watching were clearly horrified, and said so later.

In general, the overall message from these films is that birth is controlled and managed externally and with little reference to those actually going through the experience. Only after the safe delivery is the film literally 'handed back' to the parents;

the doctor places a perfect baby in the arms of the mother, and only then are the emotions of the parents allowed expression.

(b) Gender and Control

As an overlapping and an integral part of the medicalization of birth one can also point to the highly gendered power imbalances presented in the film. For example, we can often take the idea of the 'point of view' of the films quite literally—whose point of view is shown or heard, and how is it portrayed? The gendered gaze and voice of medicine is often most powerful here. Almost invariably we see shots taken between the legs of the woman giving birth, and the gaze of the camera falls on the ever-widening vagina as the head of the child emerges. The film's documentary sense of reality may beguile us into thinking that this is an 'objective' view of birth—but this is not the case. With the (very partial) exception of delivery mirrors, few pregnant women—or their accompanying partners or friends—ever see birth from this point of view. In contrast, the camera's position in many birth films is an exact analogue of the 'place' of the medical attendants in a prone-position hospital delivery.

Within this frame of reference the body of the woman has become an object of the camera and of the manipulations of medicine. Her body is intimately exposed to the camera, to the eye of medicine, and ultimately to the boys and girls in school, as a naked, vulnerable, and passive thing. This feeling is emphasized if the woman herself is not allowed a voice; if she is shown silently enduring the pain she is so obviously feeling, and if the actual voice of the sound-track is that of a male doctor describing and commenting on the progress of the birth. Even where female midwives deliver the baby, the authority of male doctors is often reinforced by the film starting with one of them giving an overview of what is to follow.

(c) Child-centredness

As described above, *The First Days of Life* has three main phases. First there are scenes of a young child with its mother, and occasionally its father, playing together in the open air.

The commentary suggests that every small act towards the child can influence its development. This takes us to the second part, which shows the development of the fetus up until the point of birth. The scenes take place entirely in an anonymous womb. Finally we see a hospital birth shot very much in the manner described above. The sequence might be summed up as: child care, child development, childbirth.

What is absent in this version of birth is the experience of the mother. We are told little about her life: her work, her home, her relationship to the baby's father, the circumstances of her pregnancy, her experience of pregnancy and of birth itself, the impact of having a child on her future life, and so on. Equally, we learn nothing about fatherhood. The exclusive focus on the child leads to a silence about birth as a social, personal, and human experience.

In *The First Days of Life* and *Everyday Miracle* this effect is strengthened by the representation of fetal development. Here we find the womb treated as if it existed apart from any actual woman. The style of presentation falls somewhere between the BBC TV nature documentary, *The World about Us*, and *2001: A Space Odyssey*—a convergence that centres on the awed scientific exploration of an alien and exotic environment. The implicit expropriation of pregnancy from its human/social context by the medical/scientific world is strengthened by the eerie sci-fi electronic music and the language of bio-engineering that is used to describe fetal growth. Indeed, the text that accompanies *The First Days of Life* notes: 'The growth of the embryo is phenomenal and fascinating, the child developing steadily in his mother's body, taking shape and leading a life that seems, in a sense, to become more and more independent of his mother . . . He floats weightlessly in his mother's womb like an astronaut in space . . .' It is not explained how a camera came to be inserted, let alone safely or painlessly, inside an apparently living pregnant woman. However, the film lets us know that this highly impersonalized 'carrier' of the child is at the same time totally responsible for the developing baby: 'Of course his heart is beating, and he is affected by the outside world, by noise, probably by his mother's emotions—he is very vulnerable.'

It would seem that pregnancy, birth, and parenthood as social and personal experiences have been pushed out of the representational process by this powerful medical framework. It is interesting to note, however, that as the high tide of medicalization has begun to ebb, partially perhaps in response to women's own protests, film-makers have begun to reinsert the personal perspective. Nevertheless, the depth of the problem can be gauged from the testimony of one health visitor who told us that she had been complaining of the frightening and upsetting character of birth films for years, to the utter incomprehension of her colleagues.

If the kinds of birth film shown in schools might now seem inappropriate even for prospective parents in an ante-natal setting, what can we say of their use and value for teenage boys and girls, most of whom are several years away from facing these experiences directly? We have seen how many pupils reacted to the films, even though they might agree in principle that birth is a subject that should be 'done' at school, as Isobel Allen (1987) notes. Behind the common-sense assumption that pupils have to know about birth, alongside other issues such as contraception, relationships, etc., is a more complex problem. We must not forget that it is to the pupils that this activity is supposedly addressed. What of their needs, interests, and feelings?

In some respects it would seem that an enormous gulf of meaning separates teenagers from the scenes depicted in birth films. They are only just beginning to negotiate the terrain of sexuality, courtship, economic and emotional dependence and independence, etc. that may bring them to the threshold of parenthood. This is not to say that they are innocent of these processes, but simply to suggest that, in addition to the silences already described, most of the birth films used in schools have nothing at all to say about the personal and social transition from adolescence to parenthood.

From this perspective it is tempting to suggest that birth films should not be used at all in secondary schools—that they are simply too insensitive to the personal and social experience of birth, and that they present the latter in such a powerful medical framework that it appears to stand simply as 'the facts', excluding all other perspectives. But we believe that this would be an over-reaction, and that films *could* be used as part of a wider educational process that recognizes and explores other frameworks. At this point many teachers and other health educators will protest that they already do so. This may be true for many, but we are also bound to say that from our observational work in schools, this claim often appears to be more rhetorical than real. Even where efforts are made to 'set birth in context', the films we have discussed here are so powerful and so dramatically intense that they overshadow both what comes before and what comes after them. In any case, the 'context' that is presented is itself often defined in biomedical terms, such as the development of the fetus, especially in the case of examined Child Development courses.

It is interesting to note that the perceived 'power' of birth films, always a factor for their critics, has undergone some transformation since they were first shown in the 1950s. Then (see Kitzinger, Chapter 5) they were felt to be 'animalistic', exposing and degrading to women—too disgusting even for fathers/husbands to watch, let alone, as we now advocate, suitable viewing for boys and girls of 14–15. This process of 'reconstructing birth', which Kitzinger describes with regard to the National Childbirth Trust, involves a degree of 'sanitization' of frightening or disturbing aspects which has been achieved by portraying birth as overseen or controlled by the medical profession—a feature that seems to have been uncritically incorporated into many of the films shown in school.

In this respect it is encouraging that more recent films (which we list in an appendix at the end of this chapter, together with other alternative resources) have overcome some of the problems we have raised. These films start from the experiences of both mothers and fathers, and their stories are told in their own words. Issues are raised as personal choices rather than as authoritative medical directives. Most importantly, these stories express the direct personal experience of the men and women concerned: the women talk about what pregnancy meant to them, how their labour started, their journey into hospital, what the medical staff were like, and the physical sensations (including pain) involved; the men talk about their feelings about becoming a father, how they received the news that birth had begun, how they felt in the delivery room, and how they thought they could help. In this way the personal is at the centre of the account, and if the medical voice enters, it does so as a participant in a social process, not only as a representative of controlling, objective science. Interestingly, the births are also presented from the mother's point of view, and the medicalized gaze is avoided. These films are intended for use in ante-natal classes, but it would be unfortunate if schools were left with more dated resources which show contemporary obstetric practice as more medicalized than it sometimes is (Chard and Richards 1977).

There is little doubt that birth and parenthood will continue to be a feature of the school curriculum. We hope that the material and the analysis presented here will help to illuminate some of the concomitant issues, and will contribute to a more sensitive handling of the topic in the class-room. Central to this must be the recognition both of the different sets of meanings that surround birth itself and of the complex issue of personal identity which mediates it for teenage girls and boys.

Appendix

Possible alternative resources for teaching about birth in the secondary school classroom

BOOKS GIVING ALTERNATIVE PERSPECTIVES ON PREGNANCY
AND BIRTH

Boyd, C. and Sellars, L., 1982, *The British Way of Birth* (London, Pan).
Kitzinger, S. and Davis, J. A., 1975, *The Place of Birth* (Oxford, Oxford University Press).
Oakley, A., 1982, *From Here to Maternity* (London, Penguin).
Phillips, A. and Rakusen, J., 1978, *Our Bodies Ourselves* (London, Penguin).
Phillips, A., 1983, *Your Body, Your Life* (London, Pandora Press).

LITERARY AND OTHER ACCOUNTS OF BIRTH

Drabble, M., 1968, *The Millstone* (London, Penguin), 90.
—— 1971, *The Waterfall* (London, Penguin), chap. 1.
Jordan, B., 1983, *Birth in Four Cultures* (London, Eden Press).
Lessing, D., 1966, *A Proper Marriage* (London, Panther), pt. 2, chap. 2.

A very useful collection of personal experiences of birth can be found in Nancy Caldwell Sorel (ed.), 1985, *Ever since Eve: Personal Reflections of Childbirth* (London, Michael Joseph).

FILMS

Having a Baby, pt. 3, 'Richards's Story'; pt. 4, 'Eileen and Jan's Stories'. Made for the Health Education Council in 1980 for use in ante-natal education. Available from CFL Vision and Concord Film Council Ltd. A fuller list of films is available from the HEA; this includes, with critical comment, some of the films described in this chapter.

References

Allen, I., 1987, *Education in Sex and Personal Relationships* (London, PSI Publications).

Baldwin, J. and Wells, H., 1980, *Active Tutorial Work* (Oxford, Blackwells, in association with Lancashire County Council).

Button, L., 1974, *Developmental Group Work with Adolescents* (London, Hodder and Stoughton).

Chard, T. and Richards, M. (eds.), 1977, *Benefits and Hazards of the New Obstetrics* (London, Heinemann).

Grafton, T. *et al.* 1983, *Preparation for Parenthood in the Secondary School Curriculum: A Report to the Department of Education and Science* (Birmingham, University of Aston, Dept. of Educational Inquiry).

Graham, H. and Oakley, A., 1981, 'Competing Ideologies of Reproduction: Medical and Maternal Perspectives on Pregnancy and Childcare', in H. Roberts (ed.), 1981, *Women, Health and Reproduction* (London, Routledge and Kegan Paul).

Hopson, B. and Scally, M., 1981, *Lifeskills Teaching* (Maidenhead, McGraw Hill).

Nash, B. (ed.), 1980, *The Complete Book of Babycare* (London, Marks and Spencer).

Oakley, A., 1979, *Becoming a Mother* (Oxford, Martin Robertson).

—— 1980, *Women Confined: Towards a Sociology of Childbirth* (Oxford: Martin Robertson).

Prendergast, S. and Prout, A., 1987, *Knowing and Learning about Parenthood* (London, Health Education Authority Research Report, 17).

Prout, A. and Prendergast, S., 1985, 'Pupils' Knowledge as a Resource in Parenthood and Family-life Education', in *Childhood*, Open University Active Learning Resource Pack PE631, developed by D. Braun and N. Eisenstadt (Milton Keynes, Open University).

Pugh, G. and De'Ath, E., 1984, *The Needs of Parents: Practice and Policy in Parent Education* (London, Macmillan).

8

Labour Relations: Midwives and Doctors on the Labour Ward

Jenny Kitzinger, Josephine Green, and Vanessa Coupland

At the Christmas review, in front of the assembled staff, the midwives mimicked the doctors, poked fun at each other, and, as the grand finale, all joined hands and sang 'The Midwives Rule the Wards' to the tune of 'Rule, Britannia!' The staff Christmas review is an event notorious for the theatrical inversion of power relations and cathartic airing of tensions, but in this case the show also demonstrated vividly the relaxed consultant–midwife relations and high midwife morale that we had noted during the previous year's research. The midwives here were proud of their autonomy, very satisfied with their role, and enjoyed considerably more leeway in their relations with doctors than their colleagues in more traditional units.

This hospital was one of six that were involved in a study to assess the implications of different medical staffing structures in obstetric units. We were investigating the effects of replacing the traditional three-tier structure of consultant, registrar, and senior house officer (SHO) with a two-tier medical hierarchy that cut out the registrar (along the lines proposed by the Short Report on medical education in 1981). Consultants voiced many reservations regarding such a move (e.g. Houghton 1983; Royal College of Obstetricians and Gynaecologists 1983). As one obstetrician declared: 'The system will not work unless it is to the patient's detriment; it is legally and morally indefensible, unless the consultant numbers are trebled.' (Valentine 1983.) Many consultants felt that

The study on which this chapter is based was funded by the Nuffield Provincial Hospital Trust and the Health Promotion Research Trust. We would also like to thank Martin Richards, Rhys Williams, John Hare, and John Harvey for their support as the grant-holders and advisory team.

working without intermediate-grade staff would downgrade their role—partly because of the necessity to come in more often when on call. As one three-tier consultant in our study said: 'I came in once for 2 simultaneous caesars, but only because the baby would have died otherwise. My job is not to come in but to be consulted.' The debate in the medical press centred on the effects of two-tier staffing on *consultants*; little was said by or about the other remaining members of the obstetric team: SHOs and midwives. In our study we spent 400 hours observing doctors and midwives on the labour wards, and interviewed 137 of the labour ward staff in the six hospitals (three two-tier and three three-tier). The results of the study as a whole are reported elsewhere (Green *et al.* 1986). In this chapter we will explore the implications of different staffing structures for relations between midwives and doctors.

There is surprisingly little research on doctor–midwife relations, with the notable exceptions of Walker (1976) and Kirkham (1987). Existing research on interprofessional relations in other areas of health care suggests that they can have important effects not only on job satisfaction, but on the quality of care that patients receive and, indeed, on how quickly they get better (Revans 1964). Furthermore, doctors, when referred to at all in discussions of midwifery and obstetrics generally, tend to be lumped together without considering the very different positions, both in terms of role and status, of consultants and SHOs. These differences imply quite distinct relationships with midwives, and it is therefore worth considering how these roles are traditionally construed before we go on to look at interstaff relationships.

In National Health Service hospitals the consultant is usually given the role of manager and leader of the medical team—someone who sets policy, is there to be consulted, but only does a very limited part of the routine work. In this 'consultant-led' model, day-to-day obstetric difficulties are the domain of the registrar. The registrar, however, is technically a doctor in training, and as such will telephone the consultant before making any major decision.

The SHO works under the direct supervision of the registrar. The SHO grade, however, is heterogeneous: it includes not only doctors intending to embark on a career in obstetics and gynaecology ('career' SHOs), but also those intending to become general practitioners ('GP' or 'vocational' trainees). Among United Kingdom graduates, GP trainees outnumber career SHOs by nearly four to one (Royal College of Obstetricians and Gynaecologists [RCOG] 1986). Career SHOs normally spend two to three years in obstetrics and gynaecology, whereas GP trainees rarely have any previous obstetric experience (apart from some minimal training as medical students) and stay in obstetrics and gynaecology for only six months.

In practice there may be variations on this traditional model, but the constant factor is that there are three grades of doctors, with much of the everyday hands-on obstetrics being performed by the middle grade. The removal of this linchpin grade inevitably leads to changes in the roles of the remaining staff. Most of what a registrar does (e.g. operative deliveries) cannot be done safely by an inexperienced SHO, and must therefore be done by the consultant. This means that consultants in two-tier hospitals might be expected to spend more time on the labour ward, and consequently see far more of the midwives. In the absence of the registrar, day-to-day decisions on the ward can become the midwives' responsibility, as they will usually be the most senior and experienced personnel on the spot. The shifts in role may, in turn, affect relationships because of the opportunity to develop closer rapport between midwives and consultants, and because, if midwives take on more decision-making power, there must be repercussions for their interactions with SHOs.

The Context of Doctor–Midwife Relations

The relations between doctors and midwives are highly charged and traditionally antagonistic (Donnison 1977). A particular potential for conflict arises out of the coexistence of two separate, yet interdependent, hierarchies. The relationship between the two is not rigidly structured, and medical and midwifery staff at all levels often have conflicting views of each other's legitimate spheres of concern. Negotiation about roles is apparent throughout the hierarchy, be it about the consultant's and the Director of Midwifery's relative influence on policy, or the SHO's and staff midwife's relative qualifications to suture. Many such disputes crystallize around the disputed territory of 'normal' versus 'abnormal' birth, 'midwives'' versus 'doctors'' cases.

Normal versus Abnormal: Drawing up the Lines of Battle

> A midwife is a person who is trained to . . . conduct normal labours on her own responsibility . . . She must be able to recognise the warning signs of abnormal or potentially abnormal conditions which necessitate referral to a doctor . . .
>
> World Health Organization 1966.

This is part of an internationally accepted definition of a midwife. However, the definition of 'normal labour' is political. There are two major competing models of labour, each of which implies a different professional relationship. One model assumes that labours are normal until proved abnormal. Most therefore start off as the responsibility of the midwife, and it is up to her to decide if and when to involve a doctor.

However, the usual medical model implies a quite different professional relationship. This model adopts the basic premiss that every labour is potentially abnormal until it is over, and that childbirth is 'the most dangerous journey in a person's lifetime' (see Schwartz, Chapter 3). The consultant must therefore take responsibility for the progress of labour, and the junior doctors and midwives must act as the consultant's deputies and in accordance with his policies. There is no room for the midwife as an independent practitioner for normal labour, since a 'normal labour' can only be recognized in retrospect.

'Normal = Natural' or 'Normal = Common'?

Normality is not a single or fixed concept for midwives. In particular we identified two distinct ways in which they interpreted 'normal labour': as 'statistically common' and as 'natural'. In the first case, normality includes such common procedures as episiotomy, intravenous drips, artificial rupture of the membranes, and electronic fetal monitoring. These are part of 'normal labour', and therefore, some midwives argue, they are the responsibility of the midwife. On the other hand, 'normal' may be used to mean 'natural'—a definition which includes breech and twin deliveries but excludes the common procedures listed above. Thus, a midwife might resist what she sees as an unnecessary induction for 'her woman' on the grounds that 'Prostin makes deliveries abnormal, I therefore refuse to put it in.' Breech and twin deliveries, which are usually defined as doctors' cases, are included within this interpretation of normal as 'natural'. A breech in itself is normal; it is only the use of forceps that makes it abnormal. Highlighting this perspective, one midwife commented: 'If the doctor's there he'll put on the forceps. Only if it's undiagnosed and the midwife has to deliver will it be normal.'

The 'natural' interpretation of 'normal' can be used both to justify midwives' resistance to medical interventions, and to maintain that they are the rightful attendants for women giving birth to twins or breech babies. Thus, midwives are able to use the definition of their role as the *attendants* of normal labour to lay claim to being the *guardians* of natural labour.

Natural and Common: Complementary or Conflicting Definitions of Normality?

The two uses of the concept of normality are in some ways complementary: together they can combine to expand the midwives' role. A midwife would need to call a doctor less often if the definition of her role as a 'practitioner in her own right for normal birth' included breeches and twins, rupturing membranes, and setting up drips.

However, the 'natural' and the 'common' definitions of normal labour can also conflict. There was concern that a strictly 'natural' interpretation could lead to some midwives 'abandoning' women once they required the slightest form of medical intervention. The 'normal = natural' definition could thus be seen to restrict the midwife's role and circumscribe the care she gives to women in labour.

On the other hand, some midwives argue that a strictly 'common' definition of 'normal' can distort traditional mid-wifery values. Anxiety was expressed that as midwives became proficient in the use of technology, they would lose the ability to 'use their ears, eyes and hands' and to support women to give birth naturally. This whole dilemma is summed up by Katz Rothman (1981: 160):

> If midwives are denied the use of available technology, then they obviously won't have it when they need it. They will have to turn over every patient who needs assistance, or even diagnosis, to a physician . . . But if she's allowed the medical technology, then what prevents the midwife from becoming a 'mini-obstetrician' as critics have claimed?

Midwives and SHOs: Conflicting Expectations

The SHOs and 'shop-floor' midwives are the members of the medical and midwifery staff who work most closely together on the labour ward; it is here that some of the general issues about doctor–midwife relations are brought sharply into focus.

In the highly status-conscious environment of the hospital, the relative position of midwife and SHO can become a matter of group negotiation. SHOs, by virtue of being doctors, take precedence over the midwives, who may be seen as 'just nurses'. However, eighteen out of twenty-four SHOs in our study were GP trainees, and thus spent only six months in obstetrics. By contrast, the midwives had specialized in obstetrics for at least eighteen months as well as having substantial practical experience: the sisters we interviewed had, on average, seventeen years' practical midwifery ex-perience, while the staff midwives had practised for an average of six and a half years. It is in this situation that the hierarchy of 'doctor' over 'nurse' most obviously runs counter to the hierarchy of skill and experience. As one consultant said: 'It's like the NCO and Lieutenant—the midwives have the experience even though the lower status.'

There was often a mismatch between SHOs' and midwives' evaluation of their own and each others' relative skills. SHOs were variously characterized by midwives as 'green as green', 'still wet behind the ears', and not knowing 'one end from the other'. Many midwives spoke pityingly of SHOs' 'illusions of superiority': 'I do feel sorry for them, they're all taught all along that they're the crème de la crème. They think they're the doctor and we're just the nurse.' The SHOs did indeed sometimes give high priority to their own medical training over and above the midwives' experience, and resented midwives' views of them as less knowledgeable: 'Some midwives think you don't know what you're saying. They try to impose on you the fact that they've been doing it for 25 years. They try to tell you that they know more than you.'

SHO–midwife interaction is thus framed both by conflicting views of each other's expertise, and by the traditional medical versus midwifery attitudes towards childbirth. Added to this is the fact that their roles overlap to some extent. Those tasks which midwives have been seeking to reclaim, such as suturing and setting up intravenous drips, are tasks which would otherwise be performed by the SHO. The SHOs in our study did not experience this loss as particularly threatening, since they saw such jobs as 'tedious and petty interruptions to sleep'.

The allocation of decision-making responsibility generates far more controversy than the issue of task distribution. This is because decision-making is seen as critical to the roles of both midwives and SHOs. Midwives in two-tier units tend to have a more extended decision-making role than their three-tier colleagues (for example, deciding when to call the consultant), and also to have more formal input into such decisions as when to accelerate a labour, and when to send a woman home.

In most hospitals, however, midwives make far more of a decision-making contribution than is formally acknowledged. SHOs may be officially responsible for many decisions, but, as one midwife said: 'You're usually putting it into *their* hands to do what *you* want them to do.' The midwives' low status inhibits them from openly expressing opinions, a situation that is exacerbated by some SHOs who argue that they, as doctors, are the only competent decision-makers: 'midwives are not medically trained so can't interpret what they see'.

This type of attitude has led most midwives to develop definite tactics for dealing with particularly arrogant SHOs. As one consultant said: 'The midwives tend to make life hell for [them]. I'm sure you've seen their little ploys. You know the sort of thing: "She seems to have a narrow sub-pubic arch". Nonsense, but it gets the SHO's adrenalin going.' None of the midwives admitted to tormenting SHOs in this way, although three of them referred mysteriously to 'ways of making sure that pride comes before a fall'. The situation is usually managed in a subtler way; most midwives stated that they tried to guide SHOs without undermining their confidence or status. Midwives, like nurses (Rushing 1965; Stein 1967; Hughes 1987), have developed particular strategies to avoid provoking overt conflict. They sought to advise the SHO without challenging the hierarchy or negating the SHOs' medical training, and they emphasized the need for gentleness and diplomacy:

If you say what you think straight some SHOs are so bolshy you have to be careful or you can make them more bolshy. They puff themselves up and pull their white coats around them . . . you can't [give your opinion directly]—you want what's best for your woman and you're not going to get it if you say directly. You just have to make them feel important and learn how to pull the right strings.

Almost every midwife could immediately provide a list of tactics of 'how to get the SHO to do what you want', it was as if they had all read the same manual on 'Gaining SHOs' Compliance': 'Instead of saying "this woman should have . . ." you get a lot more done if you watch your phraseology and say "do you think we might perhaps think about doing?". . . With some individual exceptions, midwives emphasized the politics of approaching the SHO tactfully. Some presented this as a process of humouring the junior doctors; others presented it as an elaborate game ('you have to learn to be devious') or as common politeness ('you do it as a courtesy'; 'it doesn't lower a midwife to be tactful'). Whatever the interpretation offered by different midwives, the end-result was that they were involved in a great deal of what we chose to call 'hierarchy maintenance work'.

Consultant–Midwife Relations

The consultant post represents the highest point of the medical hierarchy, and the incumbent of this position has most control over the way in which she or he wishes to work. Consultants in British hospitals have, on the whole, a common background (as far as class is concerned, and usually as far as race and gender are concerned too). However, they differ in age and experience, in their obstetric policies, in their obstetric work-loads, and in their attitudes to junior doctors and midwives. Naturally, they also differ in the extent of their other commitments; for example, their gynaecological work-load, their private work-load, their families, and their outside interests. Tied up with all of these is personality: some are easier to get on with than others.

The consultant's path crosses that of the midwife in two ways—as policy-maker and through direct contact. Whatever the consultants' personal involvement in the labour ward, their role as policy-makers is a constant feature of, and influence on, the consultant–midwife relationship. The consultant determines the policies that affect the midwife (and labouring women), and thereby attracts midwives' approval or disapproval, affection or dislike. It is here that the standard issues of normal midwifery versus abnormal medical cases come to the fore again. It is the consultant who defines, in principle, when a doctor should take over from a midwife, when drugs should be administered and procedures carried out. These policies may be seen as vague and allowing the midwife a great deal of autonomy, or as rigid and limiting the midwives' freedom. They may be seen as flexible and allowing normal (natural) labour to take its course, or as aggressive and interfering. Where consultants within the same unit had different policies, midwives sometimes felt like 'piggies in the middle': 'You've got to know each consultant's attitude and the drugs they like. But if you've got any sense you jolly well slot in and get into gear. It's worst on the actual labour ward. You have to keep remembering who each woman belongs to. You become a pawn in the political war.' One three-tier midwife was dismayed at the thought of working without registrars, because she felt that an increase in the number of consultants in the unit would add to the number of conflicting policies. She was rather horrified by the suggestion: 'You mean two extra consultants with different ideas!' However, in the two-tier system we found that better communication between consultants could lead to a convergence of policies.

The consultants also differed considerably in their attitudes towards midwives. Two-tier consultants were more positive about midwives' power on the labour ward: 'It really behoves the midwives to run the show . . . they are in charge of the labour ward'; while some of the three-tier consultants did not even see the midwives as having an independent role at all: 'the days of the midwives—in my view—managing cases themselves . . . is gone. I consider the midwives to be my juniors, my deputies.' Three-tier consultants were also generally less aware of what midwives were actually doing, let alone what they wanted. For example, one three-tier consultant said that he did not know whether or not the midwives in his hospital put up drips or took blood: 'Isn't there something against it in their training? I don't think they're allowed to stick needles in people.'

These differences in consultants' perception of the midwives' role are to a large extent a result of two-tier consultants spending much more time on the labour ward. Initially we had thought that this might result in midwives feeling that consultants were breathing down their necks. Midwives in three-tier units certainly shied away from the idea of a two-tier structure partly because they did not want the greater contact with consultants that this would imply. They were not always in harmony with their consultants' obstetric philosophies, and were therefore quite happy to have their consultants out of the way: 'We don't see the consultants much on the wards . . . but that's OK as you can gently break the doctors' orders.' Two-tier midwives, on the other hand, accepted the greater consultant involvement because they had less reason for wanting their consultants to keep away; they were less often at odds with 'the doctors' orders'. Contrary to the fears of the three-tier midwives, then, those working in the two-tier structure did not appear to find their consultants intrusive. A questionnaire sent round by the Director of Midwifery in one of the two-tier hospitals showed that none of the twenty-six midwives who responded (anonymously) thought that consultant supervision and availability for advice on the labour ward was 'too much'; twenty-three thought it was 'about right'; and three thought it was 'not enough'. No longer in awe of their consultants, two-tier midwives felt confident to talk with them relatively freely, something that few three-tier midwives could even imagine. One two-tier consultant, commenting on the advantages of frequent visits to the labour ward as opposed to the traditional consultant behaviour of just rushing in for emergencies, said: 'You can discuss things over a cup of tea with the midwives—I have a closer relationship with them than [other consultants] do. The midwives . . . really know me and like me.' The midwives in two-tier hospitals were proud of this intimacy—one told us a story of how amazed midwives from other hospitals were to see her chatting to her consultant at a conference: 'No wonder your system works if you can talk to your consultants like that', they declared.

The two-tier system itself, imposed on unwilling consultants, would not guarantee better midwife–consultant relations or increased midwifery autonomy, because the consultant's attitude is a key factor. The two-tier units that we explored represented living structures that were mediated by staff attitudes, and these units had assembled some atypical staff: quite a few independent-minded midwives had been attracted to the highest profile two-tier unit in our sample, and some traditionally minded consultants had certainly avoided two-tier units. However, at least in theory, the relationship between the staffing structure and the staff's views could be a two-way process. Midwives who accept posts in two-tier hospitals might find that the experience of working without registrars helps them to develop their skill and confidence as independent practitioners. Similarly, consultants might develop greater respect for midwives. As one consultant commented: 'In the two-tier structure you're more dependent on the midwives so you *have* to respect them.' Some two-tier consultants also come to enjoy their increased contact with women in labour, even though they did not originally choose to work in that way (Pentecost, 1983).

Relations between midwives and doctors are constantly under informal negotiation on the labour ward. The relationship between midwives and SHOs is, in particular, the focus of subtle manipulation as a result of the mismatch between midwives' skills and the SHOs status in the traditional unit.

The innovative two-tier system contains the potential for developing a more autonomous and powerful midwifery role within the hospital structure. It can also result in an increase in overt conflict between midwives and SHOs, and may be associated with improved midwife–consultant relationships. However, whether or not this potential is developed, and how specific problems arise and are resolved, depends on the attitude of the staff involved. The power of the consultants to determine the details of labour ward working means that their attitudes are crucial. The two-tier structure can provide a framework for change, but it is not, in itself, sufficient to promote midwifery autonomy or particular changes in inter-staff relationships.

References

Donnison, J., 1977, *Midwives and Medical Men: A History of Inter-Professional Rivalries and Women's Rights* (London, Heinemann).

Green, J., Kitzinger, J., and Coupland, V., 1986, 'The Division of Labour: Implications of Medical Staffing Structures for Midwives and Doctors on the Labour Ward', Child Care and Development Group, University of Cambridge, unpublished report.

Houghton, D. J., 1983, 'Is there Another Consultant Lifestyle?' *British Medical Journal*, 287, p. 562.

Hughes, D., 1987, 'When Nurse Knows Best: Some Aspects of Nurse/Doctor Interaction in a Casualty Department', Paper presented at BSA Medical Sociology Group Conference, 25–7 Sept. 1987.

Katz Rothman, B., 1981, 'Awake and Aware or False Consciousness?', in S. Romalis (ed.), *Childbirth: Alternatives to Medical Control* (Austin, University of Texas Press).

Kirkham, M. J., 1987, 'Basic Supportive Care in Labour: Interaction with and around Labouring Women', Ph.D. thesis (University of Manchester).

Pentecost, A., 1983, 'Is there Another Consultant Lifestyle?', *British Medical Journal*, 287, pp. 305–6.

Revans, R. W., 1964, *Standards for Morale: Cause and Effect in Hospitals* (London, Oxford University Press).

Royal College of Obstetricians and Gynaecologists, 1983, *Report of the Manpower Advisory Sub-Committee of the Royal College of Obstetricians and Gynaecologists* (London, RCOG).

—— 1986, 'Survey of Senior House Officers and Registrars', unpublished report.

Rushing, W. A., 1965, 'Social Influence and Social-Psychological Function of Deference: A Study of Psychiatric Nursing', in Skipper, J. K. and Leonard, R. C. (eds.), *Social Interaction and Patient Care* (Philadelphia, Lippincott).

Social Services Committee, 1981, *Medical Education with Special Reference to the Number of Doctors and the Career Structure in Hospitals* (Short Report) (London, HMSO).

Stein, L., 1967, 'The Doctor–Nurse Game', *Archives of General Psychiatry*, 16, pp. 699–703.

Valentine, B. H., 1983, 'Is there Another Consultant Lifestyle?', *British Medical Journal*, 287, p. 914.

Walker, J. F., 1976, 'Midwife or Obstetric Nurse? Some Perceptions of Midwives and Obstetricians of the Role of the Midwife', *Journal of Advanced Nursing*, 1, pp. 129–38.

World Health Organization, 1966, *The Midwife in Maternity Care* (Technical Report Series, 331; Geneva).

9

Parents and New-Born Babies
in the Labour Ward

Jo Garcia and Sally Garforth

THERE have been striking changes in the ways in which maternity hospitals deal with the social aspects of care in the post-partum period. Not only is the relationship between the mother and her new baby given increasing emphasis, but the baby's father and the wider family are more likely to be included, both in the delivery room and in the post-natal ward. This chapter uses observational and interview data from a study of maternity-unit procedures to describe in detail the labour ward policies and practices that affect the first contacts between the parents and their new baby.

Parents and their New-Born Babies

The focus of this chapter—the first encounters between new-born and parents—is an aspect of childbirth that may be very much affected by the hospital setting. Results from British studies indicate changing practice in these aspects of care. In a national sample survey carried out in 1975 (Cartwright 1979), 70 per cent of respondents reported that the baby's father was present for some or all of their labour and delivery. Among the thirty-seven hospitals in the survey with twenty or more deliveries in the sample, the proportion of deliveries at

The National Perinatal Epidemiology Unit is funded by the Department of Health and Social Security. Further funds for the study came from Birthright and the Iolanthe Trust. Our thanks go to all who helped us with the design, conduct, and analysis of the study, and especially to the midwives and patients who took part. We are grateful to our colleagues at the National Perinatal Epidemiology Unit who helped in all aspects of this project, especially Sarah Ayers, who has worked on the administration and data analysis.

which the baby's father was present at some stage varied from 20 to 95 per cent. Some comments from the women interviewed indicated that hospitals had different policies—for example, excluding fathers who had not been to classes, or during instrumental deliveries. Of the mothers in Cartwright's survey, 36 per cent reported that they were able to hold their baby before the third stage was completed. Of the remainder, half held their baby within twenty minutes. A recent sample survey of 1,500 women, carried out by the same team (Jacoby 1987), showed that in 1984 over 90 per cent of the mothers in the study had the baby's father or another companion with them for all or part of their labour, and 85 per cent were able to hold their baby straight away. Taken together, these two studies suggest that a new approach to family contact in the labour ward had already reached some hospitals at the time of the earlier study, and has become more or less standard practice in the mid-1980s.

The more recent survey also gives information about the attitudes of mothers towards these aspects of their care. Ninety per cent of respondents (who were surveyed about four months after the birth) said that they had wanted the baby's father to be with them for labour and delivery; 5 per cent did not want this, and 5 per cent had no preference. Only 2 per cent said that they did not want to hold the baby as soon as he or she was born; 93 per cent did and 5 per cent had no preference. One of the aims of the study reported in this chapter is to look in more detail at the preferences and experiences of parents with regard to this aspect of their care.

Concern about the effects of early separation on the relationship between parents and child has developed since the early 1970s (Richards 1985) and has led to a considerable volume of research. A recent review (Thomson and Westreich, 1989) of experimental studies of the consequences of restricting contact between mothers and infants in the period immediately after delivery concluded that such a procedure had no benefits. In those studies which measured the effect on breast-feeding, it was found that restricted contact was associated with lower breast-feeding rates one to three months after delivery; and, in addition, a majority of the studies which compared different policies for contact in the first two hours after delivery showed that restricted contact was associated with a reduction in the affectionate behaviour displayed by the mother to the infant (measured at a range of ages from a few days to two years).

Results of this kind should encourage care-givers to look critically at the policies for institutional maternity care in the immediate post-partum period. A recent cross-national study has indicated that restrictive policies are still the norm in many European countries (World Health Organization 1985). One problem identified by several authors (e.g. Richards 1983, 1985; Slukin *et al.* 1983) is the way in which concern about the early separation of new-born and parents can have some unwanted consequences. Part of this concern arises from the belief that there is a sensitive period immediately following delivery when a mother is able to 'bond' with her baby. If contact is not made during this period—if 'bonding' is not allowed to take place—then, it is claimed, the relationship will suffer permanent damage and many negative consequences will follow. The evidence so far does not support the idea of a sensitive period for the development of mother–infant relationships. An exaggerated idea of the importance of bonding can potentially cause great anxiety to parents who have experienced separation at what they believe to be the crucial time. The continuing relationship between parents and children may be seen as less important because of this emphasis on the first few hours of life.

Any rigid ideas about the appropriate contact between baby and parents may make it hard for the labour ward staff to respond to the needs of parents, which will certainly not be uniform. New policies, intended to facilitate contact between parents and babies, may become prescriptive, so that parents feel obliged to behave in ways that are now seen to be the norm. For example, it is now difficult for British fathers to avoid being present at the birth, as Barbour discusses in Chapter 11. Really flexible care is difficult to achieve within an institution like a hospital, even where rigid policies are avoided. Even the best policies do not automatically translate into practice, and a detailed examination of the kind of care described below may, for example, reveal conflicts between the intention to provide good care and other demands of hospital staffing, procedures, or routines.

The Policy and Practice in Midwifery Study

The data we will report on come from a national study of midwifery policies and policy-making for normal labour and post-natal care (Garcia *et al.* 1987; Garcia and Garforth, forthcoming). The study was made up of two parts. The first was a survey of the Directors of Midwifery Services in all the English health districts. This provided information about policies in the districts and the maternity units within them. It was carried out in the second half of 1984, and achieved a response rate of 93 per cent (180 out of 193 health districts). The second part was an in-depth study of aspects of policy and practice in eight health districts selected from among the 180 which took part in the survey. The aim of selection was to obtain a wide geographic spread, and to include districts which differed in their circumstances and approaches to midwifery policy and policy-making. This part of the study involved interviews with senior midwives which were intended to complement the survey results, and, most importantly, observation of labour-ward care.

Two aspects of care were chosen for observation—admission to the labour ward (Garforth and Garcia 1987), and the interval between delivery and transfer to the post-natal ward. Following the observation of a particular element of care, a short interview was sought with the midwife responsible for the care, and the next day the woman concerned was also approached to ascertain her point of view. The observation sheet and the interview schedules for mother and midwife were all partially structured and were developed in pilot studies. Before observation, consent was obtained from the midwife involved and from the woman and her companion. In each district observation was carried out during the day and at night over a period of about two weeks. There was no specific intention to observe the delivery of a woman whose admission to the labour ward had been part of the study, though in some cases this did happen. In total, sixty-two admissions and seventy-eight intervals between delivery and transfer to the post-natal ward were observed in nine consultant maternity units in the eight districts. Most of the results presented below come from the in-depth part of the study, but some national survey data will also be included. Information about the first breast-feed and about policies concerning infant feeding are the subject of another paper (Garforth and Garcia, 1989).

In studying the first hours of the baby's life we were particularly concerned with what we felt to be the social needs of parents. Although we recorded the technical aspects of the immediate post-partum period, we emphasized those actions of staff and parents that were concerned with relationships and choices. We noted information-giving by staff, and other aspects of communication between staff and parents. We tried to identify instances in which policies enabled staff to meet parents' needs, or, conversely, where they were a barrier to providing individual care. We also looked at other, less formal, constraints on staff and parents, such as attitudes, unwritten rules, and the pressures created by lack of time and space. Our own opinions and experiences were important in shaping the observation schedules and interviews that we used, and this may have led us to ask questions which some of the mothers did not find very interesting. Questions about choice are a good example. Some women were eager to talk about the scope for choice with regard to aspects of labour care, but others found the questions irrelevant. In the same way, it may be that we missed aspects of care that were of concern to the mothers but which were not drawn out by our invitation to comment generally at the end of the questionnaire. With these provisos in mind, we will turn to the detailed results of the national survey of maternity-unit policies and of the observation of care in eight health districts.

Companions in Labour

Policies about women's companions in labour were investigated in the national survey. We asked if there were any circumstances in which a woman's husband or partner might be excluded. In 40 per cent of consultant units there were no such circumstances specified in their policies, and in 6 per cent exclusion would take place only at a mother's request. General anaesthetics (10 per cent) or some other procedure (17 per cent) were given as reasons by some units, and in 22 per cent the partner could be excluded at the doctor's discretion. We also asked whether women could have additional companions. A majority of consultant units (64 per cent) allowed another adult companion *instead* of a husband or partner, and 32 per cent *in addition*. A minority of units (18 per cent) would allow a woman's children to be present for labour or delivery, with various provisos (proper supervision, for example), and a further 15 per cent said that this was possible, but not encouraged.

In our observation, which was confined to normal deliveries, we saw no instances of husbands, partners, or other companions being excluded at the time of delivery, though some women were separated from their companions during admission (Garforth and Garcia 1987). The situations of the seventy-eight women whose deliveries we observed are described in Table 9.1. Nearly three-quarters of the women had their husband or partner with them, and three women also had a companion in addition to their husband or partner. Three of the twelve women with no companion at the delivery had a husband or partner with them who chose to leave for the delivery itself but returned very soon after. In one hospital a father brought in their 18-month-old daughter who was cared for by the staff on the ward and then brought in to see her new brother soon after delivery.

TABLE 9.1. *Companions observed at delivery*

	No.	%
Husband/partner only	56	72
Husband/partner plus other (1 aunt, 1 mother, 1 friend)	3	4
Other companion only (sister, mother, or sister-in-law)	7	9
No companion	12	15
TOTAL	78	100

Out of sixty-six mothers who were asked about companions when they were interviewed, all but four were satisfied with what had happened. Five mothers had not had their husband present and were either pleased or unconcerned ('He hasn't been at any of the births—I'm not really bothered'). Twenty-nine mothers (44 per cent) had been very pleased with the presence of a companion ('I couldn't have done without him'; 'A lot more confident than if he hadn't been there'), and several mentioned previous labours and births which had been much less satisfactory in this regard ('They were a little bit strict. He kept having to be sent out when they did an internal. This time it's more relaxed'). A further twenty-eight mothers (42 per cent) made brief comments but were not especially enthusiastic. The four mothers who were not happy with what had happened included two whose husbands had wanted to be present but had not been able to because of home circumstances. Both were disappointed. The remaining two had had their husband or partner present, but were not sure that this was what they wanted ('I wasn't so sure, I didn't want anyone seeing me looking like that. But in the end I didn't mind').

The First Encounters

The first few minutes of the baby's life were recorded in some detail in our observation. Over all, the baby was delivered on to the mother's body in thirty-five (45 per cent) of the seventy-eight deliveries that we observed. In the remaining forty-three deliveries (55 per cent), the baby was placed on the delivery bed and then either moved to a cot, or resuscitation table, or given to one of the parents to hold. Some hospitals had made it their policy to ask mothers if they wanted to have the baby delivered directly on to them, and this was reflected in higher proportions of mothers receiving this kind of care. Midwives often asked mothers about this just before delivery. One mother said at interview: 'They asked me if I wanted him on my stomach. When you watch the films beforehand you think—what a mess—but you do want to hold him.' Another commented: 'As soon as he came out he was plonked on my stomach. That was another nice thing. They asked me if I wanted that.' Several parents commented, either during the delivery or at interview, that this aspect of care represented an improvement on previous deliveries. One mother said: 'As soon as she was born she flew at me. It was great. It's much better that way. I waited ages for the first one.'

In one case that was observed, however, the woman misunderstood what was being suggested when she was asked if she wanted the baby delivered on to her stomach. When she heard: 'Do you want the baby on your tummy?', she thought that she was being invited to deliver lying on her front, and was rather perplexed! This emerged only at interview, because she was too shy or perhaps too overwhelmed by labour to ask for clarification at the time.

The heads of midwifery who took part in the national survey were asked how soon the mother could hold the baby following delivery. Out of the 220 who completed a questionnaire, only four consultant maternity units suggested that the usual policy was to wait until the cord was cut before giving the baby to the mother. In 212 units (96 per cent) the mother could hold the baby at once or as soon as she wanted, and four gave some other answer (e.g. 'almost immediately').

The observation study also measured the times at which each parent first touched and held the baby. The data are summarized in Table 9.2. Seven mothers were observed to touch the baby's head before delivery, and others may have done so before we began observation. Altogether, forty mothers out of the seventy-seven for whom this information was collected (52 per cent) *touched* their babies at or before birth. The remaining thirty-seven (48 per cent) had to wait an average of 5.1 minutes (1–23 min. range). (The information was missing for one mother observed.) Thirty-four mothers (45 per cent) *held* their babies straight away, and for the remaining forty-two (55 per cent), the mean time to holding the baby was 6.8 minutes (1–60 min. range). (This information was missing for two mothers observed.) Two mothers in one hospital first held the baby against their naked skin.

Fathers took a little longer, on average, to touch and hold their babies. Fifty-nine fathers were present at delivery, and three came in just after the birth. Of these sixty-two, three did not touch their babies during the period of observation, and a

TABLE 9.2. *First touching and holding the baby*

	Mothers[a]		Fathers[b]	
	No.	%	No.	%
First touched at or				
before birth	40	52	11	18
after birth	37	48	47	77
Did not touch	0	0	3	5
First held				
straightaway	34	45	n/a	n/a
after a wait	42	55	n/a	n/a
after birth	n/a	n/a	57	93
Did not hold	n/a	n/a	4	7

[a]Total no. observed = 77 (data on holding missing for one woman)
[b]Total no. observed = 61

further one touched his baby but did not hold it. (Data were missing for one father.) So, out of fifty-eight fathers, eleven (19 per cent) touched their baby as soon as she or he was born; the remaining forty-seven (81 per cent) touched their babies 9.8 minutes after delivery on average (1–60 min. range). The fifty-seven fathers who were observed to hold their babies did so within an average of 12.8 minutes after delivery (1–60 min. range).

Although in each hospital the pattern of contact was very varied, there were signs that some hospitals were more likely to enable women to hold thir babies early on. Comparing two hospitals where times were recorded for the thirteen deliveries observed in each, we found that in the first, nine of the thirteen mothers were able to hold their babies straight away, and that the mean time for the other four (7 min.) was distorted by one long period during which a baby was being resuscitated outside the delivery room. In the second hospital, only three mothers held the baby straight away, and the other ten waited an average of six minutes. The baby was more likely to be delivered on to the mother's body in the first hospital (10/13) than in the second (4/15 deliveries).

Parents' Reactions

Note was taken of parents' comments and requests to staff about their contact with the baby. One mother, who was obviously aware of changing fashions, said 'I don't want to feel the baby's head. I just want it out. None of this sitting up and having a look!' Another, whose baby had been in her arms for a couple of minutes straight after birth but had then been passed to the father and held by him for a long time, said: 'I'm dying for a cuddle', and was then given the baby. A similar oblique request was made by a woman whose small baby had been a cause of concern. Seven minutes after birth, when she had not yet touched her, she said, 'I haven't had a chance to look at her at all.' Another mother was anxious not to be a nuisance and asked: 'Can I have her back, or will she be in your way Nurse?'. She was handed the baby at once.

In general, the parents did not pick up their babies without permission from the staff. Mothers were usually unable to reach their babies if they were in a cot, because the cot was rarely beside the bed. The examples quoted above of mothers asking for their babies were quite uncommon, and so parents depended on staff suggesting that they held their babies. The importance of this is indicated by this comment made during an interview: 'They usually tell you in the films of births to look down and touch the head. But they didn't, so I didn't.' This aspect of care is not usually a result of specific policies, nor is it likely that the staff would make a conscious decision to put the baby in a cot at the other side of the labour room. It reflects, rather, the priorities of care-givers and the pressure to get things done 'efficiently'. Putting the baby in a cot at the other side of the room may just have been part of a convenient routine.

When mothers were interviewed about the care they received, they were asked whether their first contact with the baby had been 'what they wanted'. Three-quarters of the women (55/72, 6 missing) said that it was, and some of them were very enthusiastic about this aspect: 'Marvellous, lovely . . . it was the best part of it all'; 'it was fantastic'. Two mothers, who both had to wait a long time to touch or hold their babies, made negative comments here: 'I would have

mething wrong
mething.' (The
:cial care.) The
r. My husband
r away before I
rs (21 per cent)
y positive nor
to touch or hold
for the best' or
t happen; seven

did not find the question very important, or said that they had not cared at the time. One mother might even have felt that she held the baby too soon. She commented: 'Well, I didn't mind. I wouldn't have objected if they had cleaned her up.'

Referring again to the two hospitals compared above, we find that in the one where nine of the thirteen mothers held their babies straight away (and a further two within one minute of birth), only one woman said that her first contact was not what she had wanted. Her baby was taken out to be resuscitated and was first held by her after twenty minutes. She said: 'I was a little bit concerned but they had warned me about it because they had expected it to happen.' The staff made efforts to keep her informed about the baby while this was going on, and the father went to the special care unit with the baby. In the other hospital, only three of the thirteen mothers held the baby straight away, and seven out of the thirteen said that the care was not what they had wanted.

Other Labour Ward Routines

After the initial touching and holding, the pattern of contact becomes very complex, with the baby moving between both parents, the staff, and the cot. There are various tasks to perform. The baby is usually weighed, examined, and wrapped. The mother may need stitches, and will be given a wash. The parents will be offered a cup of tea and, in most units, will be left alone with the baby for a few minutes. The midwives have to write up their notes and start to tidy the room. We looked in some detail at two further social aspects of care that we thought were important—whether the baby was separated from the parents at any stage, and the way that the first examination was carried out.

We recorded any instances in which the baby was removed from the delivery room, either temporarily or to a nursery, ward, or special care unit, without the mother. This happened in half the deliveries that we observed (35/70, 8 missing). The policies of the maternity units involved in our detailed study would suggest that this figure is probably not a good indicator of national practice. Nationally, 92 per cent of consultant units said that mothers and babies were transferred to the post-natal ward together. However, in three of the nine hospitals in the observation study (according to their stated policies), babies were routinely transferred to the post-natal ward before the mothers. In one of these three, babies were also removed from the room to be weighed, and in a fourth hospital, which was using temporary premises, some babies had to be taken out for weighing, although this was not routine. In one delivery suite the resuscitation equipment was kept in a separate room, and two of the thirteen babies whose births were observed were taken there soon after birth. Three women were separated from their babies because they needed a general anaesthetic for an incomplete third stage.

In those hospitals which had a policy of transferring the baby and mother to the post-natal ward separately, the staff did not always explain what they were doing. About fifty minutes after one delivery the nursing auxiliary asked the sister: 'Is the baby ready to go?'; the sister replied: 'Yes, she's had her injection and got her labels on.' The baby was then taken out without any kind of explanation to the parents, who subsequently discussed where she might be because her grandmother wanted to see her. Two cases were observed where a mother tried to persuade staff not to send the baby up to the ward without her. In one she succeeded and the baby stayed with her.

In those cases where mothers and babies were transferred to the post-natal ward separately, they often had to wait a long time before they saw each other again. This was because babies were often put in a nursery for the first night (at least), and so some mothers came up to the ward when their babies were already in there. Although post-natal ward care was not specifically observed or covered in the mother's interview, several mothers did comment about being separated from their babies on the post-natal ward. One said: 'They took him away to have a bath. Then I came to the ward about 6.00 or 6.30. I didn't see him until 1.00. I kept asking why. I didn't like that. I got up at 10.00 and had a look. I kept asking. I wanted him. They didn't do it on purpose. Please don't think I'm complaining. But I would have liked him to be with me a bit earlier than that.' Another mother in the same hospital had a similar experience, but did not mind because it compared favourably with a previous delivery: 'He left to be cleaned up and seen to before I did and I didn't see him again until this morning. The sister brought him in this morning.' *Interviewer*: 'Were you happy about that?' 'Yes, 'cos my other little boy, I had to keep asking for him.' In another hospital a woman said: 'They insisted on taking him away that first night so I could sleep—but I was too excited. I wanted to see him.'

For a majority of the babies whose births had been observed, a first examination was carried out by the midwife in the delivery room. The contents of this examination, and the extent to which the parents were involved in it, varied considerably both between and within hospitals. Out of seventy babies for whom this information is available, sixty (86 per cent) were examined, in a more or less formal way, in the delivery room. Of these, just over a third were examined at the mother's bedside, with some explanations being given in almost all cases; the rest were examined in another part of the delivery room, and parents were much less likely to be invited to watch and to be given explanations about the examination. There was a tendency to mention the injection of vitamin K, which was given routinely in the majority of hospitals, even when no other aspect of the examination was discussed with the parents.

For some midwives the examination was an important opportunity to reassure the parents, particularly when there had been some concern about the baby. This was done in a very sensitive way for one mother who had had a previous baby with a neural tube defect. The midwife examined the baby in the mother's arms, turning him over so that the mother could see that the spine was normal. The mother talked about this during her interview when she was asked if she had found anything particularly reassuring. Another mother, who had a child with a malformed foot, asked about the baby's feet during the examination and was reassured by the midwife.

We asked seventy-one of the mothers if they remembered their baby being examined in the delivery room and what they had thought about it. Twenty-three (32 per cent) did not remember any examination. Of the forty-eight who did, about half (twenty-five) felt interested enough to make some comment about it: 'It was good, I could see what was happening'; 'I found it quite comical—everything was counted. It was done aloud for my benefit to take my mind off the stitches'; 'Good, but I couldn't quite see'. The other twenty-three women gave single-word answers like 'OK', 'alright', 'pleased'. Only two mothers, including the one referred to above who had had a previous baby with a malformation, mentioned the examination of their babies when asked a general question about what they had found reassuring.

Relationships Between Staff and Parents

One further aspect of the labour ward that may be a reflection of the social climate in which care takes place is its lack of privacy. At no time did we observe a member of staff knocking at the door of a delivery room and waiting to be asked to enter. Many did give a quick knock before walking in, but some did not, and sometimes the doors were left open anyway. If someone did knock, it would seem strange for a parent to answer because the room is not 'theirs'. Even when parents are left alone with their baby, they never know when someone is going to come in. We did not systematically record all the members of staff who entered a delivery room during our period of observation, but one mother saw at least the following: a staff midwife, two midwife sisters, a paediatrician, an obstetric registrar, and the observer. By contrast, a mother delivering at night in a small non-teaching hospital might be cared for by only two or three members of staff—one midwife for the majority of her care, an additional one at delivery, and perhaps an auxiliary who would give her a wash.

In most places, efforts were made to provide privacy from passers-by and from other couples and visitors. In one or two cases, however, this was certainly not achieved. One mother was concerned that she had been left in a first-stage room for too long and so had frightened other women in the room who were less advanced in labour. In another hospital a woman delivered in a twin-bedded room next to a first-time mother in early labour. During the delivery the second woman's partner was asked to leave, and was not told that he could come back until some time after the first woman had had her baby. However, during the interviews following delivery, neither woman commented about what had happened. The interviewer asked each of them about it at the end of the interview: 'You had your baby with another woman in the bed next to you behind the screens. How did you feel about that?' 'Well it was her first and I thought I might put her off a bit.' And to the second mother: 'when you were in labour in the morning, that lady had her baby in the next bed beside you, didn't she. What did you think about that?' 'Well it did frighten me, because I could hear every word even though I couldn't see anything . . . I didn't want my husband to be sent out. He was out about an hour, I think, and I missed him.'

One interesting feature of this example is that the women did not react strongly to what appeared, to us, to be very unsatisfactory care. In part this is due to the fact that although the care had features which disturbed the observers (e.g. lack of privacy, unnecessary procedures, or lack of discussion and information), it was sometimes delivered by very kind and supportive midwives. In addition, mothers in some hospitals were reluctant to criticize, and also they may have had low expectations because of previous experience. The first mother in the above example concluded the interview by saying: 'They was very nice.' In another example a mother found suturing very painful, and asked the midwife who was stitching her for gas and air. She had been given some local analgesia for an episiotomy twenty minutes before, but no further local pain-relief. The midwife's response was not sympathetic. During the interview the mother did comment on the pain she had felt, adding: 'But that's necessary.' Her general comments about her care were very favourable: 'Yes, I found it all very good . . . very reassuring.'

This mother and several others commented on how reassuring it was to be told what to do: 'I needed them to tell me what to do.' Those who voiced complaints, or had reservations about their care, often added that the staff know best: 'They are qualified people, so you just don't question them'; 'Being the first time, you just get up on the bed and do what you're told, don't you.' A surprising number of women apologized or blamed themselves: 'I kept sliding down, though, but I expect that was my fault'; 'Was I good?'; 'I'm sorry to be such a nuisance'; 'Was I any trouble?'; 'I'm not letting you down, am I?'

Of the women who compared their care with previous experience, most commented that they were pleased at the increase in flexibility: 'It seems less rigid than last time— which is a positive thing. Less geared-up to the system·and more geared-up to the person'; 'It's good here. After you have had the baby they don't treat you as ill. They help you to get to know the baby'; 'Yes, it was lovely. When I had my little girl, I don't remember seeing her at all for a couple of days.'

There were occasional disputes between midwives and mothers about procedures that were carried out in labour. (Although these are not part of the care given in the period after birth, they can provide a useful indication of attitudes to care, because the urgency of the moment makes these exchanges rather sharper than any of the disagreements following delivery.) One young woman tried to stop a midwife infiltrating the perineum with a local anaesthetic, because she wanted to know what it was. She said to her mother, who was with her: 'Hold on, I'm asking her what she's doing.' Her mother was upset because she did not behave deferentially. Another woman wanted to know about a catheter which the nursing auxiliary had brought to the midwife. The woman asked: 'What's that?' *Midwife*: 'It's just a little tube.' The woman asked again: 'What's that?' *Auxiliary*: 'It's going on the trolly.' The midwife washed the woman down, saying: 'Don't talk to me, pet. Just do what I tell you.' She catheterized her. The woman asked: 'What's that for?' The midwife then gave an explanation. Three mothers in one hospital saw the syringe of Syntometrine being prepared and asked what it was. They were told that it was 'for the afterbirth', and that they should not worry and would not notice it.

Although there has been extensive research into the ways in which early contact between parents and new baby may influence their relationship both in the short and the long term, there has been less emphasis on the details of care in the immediate post-partum period, and in the interactions between staff and parents at this time. While the overall approach to contact and separation just after birth has been altered by the concern about 'bonding', specific routines for the baby, and common aspects of care for the mother, such as episiotomy repair, may have an impact on the way in which parents and new-born relate to each other. In a recent study of gastric suction in healthy new-born babies, Widstrom *et al.* (1987) showed that this intervention interfered with the subtle series of movements that took place as the baby moved towards the breast. The routine application of silver nitrate (which occurs in some countries, though not in Britain), or other eye treatments, may also affect the baby's behaviour (Wahlberg 1982). The most obvious example in our study was the policy of transferring babies separately to the post-natal ward.

Going beyond detailed policies, a range of less tangible factors emerged from our study. Hospitals differed in the layouts of their rooms, in pressures of space, and in adequacy of staffing. Midwives had very varied approaches to their priorities in the immediate post-partum period, and some were more experienced and found the tasks of clearing up and record-completion less demanding. Once the drama of birth was over, there was often a feeling of anti-climax and a sudden reduction in the amount of attention given to mothers. This was more noticeable when a woman had no companion with her. In contrast, some midwives put considerable emphasis on providing reassurance about the baby's well-being, on breast-feeding, and on the parents and other family members.

Underlying much of the care that we observed is an assumption that in those first hours of life the baby 'belongs' primarily to the hospital, and only in a limited way to the parents. Both parents and staff generally behave in accordance with this assumption. Recent changes seem to be leading away from this position, and the care that we observed certainly varied considerably, both between and within hospitals. In the more traditional hospitals the baby is caught up in a routine of wrapping and weighing, and is then moved away to the nursery to be bathed and fed. The parents' permission is not asked for and they may not even be informed. In all the hospitals the space belongs to the staff, who move freely in and out of the delivery rooms. If the staff do ask permission to enter, it is from the person responsible for care; sometimes they introduce themselves to the parents. A woman's companions are permitted to enter this space, but in no sense is it private to them and the mother.

In this study it was the midwives who largely determined the first contacts between new-born and parents. They often sought to meet parents' requests, but it was they who held the initiative: 'I'm just going to take your baby to the ward now. It's a bit cold'; 'You can feed her soon. I'd just like to have a good look at her'; 'Can we just take him up to the nursery?'; 'Here's your son, Dad. Have a look at him'. It seems likely, though we have no observational data to support this, that parents and midwives would behave very differently at a home delivery. A parent might seek advice and encouragement from a professional about approaching a new baby, but not permission. Care-givers in the parents' home would be more likely to make a genuine request to parents if they wanted to carry out some procedure involving the new baby. A midwife giving post-natal care in hospital might well tell a mother how her baby was; at home she would probably ask the mother how the baby was getting on.

Care of babies and children in other settings, such as the neonatal intensive care unit or the children's ward, is also based on the partial handing-over of responsibility from parents to care-givers. The role of parents has changed markedly in these places in recent years, so that parents are much more likely to spend time with their children and to give them some of the care they need. It is still the hospital, though, that grants this access to parents and establishes the limits of their involvement.

The idea that the baby 'belongs' to the institution may be linked to the fact that, in some cases, the mother also is accorded only partial responsibility for herself. Obstetrical procedures may be carried out without permission and sometimes even without explanation. Henderson (1984) has described the way in which midwives ruptured the membranes of women in labour. In the twenty-eight cases that she observed, consent for rupture of the membranes was obtained in only two, and of the remaining twenty-six women, seven were only told about it after the procedure had taken place. There was no discussion about rupture of membranes with any woman. Midwives assumed consent when no objection was raised by the woman, and the women themselves were almost all happy with this situation. In our study the disputes described above took place when a woman wanted to find out what was going to happen. Most midwives told mothers what they were going to do, and some asked permission.

There are several general conclusions which can be drawn from the work which we have reported on here. Firstly, contact between the parents and new-born who took part in this study, though less restricted than some parents had previously experienced, was often limited and fragmented. Secondly, the intention to facilitate contact between new-born and parents may be frustrated by conflicting demands on midwives and the low priority given to this aspect of labour ward care. Most of the midwives we observed had not looked after a woman during her pregnancy and were unlikely to see her once she left the labour ward. Systems which allow more continuity of care might change the emphasis given to the immediate post-partum period. Thirdly, any policy changes designed to give parents more access to their new babies should be assessed to see if they actually accomplish their objectives. And lastly, the possibility of adapting hospitals so that parents are more truly 'at home' is one that should be debated and explored in research.

References

Cartwright, A., 1979, *The Dignity of Labour?* (London, Tavistock).

Garcia, J., Garforth, S., and Ayers, S., 1987, 'The Policy and Practice in Midwifery Study: Introduction and Methods', *Midwifery*, 3, pp. 2–9.

——Garforth, S., forthcoming, 'Midwifery Policies and Policy-Making', in Robinson, S. and Thomson, A. (eds.), *Midwives, Research and Childbirth* (London, Chapman and Hall).

Garforth, S., Garcia, J., 1987, 'Admitting: A Weakness or a Strength? Routine Admission of a Woman in Labour', *Midwifery*, 3, pp. 10–24.

——Garcia, J., 1989, 'Breastfeeding Policies in Practice: "No Wonder they get confused"'. *Midwifery*, 5, pp. 75–83.

Henderson, C., 1984, 'Some Facets of Social Interaction Surrounding a Midwife's Decision to Rupture the Membranes', MA diss. (University of Warwick).

Jacoby, A., 1987, 'Women's Preferences for and Satisfaction with Current Procedures in Childbirth: Findings from a National Study', *Midwifery*, 3, pp. 117–24.

Richards, M., 1983, 'Parent-Child Relationships: Some General Considerations', in Davies, J., Richards, M., and Roberton, N. (eds.), *Parent–Baby Attachment in Premature Infants* (London, Croom Helm).

——1985, 'Bonding Babies', *Archives of Disease in Childhood*, 60, pp. 293–4

Slukin, W., Herbert, M. and Slukin, A., 1983, *Maternal Bonding* (Oxford, Blackwell).

Thomson, M. E. and Westreich, R., 1989, 'Restriction of Mother–Infant Contact in the Immediate Postnatal Period', in Chalmers, I., Enkin, M., and Keirse, M. (eds.), *Effective Care in Pregnancy and Childbirth* (Oxford, Oxford University Press).

Wahlberg, V., 1982, 'Reconsideration of Crede Prophylaxis', *Acta Paediatrica Scandinavica*, Supplement 295.

Widstrom, A.-M., Ransjo-Arvidson, A., Christensson, K., Matthiesen, A. S., Winberg, J. Uvnas-Moberg, K., 1987, 'Gastric Suction in Healthy Newborn Infants', *Acta Paediatrica Scandinavica* 76, pp. 566–72.

World Health Organization, 1985, *Having a Baby in Europe* (Copenhagen, WHO).

10

Women's Experiences of Caesarean Delivery

Ann Oakley and Martin Richards

ONE of the features of 'high-technology' or 'interventionist' obstetrics as it has developed in Britain and elsewhere over the last twenty years is that the changes in practice have occurred largely without the wishes of childbearing women being taken into account. This has helped to create a problem for us as authors of this chapter—namely, a relative lack of studies investigating the attitudes of women and members of their families to Caesarean delivery, and, more generally, on the social and psychological consequences of Caesarean section (see the general discussion of surveys of women's views by Jacoby and Cartwright, Chapter 13). There is a striking imbalance between this lack and the number of studies of the physiological, pathological, and epidemiological aspects of this method of delivery.

We will begin by placing the problem in a wider context and then proceed to discuss more specifically the work that is available on Caesarean section.

Caesarean Section and the Profession of Medicine

In maternity-care policy, like medical-care policy in general, a clear division has existed between the clinician's autonomy to determine treatment on the one hand, and the patient's attitudes to treatment on the other. This situation is one of potential conflict between doctor and patient. To quote Freidson (1975: 286–7; see also 1972):

The practitioner looking from his [*sic*[1]] professional vantage point, preserves his detachment by seeing the patient as a case to which he applies the general rules and categories learnt during his protracted professional training. The client, being personally involved in what happens, feels obliged to try to judge and control what is happening to him [or her]. Since he does not have the same perspective as the practitioner, he must judge what is being done to him from other than a professional point of view. While both professional worker and client are theoretically in accord with the end of their relationship—solving the client's problems—the means by which this solution is to be accomplished and the definitions of the problem itself are sources of potential difference.

Research carried out on the attitudes of practitioners and clients in the field of maternity care does indeed indicate that there are often basic differences in the definitions the two groups hold of 'the problem itself' and of the means appropriate to treating it (Cartwright 1979; Graham and Oakley 1981). Obstetricians tend to view pregnancy and birth as medical processes which can be abstracted from the totality of women's life experiences, constitute a specialist field of knowledge, and have their 'success' measured in physiological indices, i.e. mortality and physical morbidity rates. In opposition to this, many mothers retain some idea of childbearing as a natural process embedded in their personal development and social life—a process about which they possess relevant knowledge, and whose success must be approached not purely in terms of intact physical survival, but with such issues as happiness and satisfaction in mind. It should be noted, however, that women vary in their attitudes towards intervention (McIntosh 1987; Green *et al.* 1988; Reid and Garcia, 1989):

Technology of the kind involved in Caesarean section occupies a special role in the clinician's claim to unique expertise. Development of specialized techniques and equipment, whose functions and achievements can only be determined by a technical-medical élite, has historically been of great importance in establishing medicine's status as the

---

[1] If the practitioner is an obstetrician, almost 9 times out of 10 it will be a he. Despite the very significant rise in the proportion of female medical graduates in Britain, the proportion among consultant obstetricians has remained unchanged.

arbiter of health and illness. Control over technical judgement rests at the heart of the medical profession's claim to autonomy, and has also served to reduce the user of medical care to the lowest common denominator of his or her bodily existence. The dominant 'engineering approach' tends to see a person as an organism divided into discrete, separable parts. This reductionism has been a basic feature of western medicine and of the practice of obstetrics (McKeown 1976; Kennedy 1980; Scully 1980).

The professional position is put very plainly in one of the widely used midwifery texts (Myles 1981). The following quotation also illustrates the ways in which the general approach has been accepted within midwifery as well as obstetrics. (Further examples of the ways in which these issues are dealt with within obstetric texts will be found in Schwarz, Chapter 3.) First there is the claim for the necessity of intervention and reliance on professionals:

Pregnant women are inadvisedly exhorted by certain groups to demand 'natural childbirth' and to refuse any interference. But when left to nature, labour can be long, painful, exhausting to the mother and lethal to both mother and child. Women today are not aware of the disastrous results of 'natural childbirth' at the beginning of this century and in some underdeveloped countries today.

Childbirth has been made safer, shorter and easier by the very scientific procedures some misinformed women object to. Reverting to primitive methods is a retrograde step which has no justification and should not be condoned.

Having conjured up this spectre of death lurking to claim those who do not submit to professional intervention, the author then makes it clear who must make all the decisions:

To the expectant mother, labour is a very personal experience which engenders the presumption that she ought to participate in professional decisions and dictate regarding her obstetric care. But she may have little understanding of the tremendous amount of knowledge and years of experience needed in the practice of competent obstetrics. If she knew more she would realise the wisdom of having faith in professional experts and allowing them to make decisions regarding her own and her baby's well-being and safety throughout labour.

Obstetricians and midwives have theoretical knowledge, expertise, manual skill, and vast experience, which they should be given freedom to exercise. They have gleaned wisdom in the application of these professional attributes. As well as saving the lives of mothers and babies . . .

And so on in the same vein.

In the late 1960s and early 1970s long-established assumptions about the social benefits of scientific and technological advance began to be called into question (Boyle *et al.* 1977). But it is the consumer movement in health care which has provided the focus of criticism opposed to high-technology obstetrics. In recent years the debate has concentrated on Caesarean section as a key issue. Caesarean support groups have mushroomed (see e.g. Young and Mahan 1980; Johnson and Parody 1984; C/Sec. *Newsletters*); and the Maternity Alliance (1983) ran a publicity campaign drawing attention to both the high overall section rate in Britain and the wide regional variation. In 1984, the latest year for which we have a detailed breakdown of the figures, the overall Caesarean section rate in England was 10.1 per cent. Rates for individual regions varied between 9 and 12 per cent (OPCS 1987). Regional variations—or the even wider ones at district, hospital, or individual consultant level—raise many questions about the appropriateness of the use of this technique. (For a recent discussion of variations in operative delivery rates both within and between countries, and some of the determinants of the varying rates, the reader is referred to the review by Lomas and Enkin, 1989.)

Whose Baby Is it? Elective Delivery and the Control of Childbirth

Before discussing Caesarean section, there are some broad points we would like to make about elective delivery in general. The central issue in the user–provider debate about elective delivery is that of control. As one obstetrician revealingly phrased it: 'The active management of labour necessitates that obstetricians take over, not just a single aspect of delivery but responsibility for the whole process of parturition. Our control of the situation must be complete.' (Beazley 1975: 161.) This approach generates the need for such curious observations as: 'It is all too easily forgotten that mothers have the most important role to play in the management of labour.' (O'Driscoll and Meagher 1980: 90.). While the active management of labour is not the same thing as elective delivery, it could be argued that any pregnancy, labour, and delivery in which there is any intervention designed to hasten the birth of the baby is 'elective' in some sense, i.e. the timing, process, and mode of giving birth is predetermined. 'Rules' for the length of time the second stage of labour is allowed to continue, and exhortations to the mother to push, constitute interventions of this kind. Even in this latter, almost universal and apparently fairly innocuous, case, it is now being recognized, for example, that the rate of spontaneous deliveries is likely to be higher when women with an epidural are urged to push later in the second stage (Sleep *et al.* 1989).

That the timing of birth is not precisely predictable is a major source of uncertainty, both in obstetric practice and in mothers' lives. However, the evidence is that obstetricians and mothers react rather differently to this uncertainty. In short, many mothers are more prepared to tolerate it than obstetricians are. The search for a reasonably safe and efficient method of inducing labour has characterized obstetrics ever since it first became a recognizably separate speciality (Oakley 1984). The ability to control the timing of delivery adds significantly to the obstetrical claim to expertise—apart from providing what some practitioners would consider to be more comfortable conditions in which to work. In her study of induction, carried out in 1975 when the high rates for this procedure were a cause for concern, Ann Cartwright (1979)[2] asked obstetricians how the increase in inductions had affected their job satisfaction and the smooth running of maternity hospitals and departments. About half of the 379 obstetricians who took part in the study said that it had improved their job satisfaction and made the running of maternity departments easier: 'Deliveries are now more likely in "office hours" on days of mutual convenience' (Cartwright 1979: 117). The result of the policies of that period may be

---

[2] It is perhaps significant to note that induction rates have fallen since then—in response to pressures from women, some would argue—so attitudes may have changed somewhat.

seen in the daily totals of births, with marked troughs on Sundays and public holidays (Macfarlane 1978). When obstetricians and midwives were asked to estimate the proportion of women who would prefer induction, both groups overestimated the figure—the former said 36 per cent, the later 40 per cent. For the mothers themselves, 8 per cent said they would prefer an induction for a future birth—17 per cent of those who had had one for the last birth and 5 per cent of those who were not induced. Obstetricians will often take a mother's convenience into account as well as their own: 46 per cent, for instance, said that they would be prepared to induce a woman three days before her expected date so that her baby would be born before her mother returned to Australia; 64 per cent would be prepared to induce to avoid a long journey to hospital in labour. (On the other hand, only 21 per cent said they would induce purely to meet the problem of staff shortages.)

On the question of mothers' views, Cartwright (1979: 107) observes that 'The main reason for not wanting an induction was epitomized in this comment: "I'd like the baby to come naturally. I wouldn't like it to be rushed if it doesn't need to be".' In their comments about how they would prefer their childbirths to be, many women make some such reference to 'nature' as the ideal arbiter of the timing and mode of birth. In one study of British Asian women delivering in Warwickshire, 48 per cent of mothers expressed such a desire (Homans 1980). Those who advocated a 'natural' birth most strongly had experienced an unwelcome level of medical intervention in a previous birth. The main reasons why a 'natural' birth was preferred concerned (*a*) definitions of a 'proper' birth— women who had experienced induced labours with epidural analgesia and perhaps an instrumental delivery were not considered to have 'really' given birth; and (*b*) the quality of the mother–child relationship, which was felt to be inferior following an elective delivery, especially a Caesarean section. Similar findings emerged in a study of first-time motherhood in London (Oakley 1979, 1980). When questioned during pregnancy about their expectations of birth, 96 per cent of the sample voiced a desire for their labour and delivery to be without medical intervention, on the grounds that such a birth would be more natural; and 73 per cent said that they would not like to have an induction on these grounds. (In the event, 21 per cent of these women did experience an induced labour.)

The appeal to 'nature' is perhaps more complex than it first appears. Cartwright (1979) notes that some of the women who were opposed to the idea of induction nevertheless attempted to induce themselves by such traditional methods as intensive physical exercise. This suggests that a self-administered induction is considered more 'natural' because the mother herself remains in control over the timing of labour. It is important to recogize that the terms 'nature' and 'culture', or 'nature' and 'medicine' (or 'science'), do not stand in simple opposition to one another, and that their employment in the user–provider debate about elective delivery is liable to conceal the more basic issue of control over birth. This is well illustrated in our earlier quotation from Myles's (1981) midwifery textbook. Definitions of what is meant by the term 'nature' vary between different societies and between different time-periods in the same society (Hastrup 1978). One significant implication of this for the present discussion is that the opposition between 'nature' and 'medicine' exists within (and is produced by) the dominant scientific–medical debate itself.

In discussing women's views and desires, it is important to emphasize that all women do not necessarily want the same thing. A concern with the naturalness of birth is sometimes held to be a rather middle-class view. Certainly there may be some differences in the views of women according to their class background (Nelson 1983; McIntosh 1987). However, other studies suggest that attitudes about naturalness and control are not strongly class-related (Green *et al.* 1988). Some of the apparent conflict in these results may relate to geographical variation. It may be the case—but only further research can confirm this—that middle-class values are much more widely distributed through the population in the south-east of Britain than in the north, where class boundaries have remained more sharply drawn.

Surveys of women's experiences show that what the mother considers to have been an adequate discussion of induction beforehand contributes to a relatively comfortable experience of induced labour—as does good emotional support from medical staff during labour and delivery (Kitzinger 1975; Cartwright 1979). Attitudes and reactions to childbirth are, in this sense, a function of many different variables, including women's prior experiences of birth and obstetric care, their confidence (or lack of it) in their body's ability to labour spontaneously, and the degree of unpredictability that their social circumstances are able to support concerning the time of birth (see Green *et al.* 1988). These vary not only between cultures, but within them. Homans (1980), for example, showed that women from Asian communities are generally less well-informed and more 'compliant' than women from the majority community: they also received less in the way of medical intervention.

Having considered elective delivery, we will now turn our attention to Caesarean section, where we have considerably less research from Britain on which to draw for our discussion.

Caesarean Section

Considerably more research has been done in the United States than in Britain in evaluating the social and psychological costs of Caesarean section (Marieskind 1979). It is interesting to note that a sociologist and a psychologist were appointed to the Consensus Development Task Force set up in 1979 by the National Institutes of Health to examine Caesarean childbirth; one of its assignments was to consider the 'psychological effects of Caesarean delivery on the mother, infant and family' (Shearer 1981).

One reason for the lack of research is that, in Britain at least, Caesarean section is less common than induction, and thus has played less of a part in the debate about the new obstetrics. But it is probably the case that, since it involves major abdominal surgery, it is seen as a medical procedure carried out on the basis of 'need' alone. Women who might suspect that many inductions are carried out for reasons of medical convenience, and would question any suggestion that they would submit to one without strong reasons being given, might well accept a Caesarean section without resistance.

However, as with other obstetric procedures, there are very wide differences in rates both between countries and between centres within Britain (Chalmers and Richards 1977; Bergsjo *et al.* 1986; Notzan *et al.* 1987; Francome and Carson). There is every reason to think that these rates reflect obstetric attitudes and policies as much as any variation in need based on 'objective' medical criteria. While the frequency of induction appears to be falling in Britain (though the use of acceleration techniques may not be), that of Caesarean section is rising. This difference not only reflects the way in which Caesarean sections have come to be seen by many obstetricians as unproblematic and routine procedures, but also the way in which women's resistance to induction has only slowly extended to Caesarean section.

In the context of medical attitudes towards Caesarean sections, it would seem to be of some significance that they are referred to, and discussed, in a rather different way than other forms of abdominal surgery. Indeed, the term 'Caesarean section' already hints at this. We do not call it a Caesarean 'operation', Caesarean 'surgery', or even a hysterotomy, but we use the rather odd, but perhaps benign, term 'section'. This rather different way of conceptualizing the operation from other forms of abdominal surgery is also associated with a difference in the way in which the effects of Caesarean sections and other surgical procedures are seen. Thus, while it is accepted among surgeons that depression is a common consequence of major surgery (especially of emergency surgery), the same assumption is not made about a Caesarean section. In fact, however, many of the psychological consequences of surgery in general also apply to Caesarean section. These include a temporary response of emotional relief/elation at having survived the operation, worry about the mutilating effects of the operation on the body and its attractiveness to others, and a long-drawn out period of physical and psychological discomfort (Janis 1958). It is worth noting that the kinds of demands that looking after a new-born baby are likely to make involve activities that are probably forbidden to any patient on a surgical ward for some days (if not weeks) after abdominal surgery. It is presumably factors of this kind, coupled with the loss of control we discussed earlier, that account for the association between Caesarean deliveries and admission to a psychiatric hospital in the first ninety days after childbirth (Kendell *et al.* 1981).

In one of the earlier studies in the field, and one of the very few carried out in Britain, Trowell (1982) compared sixteen mothers who had unplanned Caesarean sections under general anaesthetic with a control group of spontaneously vaginally delivered women. All were having first babies, and it is clear that both the mothers and the babies in the group having Caesarean sections were normal, and that no sections were performed for pressing obstetric reasons. The spontaneously delivered babies were slightly heavier than those delivered by section (3,192 as opposed to 3,556 g.).

All the mothers and babies were seen at home one month and one year after delivery. At one month, observations showed that the Caesarean mothers looked at their babies more, but smiled less. The Caesarean babies were rated as being more tense during nappy-changing and while being dressed. Striking differences emerged from the questioning of the mothers. Those who had had sections more often remembered the birth as a bad experience, expressed doubts about their capacity to care for their baby, and were depressed or anxious. As the author comments:

The caesarean group of mothers at one month continued to remember the birth as a bad experience, feeling disappointed and disillusioned and also expressing feelings of failure as a woman and anger with the baby for not 'coming out'. These feelings may explain why at one month there was much less eye-to-eye contact between the mothers and babies in the caesarean group. . . . [They] reported experiencing considerable problems with motherhood, confirming what difficulty they had in establishing a satisfactory relationship with their child. (Trowell 1982: 48–9)

These sorts of attitudes were still present after a year, when the Caesarean mothers were more likely to describe motherhood in negative terms, more likely to delay responding to their child's crying, and gave a later age as an assessment of the stage at which they first felt their child reacted to them as a person. The Caesarean group of mothers expressed more anger in their handling of their children by shouting, smacking, and losing their tempers. There were indications that the Caesarean babies had a slower motor development (e.g. age of sitting unaided), and some interaction measures from the observations showed continuing differences between the groups; for instance, the mothers appeared less likely to start playing with them. There was evidence of a raised level of anxiety in the Caesarean-delivered babies. They did not use as much curiosity and imagination when they played with toys as the other babies did.

The groups in this study are small, and as the author herself emphasizes, it was intended to be a pilot study. There is also the problem of comparability between the two groups, and the possibility of differences beyond the mode of delivery. However, the women do not seem to have had Caesarean sections for very pressing reasons, so the groups should not be too dissimilar. With these cautions in mind, we feel it is reasonable to see the study as providing support for some of the implications of Caesarean delivery we have mentioned. Taken together with the other studies, it gives no comfort to those who would dismiss the psychological effects on either mother or child as being trivial.

The profound effects that can follow from a Caesarean section are recognized among women, and one of the more striking developments in recent years has been the growth of self-help groups offering both emotional and practical support on all sorts of matters, including the best posture for breast-feeding, and exercises to rebuild abdominal muscles. The very existence of these groups is, of course, a clear indication of psychological and social need on the part of women who have undergone these procedures. Yet even in the United States, where a similar mushrooming of Caesarean support groups has occurred, there is surprisingly little criticism of the high—and rising—Caesarean rate. This bears out our point about such surgery tending to be seen as 'necessary' by its recipients.

Even with the modern lower-segment operation, one Caesarean section is likely to be followed by another. At least on an anecdotal basis, we are familiar with instances where this fact has led to a reduction in the intended family size. How widespread such an outcome may be is not known, and we have been unable to find any British study of the effects of

Caesarean section on subsequent fertility. Data from Sweden reports more problems during subsequent pregnancies, labours, and deliveries for women who have had Caesarean sections; and that some of these problems may have been a consequence of the section itself (Hemminki 1987).

The small number of North American and European studies of the consequences of Caesarean section for mothers, their partners, and their children are in broad agreement with what has been said so far, but there are some inconsistencies. This is hardly surprising, since women's responses to obstetric surgery will vary for many individual and social reasons, and 'Caesarean section' covers a broad range of surgical procedures carried out by a variety of methods for a variety of reasons. Particular communities may have particular reactions. For instance, it has been reported that women from a Bengali community in East London have a special dislike of Caesareans, and may be rejected by their husbands on account of their 'failure' to give birth vaginally (Savage 1986). The decision to carry out the operation can be influenced by social consideration. Often an 'inverse care law' (Tudor Hart 1971) may exist, meaning that where the need is greatest the provision is smallest. Despite their privileged material and social background, we know that there are high rates of Caesarean section among women receiving private maternity care in Britain (Richards 1979). Similarly, in the United States the highest rates are found among the women with the lowest risk (Hurst and Sumey 1984; Lomas and Enkin, 1989). The operation itself may be planned or carried out as an emergency procedure. The mother may be given a general anaesthetic or an epidural. The varying circumstances of, and the procedures used for, the operation may directly affect its psychological impact on the mother (Lipson and Tilden 1980).

Most studies come to the conclusion that, in the first few post-partum days, Caesarean-delivered mothers have more difficulties in feeding their infants, and may be rather more ambivalent towards them, than those delivered vaginally (Affonso and Stichler 1978; Lipson and Tilden 1980; Hwang 1987), but others fail to find such a difference (Bradley *et al.* 1983). In many of these studies it is reported that mothers feel disappointment or even anger at being 'cheated' of a vaginal birth, and that this may be associated with depression and sometimes guilt. Others report a reduction in self-esteem (Cox and Smith 1982). Most, but not all, of these maternal effects resolve within a matter of months after the birth (Garel and Kaminski 1986). The studies that include mothers who have had either general anaesthetic or epidural Caesareans often find that the effects are more marked in the former group. One point of interest is that mothers who have had a Caesarean are somewhat slower to choose a name for their baby, a delay that the investigators interpreted as a sign of ambivalence (Marut and Mercer 1979). This study also noted instances of lowered self-esteem. Unlike the English study reported above, those from Sweden (Hwang 1987) and France (Garel *et al.* 1988) do not report any differences in the mother–infant relationship after the first few months; and Garel *et al.* (1987) suggest that long-term effects are more apparent for the mothers than for the mother–infant relationship. In this French survey, differences were found between mothers who had epidurals and those who had a general anaesthetic; the latter group experienced longer-lasting consequences, more tiredness, for example, and had more caretaking difficulties with their babies. Morgan *et al.* (1984) found that mothers are usually out of bed earlier after an epidural Caesarean, and start feeding their baby sooner. This group reports less depression and tiredness in the post-partum period, as well as a lower incidence of a wide range of complications such as infection.

Several authors have commented on the positive effects of having a father present at the operation (e.g. Cain *et al.* 1984; May and Sollid 1984). Not only may he be able to offer direct support for the mother, but he may also be able to act as a mediator with medical staff and assist in negotiations about what may happen. When a general anaesthetic is used, the father is able to give the mother an account of the birth which otherwise she may only receive in rather formal medical terms. A recent American study (Shearer *et al.* 1988) suggests that there is a growing tendency for fathers to be present at Caesarean births, and for these to be carried out with epidural anaesthesia (for this reason?).

While the mother is recovering from the surgery, the father may play a rather fuller part in the early care of the child than he might otherwise have done. This factor seems to be the reason why studies have found that the fathers of Caesarean-delivered babies are more involved in child care in the first few months (Pedersen *et al.* 1981; Hwang 1987). This effect has been cited as an explanation of the raised parental expectations of school achievement of Caesarean children found in an American study of 6–8-year-olds (Entwisle and Alexander 1987). This study found no differences in the children's school achievement or temperament. This is in line with an earlier study which found no IQ differences at age 4 (Broman *et al.* 1975).

It is clear from the studies we have reviewed that many factors affect the reactions of parents to elective delivery (see Nelson 1983). All these factors need to be taken into account when evaluating the effectiveness, safety, and acceptability of these increasingly used techniques. The negative effects of a Caesarean section on some mothers' well-being in the weeks after birth have been confirmed in a recent study of women's expectations and experiences of childbirth (Green *et al.* 1988). We will conclude the chapter with a series of quotations from some of the women who took part in that study; the quotations have been selected to illustrate the full range of experiences and feelings.

After having felt so lost and empty after the birth of my other baby because it was an elective section I now feel fulfilled and jubilant on experiencing a perfectly natural and normal birth. I now feel like a whole woman and can fully recommend this experience to other women.

Q: What would you say was the best thing about the birth?
A: Painless [Caesarean] and very quick! [epidural]
Q: What, if anything, surprised you most about the birth?
A: The feeling of elation at having the baby, that it seemed so precious from the start.

The first few weeks I was very unhappy mainly due to the Caesarean section. I was in a lot of pain and felt very helpless not being able to dash about, drive my car, etc. I found surgery a frightening experience and was worried about my wound the whole time . . . I think an abdominal wound and a new-born baby are a very difficult and stressful combination.

I was very pleased with the care I received. The theatre staff were marvellous. The lights were adjusted so I could watch the whole operation and I saw them lift the baby out. They could not have done more if they had tried.

Two previous Caesarean sections, one emergency with general anaesthetic, one elective with epidural anaesthetic. I found the latter method infinitely preferable, both physically and emotionally. My recovery was greatly aided by the fact that I remained conscious throughout the birth.

Since the birth I have felt a 'lack of achievement' and inadequate, especially at first, due to the fact that I had a Caesarean section. This was my third, and an elective section . . . I feel this lack of achievement most when friends talk of their experiences of normal deliveries. I feel I have missed out on something special, and many people are quick to point out that 'I don't know what it's like'. I have noticed that this time that no-one said 'well done' to me about the birth, with the exception of my GP.

I loved every minute of it [a Caesarean section under epidural]. [The best thing about it was] just seeing him wet and new-born, the smell of him and being able to hold him.

References

Affonso, D. and Stichler, J., 1978, 'Exploratory Study of Women's Reactions to Having Caesarean Birth', *Birth and the Family Journal*, 5, pp. 88–94.

Beazley, J., 1975, 'The Active Management of Labour', *American Journal of Obstetrics and Gynecology*, 122, pp. 161–8.

Bergsjo, P., Schmidt, E., and Pusch, D., 1986, 'Differences in the Reported Frequencies of Some Obstetrical Interventions in Europe', in Phaff, J. M. L. (ed.), *Perinatal Health Services in Europe* (London, Croom Helm).

Boyle, G., Elliott, D., and Roy, R., 1977, *The Politics of Technology* (London, Longman).

Bradley, C. F., Ross, S. E., and Warnyca, J., 1983, 'A Prospective Study of Mothers' Attitudes and Feelings Following Cesarean and Vaginal Births', *Birth*, 10, pp. 79–83.

Broman, S. H., Nichols, P. L., and Kennedy, W. A., 1975, *Preschool IQ: Prenatal and Early Development Correlates* (Hillsdale, NJ, Erlbaum).

C/Sec. *Newsletter*, 1975 *et seq.* (Cesareans/Support Education and Concern, Framingham, Mass.).

Cain, R. L. *et al.*, 1984, 'Effects of the Father's Presence or Absence During a Cesarean Delivery', *Birth*, 11, pp. 10–15.

Cartwright, A., 1979, *The Dignity of Labour?* (London, Tavistock).

Chalmers, I. and Richards, M. P. M., 1977, 'Intervention and Causal Inference in Obstetric Practice', in T. Chard and M. Richards (eds.), *Benefits and Hazards of the New Obstetrics* (Clinics in Developmental Medicine, 64; London, Heinemann).

Cox, B. and Smith, E., 1982, 'The Mother's Self-Esteem after a Caesarean Delivery', *Maternal Child Nursing*, 7, pp. 309–14.

Entwisle, D. R. and Alexander, K. L., 1987, 'Long-term Effects of Cesarean Delivery on Parents' Belief and Children's Schooling', *Developmental Psychology*, 23, pp. 676–82.

Francome, C. and Carson, D., n.d., *Can we Avoid a Caesarean Crisis?* (Occasional paper 8; London, Middlesex Polytechnic).

Freidson, E., 1972, *Profession of Medicine: A Study of the Sociology of Applied Knowledge* (New York, Dodd, Mead, and Co.).

—— 1975, 'Dilemmas in the Doctor–Patient Relationship', in C. Cox and A. Mead (eds.), *A Sociology of Medical Practice* (London, Collier-Macmillan).

Garel, M. and Kaminski, M., 1986, 'Psychosocial Outcome of Caesarean Childbirth', in Kaminski, M., Breart, G., Buekens, P., Huisjes, H. J., McIlwaine, G., and Selbmann, H. K. (eds.), *Perinatal Care and Delivery Systems: Description and Evaluation in EEC Countries* (Oxford; Oxford University Press).

——Lelong, N., and Kaminski, M., 1987, 'Psychological Consequences of Caesarean Childbirth in Primiparas', *J. Psychosomatic Obstetrics and Gynaecology*, 6, pp. 197–209.

—————— 1988, 'Follow-up Study of Psychological Consequences of Caesarean Childbirth', *Early Human Development*, 16, pp. 271–82.

Graham, H. and Oakley, A., 1981, 'Competing Ideologies of Reproduction: Medical and Maternal Perspectives on Pregnancy and Birth', in H. Roberts (ed.), *Women, Health and Reproduction* (London, Routledge and Kegan Paul).

Green, J., Coupland, V., and Kitzinger, J., 1988, 'Great Expectations: A Prospective Study of Women's Expectations and Experience of Childbirth'. Unpublished Report for the Health Promotion Research Trust and the Nuffield Provincial Hospital Trust (Child Care and Development Group, University of Cambridge).

Hastrup, K., 1978, 'The Semantics of Biology: Virginity', in S. Ardener (ed.), *Defining Females* (London, Croom Helm).

Hemminki, E., 1987, 'Pregnancy and Birth After Cesarean Section: A Survey Based on the Swedish Birth Register', *Birth*, 14, pp. 12–17.

Homans, H., 1980, 'Pregnant in Britain: A Sociological Approach to Asian and British Women's Experiences', Ph.D. thesis (University of Warwick).

Hurst, M. and Sunmey, P. S., 1984, 'Childbirth and Social Class: The Case of Cesarean Section', *Social Science and Medicine*, 18, pp. 621–31.

Hwang, C. P., 1987, 'Cesarean Childbirth in Sweden: Effects on the Mother and Father–infant Relationship', *Infant Mental Health Journal*, 8, pp. 91–9.

Janis, I. L., 1958, *Psychological Stress: Psychoanalytic and Behavioural Studies of Surgical Patients* (New York, Wiley).

Johnson, S. and Parody, K., 1984, *Birth the Caesarean Way* (Manchester, Greater Manchester Caesarean Support Network).

Kendall, R. E. *et al.*, 1981, 'The Social and Obstetric Correlates of Psychiatric Admission in the Puerperium', *Psychological Medicine*, 11, pp. 341–50.

Kennedy, I., 1980, *The Unmasking of Medicine* (Reith Lectures, London).

Kitzinger, S., 1975, *Some Mother's Experiences of Induced Labour* (London, National Childbirth Trust).

Lipson, J. G. and Tilden, V. P., 1980, 'Psychological Integration of the Cesarean Birth Experience', *American Journal of Orthopsychiatry*, 50, pp. 598–609.

Lomas, J. and Enkin, M., 1989, 'Variations in Operative Delivery Rates', in Chalmers, I., Enkin, M., and Keirse, M. (eds.), *Effective Care in Pregnancy and Childbirth* (Oxford, Oxford University Press).

Macfarlane, A., 1978, 'Variations in Numbers of Births and Perinatal Mortality by Day of Week in England and Wales', *British Medical Journal*, 2, pp. 1670–3.

McIntosh, J., 1987, 'Expectations and Experiences of Childbirth in a Sample of Working-Class Primigravidae', in Robinson, S. and Thomson, A. (eds.), *Research and the Midwife Conference Proceedings* (London, King's College).

McKeown, T., 1976, *The Role of Medicine: Dream, Mirage or Nemesis?* (London, Nuffield Provincial Hospitals Trust).

Marieskind, H. I., 1979, 'An Evaluation of Caesarean Section in the United States', Report submitted to US Department of Health, Education and Welfare.

Marut, J. S. and Mercer, R. T. 1979, 'Comparisons of Primiparas' Perceptions of Vaginal and Cesarean Births', *Nursing Research*, 28, pp. 260–6.

Maternity Alliance, 1983, *One Birth in Nine* (London, The Maternity Alliance).

May, K. A. and Sollid, D. T., 1984, 'Unanticipated Cesarean Birth from the Father's Perspective', *Birth*, 11, pp. 87–95.

Morgan, B. M. *et al.*, 1984, 'Anaesthetic Morbidity Following Caesarean Section under Epidural or General Anaesthesia', the *Lancet*, 1, pp. 328–30.

Myles, M. F., 1981, *Text Book for Midwives*, 9th edn. (Edinburgh, Churchill Livingstone).

Nelson, M. K., 1983, 'Working Class Women, Middle Class Women, and Models of Childbirth', *Social Problems*, 30/2, pp. 284–97.

Notzan, F. C. *et al.*, 1987, 'Comparisons of National Caesarean Section Rates', *New England Journal of Medicine*, 316, pp. 386–9.

Office of Population Censuses and Surveys, 1987, OPCS Monitor MB4 87/2, London.

Oakley, A., 1979, *Becoming a Mother* (Oxford, Martin Robinson).

—— 1980, *Women Confined* (Oxford, Martin Robinson).

—— 1984, *The Captured Womb* (Oxford, Blackwell).

O'Driscoll, K. and Meagher, D., 1980, *Active Management of Labour* (London, W. B. Saunders).

Pedersen, F. A. *et al.*, 1981, 'Cesarean Childbirth: Psychological

Implications for Mothers and Fathers', *Infant Mental Health Journal*, 2, pp. 259–63.

Reid, M. and Garcia, J., 1989, 'Women's Views of Care during Pregnancy and Childbirth', in Chalmers, I., Enkin, M., and Keirse, M. (eds.), *Effective Care in Pregnancy and Childbirth* (Oxford, Oxford University Press).

Richards, M. P. M., 1979, 'Perinatal Morbidity and Mortality in Private Obstetric Practice', *Journal of Maternal and Child Health*, Sept. 1979, pp. 341–5.

Savage, W., 1986, *A Savage Enquiry* (London, Virago).

Scully, D., 1980, *Men Who Control Women's Health* (Boston, Houghton Mifflin).

Shearer, E., 1981, 'NIH Consensus Development Task Force on Cesarean Childbirth: The Process and the Result', *Birth and the Family Journal*, 8, pp. 25–30.

—— Shiono, P. H., and Rhoads, G. G., 1988, 'Recent Trends in Family-Centered Maternity Care for Cesarean-Birth Families', *Birth*, 15, pp. 3–7.

Sleep, J., Roberts, J., and Chalmers, I., 1989, 'Care during the Second Stage of Labour', in Chalmers, I., Enkin, M., and Keirse, M. (eds.), *Effective Care in Pregnancy and Childbirth* (Oxford, Oxford University Press).

Trowell, J., 1982, 'Possible Effects of Emergency Caesarean Section on Mother–Child Relationship', *Early Human Development*, 7, pp. 41–51.

Tudor Hart, J., 1971, 'The Inverse Care Law', the *Lancet*, 1, pp. 405–12.

Young, D. and Mahan, C., 1980, *Unnecessary Cesareans: Ways to Avoid Them* (Minneapolis, International Childbirth Education Association).

11

Fathers: The Emergence of a New Consumer Group

Rosaline S. Barbour

THE picture of the anxious expectant father pacing the hospital waiting-room is now a thing of the past. Many fathers today attend the birth of their babies, and are sometimes actively involved as birth attendants—and, hence, as users of, and commentators on, maternity services. The growth of lay interest in this dimension of fatherhood has been paralleled by the development of a sociological and psychological literature on fathers (see e.g. Beail and McGuire 1982; Lewis 1986; and the edited collections of McKee and O'Brien 1982; Hansen and Bozett 1985; and Lewis and O'Brien 1987). However, much of the work on fathers as users of maternity services— with the notable exception of Lewis (1986)—concentrates on their intrapartum role (Perkins 1980; Brown 1982), to the exclusion of their ante-natal and post-partum involvement.

In this chapter I wish to address the question of fathers' experiences of maternity care throughout the ante-natal, intrapartum, and immediate post-natal periods. My discussion will draw on material collected in a before-and-after-interview study of eighteen first-time parents attending one large teaching hospital, and on observational data collected during field-work in four labour wards and two post-natal wards located in a variety of settings, ranging from large teaching hospitals to small general-practitioner units.

Observational work was carried out at ten clinic sessions in the large teaching hospital where respondents were booked, and yielded the following information: 68 per cent of the 364 women attending ante-natal clinics were unaccompanied (except for young children); 28 per cent were accompanied by their partners; 4 per cent by their mothers; and 0.5 per cent by a female friend. The absence of most expectant fathers is not surprising given that clinics are held during normal working hours. Informal conversations and interviews established that the majority of attending fathers were self-employed, unemployed, engaged in shift work, or on holiday.

Like Lewis (1986), I found that, of the men accompanying their partners, very few (only 8 per cent) ventured into the consulting room. This was occasionally at the suggestion of midwifery staff, but most of the men I interviewed who had attended doctors' examinations explained that they had simply followed their partners, assuming that the staff would have no objections. This assumption appeared to be valid, and I recorded no instances of men being asked to leave the consulting room and no reported conflict about their presence. Motives for attending consultations ranged from mere interest or psychological support for partners to advocacy. For example, one expectant father told me: 'We've come to see the consultant about Helen being induced . . . and, quite frankly, it'll be over my dead body.' Both this man and another attending for the same reason later revealed that the inductions were to take place, as the doctor had satisfied them with the medical explanation he had provided. As Richards (1980) has pointed out, doctors exercise a lot of power by virtue of the specialized knowledge and their skill at presenting medical arguments.

The majority of the fathers I spoke to, either in interviews or at the clinic, had attended appointments for ultrasound scans. Used as a diagnostic tool to check for abnormalities (see Reid, Chapter 16), these scans were viewed quite differently by consumers. I found, as did Antle May (1982), that these appointments were important for men forging their new identity as fathers-to-be. One expectant father told me: 'It was great to actually see the baby. Before, you know, although I knew Janet was pregnant, there was nothing to show for it. It didn't seem real, somehow.' In one case, both grandmothers-to-be had also come to hospital to watch this procedure. Appointments for scans are made in the woman's name, and men appeared to learn by word of mouth that partners were made welcome at these examinations. This was highlighted by one couple where the man had not attended. The woman commented: 'We would've gone together if it'd been mentioned. They said, "Thought your husband might've come". All the other husbands were there.'

Twelve of the eighteen men interviewed had attended two evening talks specifically aimed at fathers. These had a lecture format and dealt with general information, and one was entirely given over to the topic of pain-relief during labour and delivery. Most of the fathers had found the lectures helpful, although one complained: 'There was nothing there I didn't know from O-level biology.' Some men were clearly inhibited by the format of the talks, and one commented that the only questions at the end were put by women. There was little opportunity, then, for expectant fathers to have discussions with their peers in the same way as women did at their smaller and more informal daytime ante-natal classes. Two of the men in the sample had attended one class each. Both remarked that they felt awkward amongst the totally female attenders, and thought that the women, in turn, felt embarrassed by their presence. This was confirmed by their partners, who said that women were hesitant about holding personal discussions in their presence. However, these couples both thought that this awkwardness would be dispelled if all the women were accompanied by partners. Again, this was unlikely to happen as long as the classes were held during normal working hours.

Although two of the couples in my sample had attended couples' classes run by the National Childbirth Trust, the majority were suspicious of such groups. Their reluctance to become involved in such a way stemmed from information supplied, either first-hand from friends and acquaintances who had attended the classes, or second-hand through magazine articles and friends of friends:

From what I've heard the NCT are in favour of completely natural births. I saw a magazine article which said that the woman had felt a total failure because she hadn't had a natural delivery. I think they put too much emphasis on it. I'd rather have an open mind—I'll have pain relief if I need it. [Female partner]

Quite honestly, I don't see how me sitting cross-legged on the floor and doing breathing exercises is going to help anyone . . . We know people who've gone and they said it was a bit over the top. [Male partner]

It's replacing one dogma with another. They seem to make it into a religious experience . . . even gas and air is a bit much for them. [Male partner]

Those who had been to NCT classes, however, told me that they were keeping an open mind about pain-relief. As one man explained: 'As I see it the NCT gives you all the options and it's up to you to decide. We'll just have to see what happens.'

All of the couples I interviewed had opted for hospital deliveries, and only one had taken up the opportunity of having a domino delivery, where the baby was delivered in hospital by a community midwife, with mother and baby returning home for most of their post-partum care. Interviews revealed that couples knew very little about the possibilities that were open to them, and the majority had not heard of domino deliveries until the interviewer questioned them about their opinion on this arrangement. They expressed themselves as being happy to have the benefits of a hospital delivery, with technology and expertise on hand should they be required. By the time I talked to couples, however, such decisions had been made—either by them or for them—and what I may have been recording was simply acceptance of the status quo.

In accordance with the current orthodoxy, all but one of the men I interviewed intended to be there for the birth of his child. This is not altogether surprising, since one would expect only the most committed of fathers to be prepared to devote time to being interviewed at length about their involvement. However, I have reason to believe that, in this respect at least, they were not all that different from the general population of fathers, the majority of whom now attend the deliveries of their infants.

Fathers' attendance at deliveries is, indeed, no longer unusual: Garcia *et al.* (1985) note an increase of 60–67 per cent during the last four years at one particular hospital. My own observations in four labour wards confirm that the vast majority of women in labour are accompanied by their partners. Writing in 1977, Oakley commented: 'In the last ten years or so, it has become increasingly fashionable to admit husbands to the delivery room. What started out as a movement among middle class couples has permeated downwards until it is now the rule rather than the exception in many hospitals that the father is present.' (Oakley 1977: 203.)

Several years on, Oakley's description still appears to be valid, with the majority of the deliveries I observed involving fathers as attendants. Despite the shaky methodological and theoretical foundations of the studies carried out in the late 1960s suggesting benefits of paternal attendance, their findings appear to have been accepted at face value. Reviewing this literature, Antle May and Perrin comment that claims for the purported benefits of fathers' attendance at births have been extravagant, ranging from 'shorter and easier labors and healthier mothers and babies, to improvements in the marital relationship and subsequent parenting' (Antle May and Perrin 1985: 67).

All of the men in my sample had been subject to considerable pressure to attend the birth of their babies. Most had friends who had already been through this experience and heartily recommended it. In contrast to the fathers studied by Lewis (1986), they reported that this had not been a difficult decision to make and that they had automatically assumed they would attend. It is possible that attitudes have changed in the period between these two studies. It is also possible that the recruits to my sample were particularly committed to the concept of paternal attendance. I was also talking to fathers at a relatively late stage, when such decisions tended to have been made. My data, however, suggest that the decision had been unproblematic from the outset. Several of the women indicated that they had talked about this prior to conception, and that they would have been reluctant to have a baby were the father not to be involved in the delivery: 'I don't think I'd've been very keen to have a baby if he'd not been prepared to be there.' One father told me: 'If someone said their girlfriend had had a baby and they weren't there I'd think, "Good God—there's something wrong with them". We never had any doubts.' Most of the couples I spoke to did not question the purported benefits of paternal attendance; they described this shared experience as involving 'togetherness' and promoting 'bonding' between the father and the newly born infant.

The one couple who had not come to a decision about paternal attendance by the time of their first interview bitterly resented the pressures for him to be at the delivery which they experienced as coming from all sides; from the clinic staff as well as friends. My labour ward observations established that midwifery staff could, and did, subscribe to the belief that the father's presence at delivery was a good thing. In the encounter cited below, the labour ward midwife makes the woman account for the absence of her partner, and coaches her in the manner in which she ought to appeal to him:

MIDWIFE Is your man going to come in for the delivery, then?
WOMAN Well, I don't know. He hasna been that keen. Y'ken he's just a big coward when it comes to hospitals and that . . .
MIDWIFE Och, that's a shame, though, to miss it.
WOMAN Aye, but that's just the way he is . . . he's always hated hospitals . . . and he's the same in the dentists, anything like that.
MIDWIFE It's just as well you're no the same, eh? We just have to put up with it, don't we? We women don't have the choice.
WOMAN Aye, you're right. He might come in when it comes down to it, but I dinna ken . . .
MIDWIFE Och, that's right. You just work at him. Why should he get off that easily, eh?
WOMAN Aye, they just don't know what you go through, do they? . . . He says it's nothing to do with him. It's for the women . . .
MIDWIFE That's a good one. Tell him . . . ask him who got you into this mess, then . . .

Throughout this piece of interaction, the midwife reassures the woman that she is not making unrealistic demands on her husband. She also introduces a theme which recurred in many of the exchanges I collected as observational data: that of men as big babies, ignorant of 'women's troubles'. Some women thought that attending the delivery would be valuable experience for their partners, seen as having been sheltered up to that point:

WOMAN Hmm . . . it wouldna dae him any harm would it? . . .

to see what you go through . . . make him realize, maybe . . .

MIDWIFE   Yes . . . make him appreciate you a bit more.

OBSERVER Is he going to be there to see the baby born?

WOMAN   Too true, he is. Why should he get off scot-free? That's what I say.

It could be that the 'them and us' nature of the above conversations is merely a more palatable way of discussing the potentially embarrassing topic of 'togetherness'. Another interesting aspect of such comments, however, was that, in both the observational and the interview study, they appeared to be confined to working-class couples: it is possible that the vocabulary reflects more traditional types of relationships, relying on more segregated gender roles than middle-class relationships do. If this is the case, then the women quoted above (and their working-class midwives) have not merely taken on board the trend instigated by middle-class couples: they have adapted the rhetoric contained therein so that it reflects more accurately their own situation and relationship. In this version, paternal attendance at births remains desirable, but for different reasons.

Some work carried out in America by Nelson (1983) lends weight to this argument. Her research concluded that working-class women do not subscribe to the same model of labour and childbirth as their middle-class counterparts. Whereas middle-class women tended to embrace the concept of labour and birth as a potentially fulfilling, holistic experience, the working-class women studied by Nelson were more likely to see the time spent in the labour ward as the inevitable price to be paid for having a baby: something to be got through as painlessly as possible. If this is the case, then, it would have important implications for the nature of working-class couples' shared experience in the delivery room—a shared experience which they, and their professional attendants, may view in a negative light.

Whilst it is the acknowledgement—both by medical staff and the couple involved—of the family context in which childbirth occurs which validates the fathers' presence, the event itself, in the vast majority of cases, takes place in the hospital rather than at home, with the assistance of medical personnel rather than lay helpers, and amongst strangers rather than relatives or friends. A man is admitted to the delivery room by virtue of his relationship to the labouring woman as husband or partner, and his relationship to the fetus as biological father: his status as a participant is confirmed with reference to the family sphere rather than to the medical sphere. The father is also the representative on behalf of the extended family, and is usually the person to announce the birth to grandparents. He is the chronicler of a family event. Thus, paternal attendance represents an uneasy compromise between two contradictory views of childbirth: the medical view and the lay view.

Fathers are expected to support their labouring partners. However, as Elizabeth Perkins (1980) has amply demonstrated, their lack of knowledge of, and familiarity with, the high-technology environment of modern obstetric units places severe restrictions on their capacity to help, as does the layout of furniture in delivery rooms, where, for example, easy chairs may be provided which are not at a useful height to allow the father to participate in what is going on around him. This undoubtedly contributes to the feeling of helplessness often experienced by fathers, as Brown (1982) has also observed.

Some of the expectant fathers I interviewed defined their role at delivery in terms of general support: 'His role is to be there to support and comfort her. "You're all right, girl—give another push".' Brown also underlines the role of the father in easing communication between the medical team and the labouring woman. She described this phenomenon as involving the father explaining medical terminology to his labouring partner. This role was mentioned by the couples I interviewed: 'You're surrounded by experts who do care, but they can't pay someone just to hold her hand. And I know Ann, so if they have to give her a drug or anything and you're not thinking too clearly—if there's a decision to be made I'll be like a camera to Ann—I can relate the whole thing to her.' However, the couples in the study also suggested that the explanation could take place the other way around:

WOMAN   He's the one who can communicate what you feel.

PARTNER I'll make my presence felt if I feel they're doing some-
         thing and she can't answer for herself at the time.

This last quote describes the role of the partner as being that
of an advocate. One of the couples I interviewed explained
that the man was someone 'on the side' of the labouring
woman.

For the new father, also, attending a hospital delivery puts
what is essentially a private emotional response on public
display. He is required to live out one of the most vivid of
family experiences in an unfamiliar setting peopled by
strangers; a private and highly charged moment becomes
public property. Giving birth to a child with the father present
allows for a practical demonstration of 'family togetherness',
which Wertz and Wertz (1977) claim was pursued with
'almost religious fervour' by the post-war nuclear family in
America, and which they see as making a significant
contribution towards the widespread acceptance of the
desirability of fathers being present at the birth of their babies.
Because of the nature of labour ward work, several staff are
present throughout much of labour and delivery, and are, by
virtue of their close contact with the couple, party to their
conversations and reactions to events as they unfold. Their
relationship is thus open to scrutiny by strangers. Speaking of
those couples who fail to get what they had hoped for out of
deliveries, Elizabeth Perkins comments: 'Finally, however, a
couple's relationship is their business; they know a lot more
about it than the staff do. If they cannot make it work for them
in labour, the staff can do nothing about it.' (Perkins 1980:
22.) This serves to emphasize the possibility of failure: that the
relationship may be put to the test in the labour ward
situation and found wanting. Midwives' comments on what
they termed 'nice deliveries' show that they were sensitized to
the couple's behaviour, and, moreover, that this was an
important component of what they saw as an ideal delivery:

Now, that's what I call a nice delivery. The mother nice and calm; a
short labour, under control; no cut—only a slight tear—and they're
both just so delighted with the baby.

Oh, it makes me feel quite tearful myself. What a lovely couple—I
wish all deliveries were like that. You could see they were so fond of

each other and it's just lovely to deliver a baby to a couple like that.

Did you see them together? I felt quite embarrassed—they were obviously so pleased with themselves that they didn't care who else was there. If only all couples were as happy . . . that's the sort of thing that makes your job worthwhile, having nice deliveries.

Fathers go into hospital to witness the birth of their babies. What many of them do not realize is that the bulk of their time will in fact be taken up by 'waiting there' rather than just 'being there'. Although expectant mothers are frequently exhorted by clinic staff to 'bring something to hospital with you to read', this same activity, when indulged in by fathers, merited criticism. Fathers who read or did paperwork during the waiting period were viewed by midwives as treating the situation with less solemnity than was warranted. A midwife commented of one man who had brought some paperwork to hospital: 'He's the real executive type, that one, sitting working. You'd think he could give it a break today . . .'.

Labour is a long and frequently slow process and it is difficult to predict its culmination accurately. Fathers were often observed to ask the staff when the baby might arrive. Although they had waited nine months for the birth of their baby, now that the action had moved to the arena of the hospital they expected to be furnished with more accurate and scientific guidelines than those which were forthcoming. As one exasperated father commented to the observer: 'They keep saying they don't know when the baby'll arrive and I keep saying that I don't need to know exactly—just an idea of when . . . You'd think they'd be able to say . . . I mean, they're dealing with this every day.'

The majority of the fathers I interviewed took a fairly active role during the delivery, and help with breathing was their most common contribution. This was cited predominantly by fathers who had attended ante-natal classes, but it was also mentioned by others, indicating that women had passed on information about breathing to their partners, who had also witnessed their wives practising these exercises at home. Although some fathers performed a fairly passive role, remaining by the head of the bed and holding their partners' hands, others were more actively involved; for example, supporting their partners' legs whilst they pushed, and hence witnessing the crowning of the baby's head and the delivery.

Midwives' favourable comments about the practice of paternal attendance suggested that they saw this development as making their own jobs easier. For example, one commented: 'Labour wards used to be full of screaming women. They made a terrible noise. But now that their husbands are there that's calmed them down. They're a lot quieter now . . .'. My own observations established that fathers could be co-opted by members of the medical team, and thus became involved in supporting the latter's definition of the situation rather than their partners'. The excerpt below involves a woman in second-stage labour who seemed about to lose control:

MIDWIFE   Come on now, you're nearly there.
WOMAN   Oh, the pain's terrible . . . I . . . I can't . . .
MIDWIFE   Of course you can . . . we can just about see the baby's head when you push.
WOMAN   Huh [in disbelief] No . . . No . . . I can't . . .
MIDWIFE   [to husband, standing at the head of the bed]. See, you come down here and you can tell her. [The husband did as requested and moved to the foot of the bed. When the next contraction arrived and the woman was pushing, the midwife continued] There, did you see?
HUSBAND   Well, I'm not sure . . . I saw something.
MIDWIFE   [at the next contraction]. There, that's the head, see it?
HUSBAND   Oh yes . . . I think so . . . [To wife cheerfully] Aye, you can see the head . . . you're nearly there . . .

In this instance, the midwife, struggling to maintain control of the woman and her handling of her contractions, appeals to the husband's privileged status as trustworthy partner, and, on this occasion, he does indeed come to her rescue.

In the two post-natal wards where I carried out my observations, the role of the father changed dramatically after the birth. From then on the status of a visitor was being conferred upon him, and the time he spent in the hospital was restricted. Writing in 1964, Lomas described a situation which I found still existed in the wards where I carried out my observational work:

During this time the husband has little or no influence over the affairs of his wife and baby. He is patronised by the hospital staff who, in the same way as the general public, humorously assume him to be in a state of incompetent dither, best out of the way since liable to be a nuisance, and he accepts this practice. (Lomas 1964: 13.)

When partners arrived at visiting times, they were greeted by pristine infants, often sleeping, and giving little indication of the work involved in looking after them. All bathing and feeding demonstrations took place at other times, which meant that the mother became the expert on care of the new-born, with, one assumes, repercussions for the post-natal care of infants in the home. Lewis makes this point: 'When their wives arrive home men are at a distinct disadvantage, since not only have they had less contact with their new-born babies, they also have not had the support and guidance of the hospital staff.' (Lewis 1986: 81.)

By contrast, the couples in my interview sample enjoyed unrestricted visiting for fathers. This not only meant that fathers spent more time in hospital with their new babies, but the *nature* of this contact was also markedly different. Fathers reported having changed nappies and bathed infants, and, on several occasions, their involvement had allowed their partners to catch up on much-needed sleep. Thus, these fathers were not only learning how to perform such tasks, they were making a significant contribution to the total work involved in caring for a new baby. On occasion, they also undertook the role of organizing other visitors, thereby minimizing contact for their tired and sometimes mildly depressed partners.

It is important to bear in mind, however, that only a few fathers were able to take up the benefits of unrestricted visiting. Whilst doubtless more flexible for all concerned, unrestricted visiting allowed only those fathers on holiday, those who were self-employed, or those who were unemployed to spend long periods of time in the hospital.

Apart from one woman who had a domino delivery, all of the mothers in my sample remained in hospital for five days. Like the men studied by Lewis (1986), the majority of the fathers I interviewed took time off work to coincide with the return of mother and baby from hospital. This was un-problematic for the self-employed, but the rest of the men had to take holidays. Three of the men had jobs which allowed them to spend periods of time at home during the day.

When I interviewed the couples at home within four weeks of the mother and baby returning from hospital, it was the mothers who were doing the bulk of the work in looking after their new-born infants. This was for a variety of reasons: most of the fathers had returned to work, thereby limiting the time they spent with their families, and, in their eyes, were justifying their sleeping through night-time feeds. All of my sample of mothers were breast-feeding, a factor which obviously limited fathers' involvement, although two of the couples had plans for the woman to express milk so that the father could become involved in feeding. Couples spoke of the difficulties of sharing work equitably when only one partner was at home all day; good intentions inevitably fall victim to the restrictions which this places upon fathers' involvement. At this stage it was the woman alone who had contact with health-care professionals through home visits and attendance at baby clinics.

If we compare fathers' ante-natal, intrapartum, and post-partum involvement, we find that it is within the sphere of labour and delivery that they have made the most significant inroads into what was originally women's territory and, more recently, medical territory. Their involvement has become established in the one dramatic event rather than in the slower, unfolding process of the ante-natal and post-partum periods.

As Lewis (1986) laments, the changes in hospital policies with regard to paternal attendance at deliveries are not documented. Nor are the more piecemeal moves towards the ante-natal and post-natal involvement of fathers. Nevertheless, progressive hospital policies and individual obstetricians and midwives have had considerable influence in achieving this participation. As Lewis points out, the progressive view on paternal attendance was being promoted in medical circles *before* it gained widespread support from the media or expectant couples. In my own study, the clearest example of this was the introduction of unrestricted visiting at the hospital from which my interview sample was drawn.

Midwives at this hospital also sometimes suggested that expectant fathers should attend ante-natal consultations.

Antle May and Perrin (1985) attribute the origins of today's more active role for fathers to the natural childbirth movement which developed in the United States in the 1940s. It was not until later, however, that this group and its ideas gained more general acceptance. Also writing of the American situation, Nelson argues that the growth of the movement was associated with several parallel developments:

In the early 1960's middle class women were not very interested in childbirth; in the early 1970's only elite portions of the middle class took childbirth classes or attempted to define birth independently of the prevailing high-technology, medical model. The change came with the convergence of (and occasional tension among) four social movements: (1) the natural childbirth movement; (2) feminism; (3) consumerism and (4) 'back to nature' romanticism. (Nelson 1983: 295.)

In this country these same movements, or their equivalents, have had some input. The National Childbirth Trust has undoubtedly exerted some influence over hospital policies (see Kitzinger, Chapter 5). But, as Lewis points out: 'Fathers have been included at hospital delivery at the same time that birth has become increasingly "unnatural".' (Lewis 1986: 56.) Clearly the development of fathers' involvement is a complex issue, and no one explanation, on its own, can account for the situation described in this chapter.

However, it will be interesting to see how paternal involvement develops in the future. Now that fathers have consolidated their position with regard to labour and delivery, it will be important to monitor the progress of their involvement as service-users in relation to the ante-natal and post-natal periods.

References

Antle May, K., 1982, 'Three Phases of Father Involvement in Pregnancy', *Nursing Research*, 31/6, pp. 337–42.
——and Perrin, S. P., 1985, 'Prelude, Pregnancy and Birth', in S. M. H. Hanson and F. W. Bozett (eds.), *Dimensions of Fatherhood* (Beverley Hills, Sage).
Beail, N. and McGuire, J., 1982, *Fathers: Psychological Perspectives* (London, Junction Books).
Brown, A., 1982, 'Fathers in the Labour Ward: Medical and Lay Accounts', in L. McKee and M. O'Brien (eds.), *The Father Figure* (London, Tavistock).
Garcia, J. *et al.*, 1985, 'Mothers' Views of Continuous Electronic Fetal Heart Monitoring and Intermittent Auscultation in a Randomized Controlled Trial', *Birth*, 12, pp. 79–85.
Hanson, S. M. H., and Bozett, F. W. (eds.), 1985, *Dimensions of Fatherhood* (Beverley Hills, Sage).
Lewis, C., 1986, *Becoming a Father* (Milton Keynes, Open University Press).
——and O'Brien, M. (eds.), 1987, *Reassessing Fatherhood* (London, Sage).
Lomas, P., 1964, 'Childbirth Rituals', *New Society*, 4 (118).
McKee, L. and O'Brien, M. (eds.), 1982, *The Father Figure* (London, Tavistock).
Nelson, M. K., 1983, 'Working-Class Women, Middle-Class Women and Models of Childbirth', *Social Problems*, 30/3, pp. 284–97.
Oakley, A., 1977, *From Here to Maternity: Becoming a Mother* (London, Penguin).
Perkins, E. R., 1980, *Men on the Labour Ward* (Leverhulme Health Education Project, University of Nottingham Occasional Paper 22).
Richards, M., 1980, 'Husbands Becoming Fathers', Paper presented at a symposium organized by the UK Marriage Research Centre on the impact of children on marriage, 23 April 1980.
Wertz, R. and Wertz, D., 1977, *Lying-in: A History of Childbirth in America* (New York, The Free Press).

12

Recent Debate on the Place of Birth

Rona Campbell and Alison Macfarlane

Britain is unusual, although not unique among Western
nations, in not regarding the hospital as the only
acceptable place to be born

Smith 1970: 15.

It has been suggested that the move towards 100 per cent
hospital confinement removes from women the possibility
of choice. One is very conscious of the need to involve the
consumer in any form of personal service, but with the
greatest respect one might suggest that the majority of
women are not in a sufficiently informed position to
make such a choice.

Fox 1976: 11.

THE move from home to hospital births has taken place over
a period of seventy years, but a distinctive and apparently
final phase in the process has occurred since 1970. This has
also coincided with the much more recent change from births
in small maternity units to departments in large obstetric
hospitals. We have already reviewed the evidence—or to be
more precise, the lack of evidence—to support these policies
in our *Where to be Born?* (Campbell and Macfarlane 1987), so
we will not repeat the exercise here. Instead we will describe
the debates which have taken place over the past eighteen
years, and the arguments that have been put forward by
supporters and opponents of these changes.

The publication in 1970 of a report by the Standing Maternity
and Midwifery Advisory Committee (Chairman: J. Peel)
marked an important watershed in policy on the place of
birth. It appeared at the end of a period during which the

birth-rate had been declining whilst the number of hospital maternity beds had risen. Although previous expert committees had advocated increasing the proportion of hospital deliveries (Royal College of Obstetricians and Gynaecologists 1944; Ministry of Health 1959), the Peel Committee was the first to propose that the maternity service should no longer offer the option of home delivery. In its report the committee stated that: 'We consider that the resources of modern medicine should be available to all mothers and babies, and we think that sufficient facilities should be provided to allow for 100% hospital delivery. The greater safety of hospital confinement for mother and child justifies this objective.' (Standing Maternity and Midwifery Advisory Committee 1970: 60.)

Aside from the proposal to provide universal hospital delivery, this statement contains two other important points. Firstly, safety is established as the only criterion by which places of delivery should be judged; and secondly, it asserts, without any supporting evidence, that a hospital delivery is safer for all women and their babies. Much of the debate on place of birth during the subsequent decade was largely focused around these two points.

Place of Birth and the Quality of Care

For women and the groups that sought to represent them, the question of where a baby should be born seemed, in the early 1970s, to be focused not so much on safety, but rather on the quality of care received and the emotional satisfaction associated with the birth. Many opinions expressed in the press and through the media at this time tended to suggest that a home delivery offered a more rewarding experience for the parents, because the kind of care provided by community midwives and family doctors was more personal. For example, writing in *The Times*, Margaret Allen describes her first delivery in hospital as one in which she 'felt physically, mentally and emotionally assaulted', while her second birth at home was 'simply a slightly untidy morning at home' (Allen 1973: 8).

Jean Robinson took up the theme of the quality of maternity care when she wrote in an article in *The Times*:

Whereas doctors, understandably and properly, judge quality of treatment by perinatal and maternal mortality rates, they may not fully have understood that mothers also judge maternity care in terms of the quality of relationship fostered between them and their babies and they may even be willing to take greater physical risks to ensure this. It is because some hospitals are neglecting patients' emotional needs that the loss of a domiciliary midwifery service for low risk cases is so bitterly regretted. (Robinson 1974: 6.)

A number of surveys undertaken at this time confirmed that these press reports were not merely isolated anecdotes. At least 80 per cent of the women included in these surveys who had experienced both home and hospital deliveries said that they preferred giving birth at home. Between 34 and 40 per cent of those stating a preference for home delivery expressed a dislike of hospitals. Interestingly, the increasingly liberal use of induction was not mentioned as a major reason for disliking hospital delivery (Richards *et al.* 1970; Goldthorpe and Richman 1974; AIMS *Quarterly Newsletter* Mar. 1975).

Several pressure groups took a very active part in the debate. The publication of a report on users' views of the National Health Service in Oxford in 1974 recorded a considerable degree of dissatisfaction with the maternity services, and stimulated a good deal of debate (Robinson 1974). In the same year the Society to Support Home Confinements was formed in Durham, and in 1976 the National Childbirth Trust formed its multidisciplinary Study Group on Home Confinements. This debate on place of birth was taking place at a time when new developments were being introduced in obstetrics, particularly in the technological management of labour. During the mid-1970s, however, user groups expressed increasing concern about the possible misuse of induction for social rather than medical reasons (Jordan 1974; Robinson 1974).

Disquiet about the use of induction was also beginning to be voiced by the medical profession itself. An editorial published in the *Lancet* in 1974 was unswerving in its condemnation of induction for social reasons, stating that: 'induction on the grounds of social convenience is a pernicious practice which has no place in modern obstetric care' (The *Lancet* 1974: 1184). Similar views were being expressed by midwives (Robinson 1974). Indeed, in 1976 two student midwives were so unhappy about what they saw as a 'surge in obstetric interference' that they convened the first meeting of what was later to be named the Association of Radical Midwives (Scruggs 1978). The professed aim of the group was then, and remains, 'to restore the role of the midwife for the benefit of the childbearing woman and her baby' (Association of Radical Midwives 1978).

This backlash against the widespread use of induction seemed to shift the emphasis of the debate on place of birth, as Dr Luke Zander, a general practitioner, observed when he wrote: 'Whereas previously the motivation for home confinement was largely focused on the desire of some mothers to enjoy the extra benefits that a delivery safely conducted in their home could provide, one now senses that the motivation is increasingly the more negative one of wishing to avoid hospital confinement.' (Zander 1976: 14.)

Safety and the Place of Birth

Although the Peel Committee failed to produce any evidence to substantiate the claim that a hospital delivery was always safer, it did, in a separate paragraph, draw attention to the fall in the overall perinatal mortality rate, and the increase in the proportion of hospital deliveries. In an influential book on the effectiveness and efficiency of the National Health Service published shortly after the Peel Report, Archie Cochrane warned of the dangers of assuming that the coincidence between these two time-trends implied a causal relationship. Instead, he advocated the randomized controlled trial as the only rigorous way of establishing causality (Cochrane 1972). Regrettably, this call went largely unheeded, and rational debate about the place of birth has continued to be hampered by a lack of experimental evidence.

In questioning the existence of a direct link between the decline in perinatal mortality and the increase in institutional delivery, some people pointed to the Dutch maternity system. In the mid-1970s The Netherlands had the second lowest perinatal mortality rate in the world, even though approximately half of its deliveries took place at home. Others dismissed this argument on the grounds that 'the better performance of Dutch women is closely related to their superior height and good health' (*British Medical Journal* 1976: 55). Finally, it was suggested that direct comparisons were probably inappropriate. As the Study Group on Home Confinements pointed out, although Sweden had 100 per cent hospital delivery and the lowest perinatal mortality rate in the world, factors other than the place of delivery were probably responsible for the decline in its perinatal mortality (Study Group on Home Confinements 1976).

By the mid-1970s the results of a number of studies had been published which did tend to suggest that the relationship between the hospital delivery rate and the decline in perinatal mortality was spurious (Chalmers *et al.* 1976; Barron *et al.* 1977; Ashford 1978). These findings did not support the prevailing view at the time, and, as we show later in the chapter, they are still largely ignored by policy-making bodies.

Selection of Higher-Risk Women for Hospital Delivery

The prevailing views about the safety of hospital birth may have been coloured by experience in the 1950s and 1960s, when the demand for hospital beds outstripped supply. During the 1950s, reports by the Ministry of Health repeatedly mentioned the rising demand for hospital delivery (Campbell and Macfarlane 1987). The problem, therefore, was how to select the women who, for medical and social reasons, needed to give birth in hospital.

A study of 1.5 million children born in England and Wales in 1949 and 1950 had found above-average rates of stillbirth and infant death among babies born to women over 35 years of age, and to younger women with large families (Heady *et al.* 1955). Additional analyses also showed that perinatal mortality was lowest among babies born to women married to men in social class I, and that it increased as one moved across the class spectrum, so that it was highest for babies with fathers in social class V. Babies who had the highest risk of infant death were underrepresented among those born in hospital (Heady and Morris 1956).

These findings were noted in the Chief Medical Officer's reports for 1955 and 1956, together with instructions to general practitioners and hospitals to refer selectively women in these 'vulnerable groups' for hospital delivery. It was assumed that the risk of death for babies born to women in the 'vulnerable groups' would be reduced by delivery in hospital, and, correspondingly, that women whose babies were in the groups with low mortality could be safely delivered at home.

Despite continued exhortations by the Ministry of Health throughout the 1960s and the 1970s, a number of studies undertaken before 1970 had shown that selection remained poor. This theme was revived in 1976 with the publication of the results of a study of 155 home births. The authors claimed not only that their study demonstrated the inability of general practitioners to adhere to recognized risk criteria when booking women for home delivery, but also that the criteria themselves could not predict perinatal problems with sufficient accuracy (Cox *et al.* 1976). This study was methodologically flawed, however: no distinction was made between planned and unplanned births; nor was there any attempt to compare the outcomes for mothers delivering at home with those of a similar group of women delivering in hospital. The results of the study were published in the *British Medical Journal*, together with an anonymous editorial entitled 'A Place to be Born' (*British Medical Journal* 1976). The intensity of the debate at this time can be judged by the fact that, following publication of this editorial and the paper by Cox *et al.* the journal received a massive amount of correspondence, and during the subsequent three months fourteen letters on the subject were published.

The response of health professionals to the public debate on place of birth at this time was varied. As a group, however, obstetricians seemed to be satisfied that hospitals were the safest place to give birth, and that safety was the paramount, if not the only criterion, on which the argument should be based. Thus, the Study Group on Home Confinements was accused of introducing 'nebulous factors' when it suggested that, if 'physical safety measured in terms of mortality and morbidity becomes the over-riding preoccupation there is a real danger that other important factors will be disregarded' (Reid 1976: 396; Study Group on Home Confinements 1976: 279). The more conservative members of the medical profession clearly resented the media interest. As they saw it, 'the trend inside journalism for self-appointed and self-taught experts to investigate a subject and reach an opinion on the merits or demerits of one form of medical treatment' amounted to journalists wielding 'power without authority' (*British Medical Journal* 1975: 539). Attempts were made by some professionals, not all of whom were obstetricians, to dismiss the criticisms voiced by women by using such pejorative terms as 'village Illiches', 'vociferous lobby', 'back to nature cult', and 'small minority' (Brewer 1979: 256; *British Medical Journal* 1 (1976), 55; Cox *et al.* 1976: 85; *British Medical Journal*, 2 (1976), 729), but this approach was challenged by others, who felt that 'It would be easy to dismiss these pleas as a minority, back-to-Nature fringe, were it not that the medical evidence is equivocal.' (The *Lancet* 1974: 1183.) Debate at this time seems to have been very polarized, being conducted in terms of home versus hospital (Zander 1976), and woman versus obstetrician. Viewed from a theoretical perspective, this is not surprising. Sociologists had already identified that two different paradigms of pregnancy were operating; one upholding pregnancy and childbirth as natural and normal processes in which intervention was rarely necessary; the other seeing parturition as a hazardous event requiring high-powered medical supervision (Comaroff 1977; Macintyre 1977). The phasing-out of home delivery and the increasing use of techniques for the active management of labour suggested that a shift from the former to the latter paradigm was under way, and that pregnancy and childbirth were becoming increasingly medicalized (Oakley 1975).

The oversimplification of the debate into the two extremes of home and hospital undoubtedly contributed to this polarization. Discussion of the merits and demerits of deliveries in general-practitioner beds and units only surfaced occasionally (Gervis and Sutherland 1976; Hudson 1976). Towards the end of the decade some obstetricians were beginning to accept the criticisms about the impersonal, paternalistic nature of obstetric care in hospital. On the question of safety, however, the medical profession remained convinced that hospital deliveries were best. This conviction still seemed to be based on the belief that the rise in the proportion of hospital deliveries was directly responsible for the observed decline in maternal and perinatal mortality, in spite of mounting evidence that the association was probably coincidental (The *Lancet* 1975; Campbell 1976).

Debate during the period 1970 to 1977 could be said to be more opinionated than informed. Pressure groups had drawn attention to the differences in the reports of women delivering in hospital and at home, and thus forced the medical and midwifery professions to re-examine their treatment of women giving birth in hospital. What they had failed to do, however, was to launch an attack on the established assumption that a hospital delivery was safer for all women.

Hospital Delivery Safer for All Women?

The challenge to this assumption came from Marjorie Tew, a statistician working in the Department of Community Health at Nottingham University Medical School. While teaching a course in epidemiology, Marjorie Tew set herself and the students an exercise to see how much they could find out about maternal and perinatal mortality from published data. Expecting to find evidence to support the conventional wisdom that a hospital delivery was safer for all women, Marjorie Tew was astonished to find 'that maternal and fetal death rates for comparable groups were always higher in hospital than at home whether the predicted risk, on account of the mother's age or size of family was high or low, and also that the years when births in public hospitals had increased most were not the years when mortality rates decreased most' (Tew 1987).

Marjorie Tew's initial attempts to have these findings published in a medical journal were unsuccessful. She was told by the editors that they would be of no interest to the readership. When the results eventually appeared in *New*

Society in 1977, however, they attracted a considerable amount of attention (Tew 1977), and their publication was even reported in the national press (*The Times* 1977). What is more, the status of the correspondents whose letters subsequently appeared in *New Society* indicate interest from the very highest of academic and government circles (Cartwright 1977; Whitehead and Ford 1977). When the Department of Community Health in Nottingham failed to renew her contract in 1976 (Tew 1987), Marjorie Tew was not alone in interpreting this as a further indication of the hostility and anger with which her findings had been received.

Most of the considered criticisms of Marjorie Tew's initial work concerned the difficulty in controlling for the selective factors which result in different women giving birth in different places (James 1977; Leiberman 1977; Williams 1977). Two examples of how these selection biases may operate were given by one correspondent, who wrote:

Marjorie Tew's implication that hospital fatalities are due to the treatment, rather than to the selection of cases, is seen to be silly when one considers that a proportion of hospital stillbirths occur in women who have been admitted for the very reason that the foetus is already dead. Hospital delivery is always arranged if possible in cases of such lethal congenital malformations as anencephaly. (James 1977: 248.)

Marjorie Tew was not the only person to challenge the received wisdom that hospital deliveries were safer than home births. In 1978 the work of the Study Group on Home Confinements culminated in the publication of a book entitled *The Place of Birth*. The editors, social anthropologist Sheila Kitzinger and paediatrician John Davis, clearly saw this book as a way of stimulating and informing debate on the place of birth, as this extract from their preface shows:

We question therefore the policy whereby many women are being deprived of the right and opportunity to give birth to their babies in their own homes (when they want to do so) on the grounds that this represents for them an unacceptable risk. What the order of this risk is; what the evidence on which it is estimated; how far it is inherent in home delivery and unavoidable in hospital delivery; and whether the government, acting on the advice of the obstetric establishment, has the duty or right to dictate to women and their attendants what risks they should or should not take, rather then letting them judge the evidence for themselves, the editors will be content to let their readers decide. (Kitzinger and Davis 1978: vi.)

In 1976 the government proposed a reduction in the provision of maternity services in response to the falling birthrate (Department of Health and Social Security 1976). Shortly after this, the Spastics Society mounted a campaign in which it claimed that, because of the inadequacies of the maternity services, babies born in Britain ran a far greater risk of perinatal death or handicap than many of their European neighbours (Macfarlane 1981). In seeking to defend the maternity services, clinicians latched on to the arguments put forward by the Spastics Society without considering the statistical merits of the evidence (Chalmers *et al.* 1980). In spite of the fact that national perinatal mortality rates for England and Wales continued to decline, public concern became so great that in November 1978 the Social Services and Employment Subcommittee of the House of Commons initiated an inquiry into perinatal and neonatal mortality (Macfarlane 1981). The committee, reconstituted after the 1979 general election and chaired by the Labour MP Renee Short, echoed the views of earlier committees when it recommended that: 'An increasing number of mothers be delivered in large units; selection of patients is improved for small consultant units and isolated GP units; and that home delivery is phased out further.' (Social Services Committee 1980.) In its report the Social Services Committee reproduced a graph (see Figure 12. 1) from an article published in *Population Trends*, the house journal of the Office of Population Censuses and Surveys. This showed a rise in the perinatal mortality rate for births at home. The author of the article warned that 'rates for place of confinement (for example, in hospital or at home) cannot easily be interpreted' (Macdonald Davies 1980), but unfortunately the warning went unheeded, and these data were taken at face value by the Social Services Committee.

Critics of the committee's interpretation suggested that the decline in the overall numbers of *planned* home births might mean that the rise in perinatal mortality for births at home

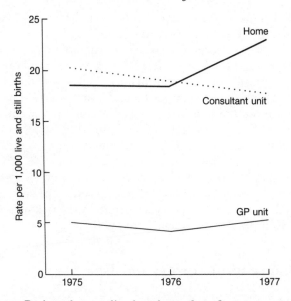

FIG. 12.1 Perinatal mortality by place of confinement, 1975–7. MacDonald-Davies, I., 1980, 'Perinatal and Infant Death Rates: Social and Biological Factors', *Population Trends*, 19, pp. 19–21, (HMSO). Reproduced by permission of OPCS.

could be accounted for by an increase in the proportion of *unplanned* births occurring there (Tew 1981; Campbell *et al.* 1982). The findings of a survey of all home births in 1979 supported this thesis, and showed the perinatal mortality rate for planned home births to be very low (Campbell *et al.* 1984).

Data presented in the Social Services Committee's report to illustrate the relationship between the size of obstetric units and stillbirth rates (for 1978) failed to support the committee's recommendations. Instead, they showed that stillbirth rates were uniformly low for isolated general-practitioner units, regardless of size. Stillbirth rates for consultant units actually rose as the volume of deliveries undertaken increased (Campbell and Macfarlane 1987).

Since her initial work, Marjorie Tew has (entirely at her own expense) continued to refine and extend her original analyses. Undoubtedly, her most important contribution has been a reanalysis of data collected in the 1970 British Births

Survey. Using two risk-scores constructed by the researchers who carried out that survey, Marjorie Tew has demonstrated that, except for women who, according to the scores, were deemed to be at the highest level of risk of perinatal problems, perinatal mortality was significantly lower for those giving birth at home or in isolated general-practitioner units (Tew 1985). Doubts have been expressed about the reliability and validity of the risk-scores, and about the fact that deaths resulting from congenital malformations had not been excluded from the analysis. Nevertheless, this work lends no support to the argument that perinatal mortality rates in hospitals, at least prior to 1975, were higher only because the women who delivered there were at a greater pre-delivery risk of perinatal death (Campbell and Macfarlane 1986).

The Stance of the Professionals

Since the late 1970s, obstetricians have increasingly acknowledged women's demands for a better quality of obstetric care. Indeed, by equating better care with more fully trained specialists rather than house officers and registrars, obstetricians were able to translate these demands into a call for more consultant obstetric posts (Royal College of Obstetricians and Gynaecologists 1983).

The obstetric community welcomed the report of the Social Services Committee, and remained steadfast in its view that a policy of 100 per cent hospital delivery should be pursued in the interests of safety. The report of the Royal College of Obstetricians' working party on ante-natal and intrapartum care noted that: 'The Peel Report provided a major impetus for confinement being in hospital and we do not think this trend should change. Even in low risk cases there is evidence that the risk of developing an abnormality during labour is approximately 10%, and we remain convinced that all confinements should take place in hospital.' (Royal College of Obstetricians and Gynaecologists 1982: 24.) In addition, this report also endorsed a recommendation made by a joint working party of the Royal College of General Practitioners and the Royal College of Obstetricians and Gynaecologists, namely, that general practitioners should only deliver carefully selected women in facilities adjacent to consultant obstetric units (Royal College of Obstetricians and Gynaecologists and Royal College of General Practitioners 1981; Royal College of Obstetricians and Gynaecologists 1982).

The position of midwives and health visitors has always been markedly different from that of their obstetric colleagues. Midwives and health visitors have been as much concerned with continuity of care, adequate support, and informed choice for parturient women as with safety. In a joint statement released in 1983 the Royal College of Midwives and the Health Visitors' Association stated that: 'The midwife should ensure that each pregnant woman is enabled to make an informed choice about the place of her confinement. At present this freedom of choice is regrettably curtailed. There are seldom sufficient midwives to allow for even a limited choice and home delivery is often inhibited by inadequate medical cover.' (Health Visitors' Association and Royal College of Midwives 1983: 1.) In its most recent policy document, *Towards a Healthy Nation*, the Royal College of Midwives has also explicitly acknowledged that 'there is some doubt about the assumption that the safest place for delivery of all women is the consultant unit' (Royal College of Midwives 1987: 9).

The Impact of Research on Recent Debate

Debate since the late 1970s, although just as intense as that which followed the recommendations of the Peel Report, has been better informed and less polarized. Discussions have not simply focused on the home versus hospital divide, but on the relative merits and demerits of all places of birth. The fact that this is so owes much to the work of individuals like Marjorie Tew and groups of researchers such as the National Perinatal Epidemiology Unit and the Study Group on Home Confinements. In addition, there has been an increasing awareness of the need for the rigorous scientific evalution of many obstetric and midwifery procedures (Macdonald 1987; Royal College of Midwives 1987). As a result, randomized trials are now being used to test the efficacy of a wide variety of new and existing ways of providing maternity care.

An experimental approach is the only way to eliminate the selection biases which make it so difficult to interpret observational studies of the benefits and disadvantages of different places of birth. While it is impractical, because the number of deaths is so small, to undertake such a comparison of outcomes for different places of birth in terms of perinatal mortality, there are plans afoot to use this approach to produce unbiased comparisons of parents' views about, and the morbidity associated with, different places of birth.

Recent Policy on Place of Birth

In spite of this, debate has continued against a background of the steady erosion of choice about the place of birth, encouraged by further policy recommendations which seem to have been formulated without any objective review of the evidence on the relative risks and benefits (Campbell and Macfarlane 1987). It is particularly sad to note that, many years after evidence had been produced which demonstrated that there was almost certainly no causal link between the decline in perinatal mortality and the increase in hospital delivery, the reverse was still being cited as a matter of fact by the chairperson of the influential Maternity Services Advisory Committee when she wrote in the introduction to the committee's second report: 'The practice of delivering nearly all babies in hospital has contributed to the dramatic reduction in stillbirths and neonatal deaths and to the avoidance of many child handicaps.' (Maternity Services Advisory Committee 1984: v.) This committee went on to recommend that: 'As unforseen complications can occur in any birth, every mother should be encouraged to have her baby in a maternity unit where emergency facilities are readily available.' (Maternity Services Advisory Committee 1984: 23.) Even after we had challenged this in *Where to be Born?*, partially funded by the DHSS as part of its programme of health-services research, the Department still stated in response to a question about its policy for maternity services:

Our objectives in the maternity services are healthy babies born whenever possible at full term to healthy mothers. We aim to minimise the risks to babies by encouraging delivery in hospital preferably with access to the full range of facilities which are likely to be found only on district general hospital sites. We aim to support the services outside hospital both ante- and post-natal by increasing the number of qualified staff and by other measures.

As a result there has been a fall in perinatal mortality rate in England from 14.6 per thousand births in 1979 to 9.8 in 1985. During the same period the maternal mortality rate per thousand live and stillbirths declined from 0.11 to 0.07. (Hansard 1987: 919.)

It is not difficult to detect which of the protagonists in the debate has enjoyed almost exclusive influence over policy on place of delivery. In the past, recommendations from the Royal College of Obstetricians and Gynaecologists have habitually reappeared in subsequent government policy documents (Campbell and Macfarlane 1987). This happened, for example, with the recommendation made by the Maternity Services Advisory Committee. Two years previously, in the College's report on ante-natal and intrapartum care, it was noted that: 'In the present state of knowledge it is not possible to predict with accuracy which labours will be uncomplicated. It is therefore hoped that few, if any, pregnant women will be delivered at home.' (Royal College of Obstetricians and Gynaecologists 1982: 9.) More recently, the Association of Anaesthetists issued a report recommending immediate withdrawal of anaesthetic cover from small units with infrequent requests for anaesthesia, and that in the longer term: 'small obstetric units which offer a substandard level of anaesthetic service should be closed, amalgamated or relocated to within a District General Hospital or unit where full services are available. A single unit in each District is strongly recommended.' (Association of Anaesthetists 1987: 1.) This report referred to the contribution of anaesthetic problems to maternal mortality, but presented no evidence that such deaths were more likely to occur in small units in general, or in isolated general-practitioner units in particular. Indeed, the DHSS seems to be unable to answer this question itself (Hansard 1988: 850).

Commercial interests have also been more obvious in the

last few years. An example of this was witnessed in 1980, during a press launch of the Social Services Committee's first report on perinatal and neonatal mortality (Social Services Committee 1980). This contained a recommendation that continuous fetal monitoring of the baby during labour should be routine. During the press launch a member of the committee actually spelt out the name of a British firm from which the requisite equipment could be purchased (Macfarlane 1981). Alternative medicine is also a lucrative enterprise. This was very evident at the First International Conference on Home Birth held in October 1987, when stalls selling a veritable plethora of alternative aids for childbearing women could be seen to be doing a roaring trade.

The National Health Service has at times shown itself unwilling to accommodate the wishes of those women desiring a home birth, or a delivery involving a minimum of intervention, or, indeed, to allow obstetricians and midwives wishing to offer this type of care to do so. As a result, some people have turned to the private sector. What seems certain is that this debate will continue unresolved for the forseeable future, because the profound 'clash of values' between the main protagonists remains (Oakley 1987). Many groups representing women's interests, and some representing midwives', maintain that every woman has the right to a safe birth and one in which informed decisions about how and where to give birth are ultimately made by the childbearing woman herself. The prevailing view amongst most obstetricians continues to be that safety remains the paramount consideration (Royal College of Obstetricians and Gynaecologists 1982).

This clash was highlighted recently by a gynaecologist writing 'in defence of obstetricians' when he observed that: 'Many obstetricians feel under attack, from consumer associations on the one hand and increasing litigation on the other. When a pregnant patient presents a list of demands and insists on her chosen method of delivery, has the obstetrician the right to claim that he can offer any special expertise and useful advice?' (Macdonald 1987: 833.) The answer, as far as Mr Macdonald was concerned, was that 'Obstetricians and neonatal paediatricians are doing a good job', and if the patient is not prepared to take the expert advice of an obstetrician, then 'Such a patient should be invited to consult another doctor who may be more in tune with her ideas.' (Macdonald 1987.)

As we have noted throughout this chapter, much of the debate has been conducted in terms of safety. Although the word has been used often, it is rarely defined, and it is tempting to ask: safety for whom? The stated rationale of a policy that all women should give birth in hospital is that this affords the safest environment. Unlike home, hospitals for most women are alien environments over which they have almost no control. This is not so for obstetricians and hospital midwives. Thus, it might be suggested that when obstetricians recommend that the wishes of women should be met, but only 'within the confines of safety', this means—at least in part—within the confines of an environment in which the obstetrician feels 'safe' (Royal College of Obstetricians and Gynaecologists 1982). A second reason for the likely continuation of this debate is that the case against home delivery is non-proven in scientific terms. Nevertheless, as Luke Zander points out: 'The reluctance of the obstetric establishment to consider the implications of objective evidence which runs counter to their preconceived assumptions—without refuting them on statistical grounds—must cast doubts in some minds as to whether the reasons for their decisions stem in part from intraprofessional self-interest, as well as a concern for patient care.' (Zander 1984: 128.)

References

AIMS *Quarterly Newsletter*, Mar. 1975, p. 5.

Allen, M., 1973, *The Times*, 13 Aug. 1973, p. 8.

Ashford, J. R., 1978, 'Policies for Maternity Care in England and Wales: Too Fast Too Far?' in Kitzinger, S. and Davis, J. (eds.), *The Place of Birth* (Oxford, Oxford University Press).

Association of Anaesthetists, 1987, *Anaesthetic Services for Obstetrics: A Plan for the Future* (London, The Association of Anaethetists of Great Britain and Ireland).

Association of Radical Midwives, *Newsletter*, 3 June 1978.

Barron, S. L., Thomson, A. M., and Philips, P. R., 1977, 'Home and Hospital Confinement in Newcastle-upon-Tyne 1960–1969', *British Journal of Obstetrics and Gynaecology*, 84, pp. 401–11.

Brewer, C., 1979, 'Risks in being Born', *New Society*, 1 Nov. 1979, pp. 256–7.

British Medical Journal, 1975, editorial, 'Medicine on Television', 2, p. 539.

—— 1976, editorial, 'A Place to be Born', 1, pp. 55–6; editorial, 'Induction of Labour', 1, pp. 729–30.

Campbell, A. G. M., 1976, Letter to the *British Medical Journal*, 1, p. 279.

Campbell, R. and Macfarlane, A., 1986, 'Place of Delivery: A Review', *Br J Obstet & Gynaecol*, 93, pp. 675–83.

—— —— 1987, *Where to be Born? The Debate and the Evidence* (Oxford, National Perinatal Epidemiology Unit).

Campbell, R., Macdonald Davies, I., and Macfarlane, A., 1982, 'Perinatal Mortality and Place of Delivery', *Population Trends*, 28, pp. 9–12 (HMSO).

—— —— —— and Beral, V., 1984, 'Home Births in England and Wales: Perinatal Mortality According to Intended Place of Delivery', *British Medical Journal*, 289, pp. 721–4.

Cartwright, A., 1977, Letter to *New Society*, 39, p. 749.

Chalmers, I., 1978, 'Implications of the Current Debate on Obstetric Practice', in Kitzinger, S. and Davis, J. A. (eds.), *The Place of Birth* (Oxford, Oxford University Press).

—— Oakley, A., and Macfarlane, A., 1980, 'Perinatal Health Services: An Immodest Proposal', *British Medical Journal*, 1, pp. 842–5.

—— Zlosnik, J. E., Johns, K. A., and Campbell, H., 1976,

'Obstetric Practice and Outcome of Pregnancy in Cardiff Residents 1965–1973', *British Medical Journal*, 1, pp. 735–8.

Cochrane, A. L., 1972, *Effectiveness and Efficiency: Random Reflections on the Health Service* (London, Nuffield Provincial Hospitals Trust).

Comaroff, J., 1977, 'Conflicting Paradigms of Pregnancy: Managing Ambiguities in Antenatal Encounters', in Davis, A. and Horobin, G. (eds.), *Medical Encounters: Experience of Illness and Treatment* (London, Croom Helm).

Cox, C. A., Fox, J. S., Zinkin, P. M., and Mathews, A. E. B., 1976, 'Critical Appraisal of Domiciliary Obstetrics and Neonatal Practice', *British Medical Journal*, 1, pp. 84–6.

Department of Health and Social Security, 1976, *Priorities for Health and Personnel Social Services in England* (London, HMSO).

Fox, J. S., 1976, 'Home v. Hospital Delivery', *Journal of Maternal and Child Health*, 1, pp. 10–16.

Gervis, J. H. and Sutherland, R. A., 1976, Letter to the *British Medical Journal*, 1, p. 342.

Goldthorpe, W. O. and Richman, J., 1974, 'Maternal Attitudes to Unintended Home Confinements: A Case Study of the Effects of a Hospital Strike upon Domiciliary Confinements', *Practitioner*, 212, pp. 845–53.

Hansard, 1987, House of Commons, *Parliamentary Debates*, 121, col. 919W.

——1988, House of Commons, *Parliamentary Debates*, 125, col. 850W.

Heady, J. A. and Morris, J. N., 1956, 'Social and Biological Factors in Infant Mortality, vi. Mothers who Have their Babies in Hospitals and Nursing Homes', *British Journal of Preventive and Social Medicine*, 10, pp. 97–106.

——Daly, C., and Morris, J. N., 1955, 'Social and Biological Factors in Infant Mortality, ii. Variations of Mortality with Mother's Age and Parity', the *Lancet*, 2, pp. 395–7.

Health Visitors' Association and Royal College of Midwives, 1983, *Joint Statement on the Post-Natal Period* (London, HVA and RCM).

Hudson, C. K., 1976, Letter to the *British Medical Journal*, 1, pp. 216–17.

James, R., 1977, Letter to *New Society*, 39, p. 248.

Jordan, P., 1974, 'Bitter Row over Induced Birth', the *Guardian*, 9 Dec. 1974.

Kitzinger, S. and Davis, J. A., 1978, *The Place of Birth* (Oxford, Oxford University Press).

The *Lancet*, 1974, editorial, 'A Time to be Born', 2, pp. 1183–4.

——1975, editorial, 'The Cold Facts of Childbirth', 2, p. 963.

Leiberman, P. J., 1977, Letter to *New Society*, 39, p. 249.

Macdonald, R. R., 1987, 'In Defence of the Obstetrician', *British Journal of Obstetrics and Gynaecology*, 94, pp. 833–5.

Macdonald Davies, I., 1980, 'Perinatal and Infant Death Rates: Social and Biological Factors', *Population Trends*, 19, pp. 19–21 (HMSO).

Macfarlane, A., 1981, 'Birth Death and Handicap: Saving Money, Spending Lives', *Science for People*, 48, pp. 9–13.

Macintyre, S., 1977, 'The Management of Childbirth: A Review of Sociological and Research Issues', *Social Science and Medicine*, 2, pp. 477–84.

Maternity Services Advisory Committee, 1984, *Maternity Care in Action, ii. Care during Childbirth (Intrapartum Care): A Guide to Good Practice and a Plan for Action* (London, HMSO).

Ministry of Health, 1959, *Report of the Maternity Services Committee* (Cranbrook Committee) (London, HMSO).

Oakley, A., 1975, 'The Trap of Medicalised Motherhood', *New Society*, 34, pp. 639–41.

—— 1987, 'Home Birth: A Class Privilege', *New Society*, 82/1297, p. 7.

Reid, M., 1976, Letter to the *British Medical Journal*, 1, pp. 395–6.

Richards, I. D. G., Donald, E. M., and Hamilton, F. M. W., 1970, 'Use of Maternity Care in Glasgow', in G. McLachlan and R. Shegog (eds.), *In the Beginning* (London, Oxford University Press).

Robinson, J., 1974, 'Active Management of Childbirth "Reduces Hazards and Anxiety"', *The Times*, 12 Aug. 1974, p. 6.

Royal College of Obstetricians and Gynaecologists, 1944, *Report on a National Maternity Service* (London, RCOG).

—— 1982, *Report of the RCOG Working Party on Antenatal and Intrapartum Care* (London, RCOG).

—— 1983, *Report of the Manpower Advisory Sub-Committee of the Royal College of Obstetricians and Gynaecologists* (London, RCOG).

—— and Royal College of General Practitioners, 1981, *Report on Training for Obstetrics and Gynaecology for General Practitioners by a Joint Working Party of the RCOG and RCGP* (London, RCOG and RCGP).

Royal College of Midwives, 1987, *Towards a Healthy Nation* (London, RCM).

Scruggs, M., 1978, 'Labour Pains: How the Association of Radical Midwives was Born', Association of Radical Midwives *Newsletter*, 6 June 1978.

Smith, A., 1970, 'Progress in the 1960s and Problems for the 1970s', in G. McLachlan and R. Shegog (eds.), *In the Beginning* (London, Oxford University Press).

Social Services Committee, *Perinatal and Neonatal Mortality* (Second report, 1979–80; London, HMSO).

Standing Maternity and Midwifery Advisory Committee, 1970, *Domiciliary Midwifery and Maternity Bed Needs* (Peel Committee) (London, HMSO).

Study Group on Home Confinements, 1976, Letter to the *British Medical Journal*, 1, p. 279.

Tew, M., 1977, 'Where to be Born?', *New Society*, 39, pp. 120–1.

—— 1981, 'Effects of Scientific Obstetrics on Perinatal Mortality', *Health and Social Services Journal*, 91, pp. 444–6.

—— 1985, 'Place of Birth and Perinatal Mortality', *Journal of the Royal College of General Practitioners*, 35, pp. 390–4.

——1987, 'Is Home Birth Less Safe', Paper presented at the First International Conference on Home Birth, 24–5 Oct. 1987, London.

The Times, 20 Jan. 1977, p. 3.

Whitehead, F. E. and Ford, G. R., 1977, Letter to *New Society*, 39, pp. 748–9.

Williams, S., 1977, Letter to *New Society*, 39, p. 412.

Zander, L., 1976, 'Home v. Hospital Delivery', *Journal of Maternal and Child Health* 1, pp. 14–20.

—— 1984, 'The Significance of the Home Delivery Issue', in Zander, L. and Chamberlain, G. (eds.), *Pregnancy Care for the 1980s* (London, The Royal Society of Medicine and The Macmillan Press).

13

Finding out about the Views and Experiences of Maternity-Service Users

Ann Jacoby and Ann Cartwright

THE changes in maternity care which have taken place since the 1950s (see Robinson, Chapter 4, and Schwarz, Chapter 3), and the resulting medicalization of childbirth, have been the focus of considerable public debate, in particular over such issues as the loss of the option of delivery at home and the frequency of obstetric interventions during labour and child-birth. The proliferation of pressure groups in this area (see Durward and Evans, Chapter 14) is a clear indication of the need to monitor these changes. One way of doing so is by surveys of maternity-services users.

In two important ways, finding out about the views and experiences of women using the maternity services is straight-forward and relatively easy. Firstly, women who are pregnant, and those who have recently had a baby, are, for the most part, eager to describe their experiences and to share their views on the way they were treated: response rates to such studies are generally good. Secondly, there is an excellent sampling frame, based on birth registration, for retrospective studies. However, the survey approach does have drawbacks; and it is these limitations and methods, together with a discussion of the scope of such surveys and the ways in which they could be made more effective, that are the subject of this chapter.

Background

In their review of consumer feedback for the National Health Service (NHS), Jones, Leneman, and MacLean (1987: 9) write that: 'During the past ten years the consumer movement, not only within the NHS, but in the world at large, has been accelerating to an unprecedented extent.' In maternity care, rapid technological developments and changes in patterns of care have provided the stimulus for consumer surveys. In a later chapter of this book (Chapter 14), Durward and Evans point out that both the major user groups in this area, the National Childbirth Trust and the Association for Improvements in Maternity Services, 'grew up around particular concerns about the ways in which NHS maternity care was developing, and its treatment of pregnant women and mothers'.

The report of the Maternity Services Advisory Committee (1982) and the Griffiths Report (1983) on management in the NHS both acknowledge the need to take consumers' views into account. Griffiths writes that it should be central to the approach of management to 'ascertain how well the service is being delivered at local level by obtaining the experience and perceptions of patients and the community . . .'. In our view, regular systematic surveys of a random sample of women who have recently had a baby or a stillbirth would be a useful and practical way of auditing many aspects of the maternity services at both local and national level. Ascertaining the views of the women involved is also an important, although at one time neglected, aspect of randomized control trials of obstetric procedures.

Surveys of maternity services have been undertaken by academic researchers, the media, health authorities, and Community Health Councils. Their aims, coverage, and methods have varied widely and are discussed later in this chapter. First, however, we consider the limitations and difficulties of surveys of this kind.

Limits of the Survey Approach

Women who have had babies are a potential source of a great deal of information about the processes and procedures involved. Studies and comparisons have shown that for the most part they report their experiences accurately (Cartwright and Smith 1979; Joffe and Grisso 1985; and Martin 1987). The main limitations are that they may not be aware of some of the procedures carried out (e.g. alpha fetoprotein tests); there are likely to be some problems of interpretation and definition (e.g. over the point at which they went into labour, and over acceleration or induction); and there will be some difficulties over recall (e.g. of the number and stages of ante-natal visits). There may be some under-reporting of such incidents as terminations of pregnancy, probably because women may want to forget or conceal these. Despite these difficulties, for many of the events that are recorded in hospital records we know that women are a *reliable* source of information, and for other events not systematically recorded in the records (e.g. length of time breast-feeding (see Martin and Monk 1982)), they are the *only possible* source.

Surveys of women who have had, or who are in the process of having, babies are also the way to find out about attitudes to, and satisfaction with, maternity services. Here too there are problems in collecting and interpreting the data. Satisfaction is difficult to define and to measure in a meaningful way, and there are complications over the timing of data collection. Stimson and Webb (1975) suggest that satisfaction with care is related to patients' perception of its outcome and the extent to which it meets their expectations. In the context of childbirth, women expect to produce a healthy baby, and their expressions of satisfaction may be coloured by whether or not this is the case. Thus Riley (1977) argues that many women 'may not mind greatly about what has happened to them, especially in their relief and pleasure at having produced an intact child . . . they may be so delighted to have produced a healthy child that other considerations pale into insignificance'.

A repeated finding from studies of users of services is that general questions tend to elicit high. levels of expressed satisfaction with care. For example, Jacoby (1987) found that the great majority of women said that they were satisfied with the way their labours were managed, whether or not their reported preferences over particular procedures were met. In a survey of women's experiences of ante-natal care by South-East Hampshire Community Health Council (1985), the majority of women said that they were either satisfied (42 per cent) or very satisfied (54 per cent), when asked to comment on their overall opinion of the care. However, almost three-quarters of the sample made detailed and explicit suggestions about the ways in which it could be improved. Locker and Dunt (1978) conclude from evidence of this kind that 'global evaluations are inadequate measures of consumer opinion since the majority of studies indicate that the level of satisfaction expressed varies with different aspects of medical care. Global evaluations which ask respondents how satisfied they are in general tend to mask these differentials . . .'. A number of questions related to specific aspects of care may be a better way of assessing satisfaction.

Another problem in carrying out maternity-care studies is the timing of data collection. Women approached post-natally may find it difficult to recall details of their ante-natal care, and their reports may be coloured by subsequent events. There are also problems about collecting information about women's views of their ante-natal care during their pregnancy; in addition to the difficulty of obtaining a representative sample, it is possible that women's thoughts may be dominated by immediate events to such an extent that they cannot put their opinions into perspective.

There is evidence that women's perceptions of their labour and delivery change over time, perhaps as they attempt to rationalize their childbirth experiences (Shaw 1985). One study to address this problem was carried out by Bennett (1985). Seventy-two women who had been interviewed three weeks post-partum were reinterviewed two years after the birth, and a comparison made of their ratings of the procedures they had undergone. There was a significant decrease after two years in the women's satisfaction-ratings of their medical and preparation procedures, and the author concluded that time of interview is 'an important factor when women's ratings are to be included in evaluations of obstetric procedures'.

Another feature of the way in which data collection may affect reported levels of satisfaction is the extent to which the researcher is seen as being identified with the service. Women who are approached in, for example, the ante-natal clinic or the post-natal hospital ward may be reluctant to express their views and dissatisfactions. In such situations, Fitzpatrick (1984) suggests, there may be 'quite strong pressures on patients to express socially acceptable views when talking about health care'. He concludes that: 'it may be that patients make less use of socially desirable answers if the researcher is less identified with the health care service that is being discussed'.

Studies of maternity-service users have focused not only on their experiences and satisfaction with care, but also on their preferences: 'Preferences are more difficult to study than satisfactions because they are not usually based on experiences of the possible alternatives.' (Cartwright 1983: 106.) A study carried out by the Institute for Social Studies in Medical Care reported that 76 per cent of the few women who had experienced both a home and a hospital birth preferred the former (Cartwright 1979). But there was evidence that women tend to say that they 'prefer' whatever type of care they had, and so they cannot realistically be asked to make choices about, or state preferences for, procedures of which they have no experience. Ninety-one per cent of the women on that study who had their last baby at home said that they would prefer to have their next baby at home as well, compared with 15 per cent of those who had their baby in hospital (O'Brien 1978). There was a similar pattern for those women who did or did not have epidural anaesthesia, although not for women whose labour had been induced. The study concluded that: 'Generally, women are conservative in that they tend to opt for things they have experienced.' (Cartwright 1979: 114.) These findings about care during labour and delivery are parallelled in Porter and Macintyre's research (1984) into women's satisfaction with ante-natal care. They, too, found that if women expressed a preference about care, it tended to be for the things they had experienced.

It has been suggested that women may be dissatisfied with their care but too deferential to say so. This may well be the result of their dependence upon medical expertise. Martin (1986) points out that: 'The nature of many human services also places consumers in a relatively weak position . . . Professional staff delivering services generally possess specialised knowledge which clients do not have, and clients are highly dependent upon the judgements and actions of professional staff . . .'. Thus women may accept procedures in maternity care because they are assured by clinical staff that such procedures are medically desirable for them or their baby; when questioned, they may then even say that they 'preferred' to have them.

The points we have discussed here suggest that data from surveys need to be interpreted with care, and that it can be made more useful by focusing questions on specific issues rather than on general satisfactions.

Sampling

It is an easy task to identify the users of maternity services, because birth registrations, compulsory within forty-two days of the birth, are an excellent sampling-frame for either national or local studies. The registration of stillbirths identifies another important group of users, though here there may be some problems over the borderline with late spontaneous abortions, as, formally, a fetus must have reached twenty-eight weeks of gestation to be registered. Obviously, both of these registers only identify users retrospectively. The Office of Population Censuses and Surveys (OPCS) can do this within two to three months of registration, and the average interval between birth and registration is just under two weeks, with 98 per cent being registered within six weeks (Cartwright 1986*b*). Further information on the non-confidential part of the registration form makes it possible to identify such groups as home births, births in a particular hospital, those for which no father was identified, and births to mothers born in different countries or in different parts of England. Both live and stillbirths are reported to the District Medical Officer within thirty-six hours, and these notifications are one way of identifying mothers at an earlier stage. But access to these would be controlled by the District Medical Officer, and his or her willingness to grant such access to researchers is likely to vary.

If contact with users of ante-natal services is wanted before the baby is born—for instance, to look at women's reactions to particular procedures—then it is necessary to identify the women through the relevant service. Farrant (1980, 1983, 1985) used this approach in her study of pre-natal screening. For prospective studies, following women through the whole process of becoming a mother, as Oakley (1979) did, women have to be identified through the ante-natal services. This approach is being used by the OPCS in their work to develop a standardized survey-methodology for use by district health authorities (Mason, 1989). Hospital records of women booked for delivery in particular weeks are being used as a sampling-frame. For such an approach, obtaining the agreement of the doctors and the ethics committees, and working out an acceptable strategy, takes time; and pregnant women who, for whatever reason, do not make use of ante-natal services cannot be included.

Interview versus Postal Studies, and Response Rates

Postal surveys generally elicit lower response rates than interviews, but they are much cheaper, and since interview studies are invariably clustered to keep down costs, a greater geographical spread can be achieved using this approach. Another advantage is that there is no 'interviewer' effect, and no need to ensure that interviewers are adequately trained and follow instructions correctly. On the other hand, postal studies are generally restricted to those subjects that can be covered in structured questionnaires; in-depth, qualitative data need interviews.

With two reminders, it is possible to obtain response rates to national postal studies of around 80 per cent (Cartwright 1986a). This compares with response rates of 88 and 91 per cent to interview studies based on similar samples (Cartwright 1976 and 1979). Interviews cost between twenty and fifty times as much as postal surveys (the expenses for interviews increase with the spread of the sample) (Cartwright 1986b), but the costs of analysis, sampling, and administration can be roughly the same for both approaches if most of the answers on the postal questionnaire are precoded—i.e. mothers are asked to ring the number next to the answer that applies to them, rather than tick boxes—a procedure which does not appear to affect response rates (Cartwright 1986*a*).

In one of a series of studies carried out by the Institute for Social Studies in Medical Care to assess the feasibility of monitoring maternity services by sending postal questionnaires to mothers, a comparison was made of the response rates and the nature of replies to interviews and postal questionnaires (Cartwright 1988). A sample of 800 births was allocated at random to either an interview or a postal approach. The topics covered a range of factual experiences and attitudes to treatment during pregnancy, labour, delivery, and the post-partum period. The response rate for the interviews was substantially higher: 92 per cent, as opposed to 75 per cent for the postal study. However, comparison of the information revealed no major differences in the nature of responses.

In another study in the series, in which a nationally representative sample of 3,200 women was approached using a postal questionnaire, a response rate of 79 per cent was achieved after two reminders. A number of biases were identified among those who replied (Cartwright 1986*b*). Response rates from women born in Asia and Africa were substantially lower (42 and 64 per cent respectively) than those from women born in the UK (83 per cent). (Language problems probably contributed to this difference.) The 6 per cent of births for which no father was entered on the birth registration forms also had a significantly lower response: 69 per cent, compared with 81 per cent for others. The response rate was higher for the middle class than for the working class (defined according to the occupation of the baby's father): 86 per cent compared with 76 per cent. There were also wide variations between the ten study areas that were used in this project which could only be partly explained by differences in the mother's country of birth and the social class distribution.

A third study in the series compared responders and non-responders to a postal questionnaire; information from hospital records was available for both groups (Cartwright 1986*b*). This again showed response biases related to ethnic origin. In addition, there were differences associated with complications for the baby: only 52 per cent of those mothers whose babies weighed less than 2,500 g. at birth responded, and 50 per cent of those whose baby was not discharged with them. Those who attended for ante-natal care relatively late were less likely to respond than those attending earlier in their pregnancy. Response rates declined from 82 per cent for those first attending when they were less than twelve weeks pregnant, to 64 per cent for those who first attended at twenty or more weeks. These biases do not, in our opinion, invalidate the use of a postal approach, but they do enable its limitations to be recognized and taken into account when making generalizations from the results of such studies.

To study an ethnic minority whose understanding of English is poor needs a different approach. Interviews using an interpreter tend to be unsatisfactory, and it will usually be necessary to recruit and train interviewers who are fluent in the appropriate languages.

Response to postal questionnaires were unaffected by differences in approach, such as the use of a personalized letter or a different form of address (Cartwright 1986*a*). More importantly, when a long questionnaire with twenty-four A5 pages and around 110 questions was compared with a short one of eight pages and 35 questions, no association was found between response rates and length. This means that a wide range of topics can be covered.

Range and Nature of Recent Studies

Recent studies have ranged from national ones, both random and non-random, to local ones, the impetus for which has generally been a planned change in the provision of local services or anxiety about their adequacy and efficiency. Some studies have focused on specific aspects of maternity care. Several small-scale, in-depth studies have tried to assess what pregnancy and the processes of childbirth mean to women. Women's views and experiences of procedures have recently become a feature of randomized controlled trials.

Local Studies

Health authorities and Community Health Councils (CHCs, set up in 1974 to represent consumers in the Health Service) have undertaken a number of surveys in this area, often generated by a specific local issue about provision of care. A survey in Newcastle (Clayton 1979) interviewed mothers in their homes about one month after delivery, and achieved a response rate of 86 per cent. Another survey, carried out by Kidderminster CHC (1978), interviewed 85 per cent of a sample of women who gave birth within a specified period of time. This survey also attempted to obtain the views of professionals: fifty-five GPs and sixty-three midwives were sent a postal questionnaire; the response rates for the two groups were 65 and 75 per cent respectively. Over 80 per cent of women approached for interview in ante-natal clinics responded to a survey by Central Nottingham CHC (1986). Postal surveys have generally achieved lower response rates of around 75 per cent (see e.g. South-East Hampshire CHC 1985; Hampstead Health Authority 1987). Bexley CHC (1979) achieved a response rate of only 27 per cent to a postal questionnaire—it is not clear from the report whether reminders were sent out to the women canvassed.

Poor response rates are not the only potential source of difficulty for these surveys. West Birmingham CHC (1984) had problems in trying to obtain a random sample of women attending an ante-natal clinic in the district; to protect confidentiality, the hospital management insisted that hospital staff rather than CHC personnel should implement the sampling scheme. The authors of the report admit that several errors occurred as a result of this, and point out that this was partly because hospital staff had to carry out the sampling procedures in addition to their normal clinical and adminis-trative duties. However, they conclude that these errors do not invalidate the sample or the study findings.

In a review of Community Health Council studies of ante-natal care, Garcia (1981) points out that: 'These surveys are very varied in the method of recruiting interviewers, the subjects covered and the proportion of the appropriate population surveyed. The reports themselves are also variable in their style and completeness.' Nevertheless, such local studies have provided valuable insights into specific local needs or into local variations in care, for example, between different hospitals and clinics. Furthermore, a number of common themes have emerged from these studies; in particular, dissatisfaction with waiting times at clinics, lack of continuity of care, and problems over communication, information, and explanation (ACHCEW 1987).

In-Depth Studies

There have been a number of in-depth prospective studies of pregnancy and childbirth (see Graham and McKee 1980; Macintyre 1981). Although focusing primarily on the meaning of pregnancy to the women experiencing it, and the processes involved in assuming the role of motherhood, such studies have highlighted some important issues about maternity care. Oakley (1979, 1980) interviewed sixty-six first-time mothers, twice ante-natally and twice post-natally, about social and medical aspects of the transition to motherhood. The women were selected from one hospital in London, they were all aged between 19 and 32 at the time of delivery, and they were all born in Britain, Ireland, or North America. Oakley acknowledges that the sample was biased towards middle-class women. (Other studies have shown different attitudes and expectations about childbirth among working-class women (Nelson 1983; McIntosh 1987). From the interview material, Oakley identified a number of responses to the birth process which she related both to social variables in the women's lives and to the medical-technological aspects of their birth experiences. She then uses this to form the basis of her recommendations for future developments in childbirth, and to suggest hypotheses which could be applied to larger, more representative populations.

Studies of Specific Aspects of Care

Some studies of women's experiences have focused upon specific aspects of pregnancy and childbirth. For example, Kitzinger (1975) compared reports of 614 induced labours and 224 non-induced ones among women attending National

Childbirth Trust (NCT) ante-natal classes. There was a bias in the sample for this study, since attendance at NCT classes is heavily weighted towards middle-class women. However, a national study of a random sample of recent mothers (Cartwright 1979) produced similar results. Kitzinger (1987) has also explored women's views about epidural anaesthesia.

Another study to focus on one particular aspect of care was Farrant's analysis of women's experiences of pre-natal screening (Farrant, 1980, 1983, 1985). Sixty-two women in one hospital who had a raised maternal serum AFP level, and seventy-three who had undergone amniocentesis in early pregnancy because of their age or their obstetric or family history, were interviewed about their experiences, attitudes, and needs. Oakley and Richards (see Chapter 10) have drawn attention to the paucity of research into mothers' views on specific obstetric procedures—Caesarean sections in particular. It is encouraging to note the emphasis that is now being placed on the importance of taking their attitudes into account in randomized controlled trials.

Randomized Controlled Trials

If the risks and benefits of new procedures or treatments are to be properly assessed, randomized controlled trials should take account not only of their desired outcome and physical side-effects, but also of women's preferences and the possible anxieties created. One study in which this is being done is the Multicentre Fetal Movements Trial (Grant *et al.*, 1989) at the National Perinatal Epidemiology Unit. The aim of this trial is to evaluate a policy of fetal-movement counting, backed by appropriate clinical action. Over 60,000 women have been randomized to take part, either as counters or as controls. The main outcome-measure is ante-partum stillbirths, but the women's feelings of anxiety, reassurance, confidence, and satisfaction with care have also been assessed by means of a postal questionnaire sent to them about two weeks after delivery.

Another randomized control trial in progress has been designed to test the hypothesis that social-support intervention by midwives to women at above-average risk of a low birthweight delivery is able to increase birth weight (Social Support and Pregnancy Outcome Project, *Newsletter*, 2 (Jan. 1987)). The main outcomes to be analysed are birth weight, maternal and infant morbidity, maternal psychological condition, and maternal satisfaction with care. In addition to information taken from the women's hospital case-notes, data is also being collected by means of a postal questionnaire sent to the mothers at around six weeks after the birth. Other recent trials to take account of the views of the participants include a comparison of continuous intrapartum fetal heart-rate monitoring with intermittent auscultation (Garcia *et al.* 1985*a*); an assessment of a policy of women holding their own obstetric records (Elbourne *et al.* 1987); and a study of instrumental delivery using vacuum extraction and forceps (Garcia *et al.* 1985*b*). (The authors of this last study acknowledge that the women selected for interview did not represent a random sample of those taking part in the trial, but depended on the number of women available for interview at any time and the commitments of the interviewer.)

The involvement of childbirth education organizations in randomized controlled trials has been a recent development in Britain (Beech 1986; *New Generation* Dec. 1987). For example, the Medical Research Council has recently asked AIMS (Association for Improvements in the Maternity Services) to formulate a follow-up questionnaire for women taking part in a multicentre trial of amniocentesis and chorionic villi sampling (Beech, personal communication).

National studies

The only national random studies that we know of in this subject-area are the two carried out at the Institute for Social Studies in Medical Care, discussed earlier in this chapter. Two national non-random studies of maternity services are also worth mentioning. *The British Way of Birth* (Boyd and Sellers 1982) was compiled by asking those viewers of a television programme who were at least three months pregnant to take part in a survey. Nearly 10,000 letters were received in response to the request, and nearly 6,000 women returned a questionnaire. Taking into account the number of women pregnant at the time, this could be interpreted as an approximate participation rate of 2 per cent. The authors acknowledge that the women who replied were a self-selected group, and that lower-class women and young women were underrepresented. A further bias not identified in the report was the underrepresentation of single women. Another non-random survey was carried out by *Parents* magazine—nearly 7½ thousand readers replied to its 1983 birth survey. In spite of inevitable biases due to their non-randomness, both these surveys highlighted important issues about maternity care that had also been identified by surveys based on random samples: the difficulty experienced by women who want to have more choice and control over how they give birth; dissatisfaction with information and advice; and dissatisfaction because of the lack of continuity in care.

Finding out about the views and experiences of the users of maternity services is important in alerting providers to any shortcomings in those services. Such surveys can act as an audit of the sensitivity and efficiency of the services. They can also contribute substantially to the evaluation of techniques and procedures by monitoring their effects on the women who receive them.

Surveys have been conducted in a variety of ways, on both representative and highly selected samples, and at different stages of the childbearing process. In spite of this variability, a number of common themes emerge: lack of understanding by staff; poor communication; long waits for routine and apparently superficial ante-natal care; and lack of choice in the type of care available. They also demonstrate once again the truth of the inverse care law: 'the availability of good medical care tends to vary inversely with the need for it in the population served' (Hart 1971), with the more vulnerable and disadvantaged mothers receiving poorer treatment.

It would seem to us that, for the most part, we need action to correct these inadequacies rather than more research to demonstrate them. At the same time, however, there is a case for using repeat studies on a regular national basis to monitor the effectiveness of action and to identify other changes, particularly at a time of considerable and increasing pressure on the maternity services.

References

Association of Community Health Councils in England and Wales, 1987, *Antenatal Care: Still Waiting for Action* (London, ACHCEW).

Beech, B., 1986, 'Consumer View of Randomised Trials of Chorionic Villus Sampling', the *Lancet*, 1, p. 1157.

Bennett, A., 1985, 'The Birth of a First Child: Do Women's Reports Change over Time?', *Birth*, 12, pp. 153–8.

Bexley Community Health Council, 1979, Report of a Survey of Maternity Services in Bexley Health District.

Boyd, C. and Sellers, L., 1982, *The British Way of Birth* (London, Pan Books).

Cartwright, A., 1976, *How many Children?* (London, Routledge and Kegan Paul).

—— 1979, *The Dignity of Labour?* (London, Tavistock).

—— 1983, *Health Surveys: In Practice and in Potential* (London, King Edward's Hospital Fund).

—— 1986a, 'Some Experiments with Factors that Might Affect the Response of Mothers to a Postal Questionnaire', *Statistics in Medicine*, 5, pp. 607–17.

—— 1986b, 'Who Responds to Postal Questionnaires?', *Journal of Epidemiology and Community Health*, 40, pp. 267–73.

—— 1988, 'Interviews or Postal Questionnaires? Comparisons of Data about Women's Experience with Maternity Services', *The Milbank Quarterly*, 66, pp. 172–89.

Cartwright, A. and Smith, C., 1979, 'Some Comparisons of Data from Medical Records and from Interviews with Women who had Recently Had a Live Birth or Stillbirth', *Journal of Biosocial Science*, 11, pp. 49–64.

Central Nottinghamshire Community Health Council, 1986, A Survey of Antenatal Care Services in the Central Nottinghamshire Health District.

Clayton, S., 1979, 'Maternity Care: Some Patients' Views', Report of a survey carried out under the aegis of the Newcastle CHC.

Elbourne, D. *et al.*, 1987, 'The Newbury Maternity Care Study: A Randomised Controlled Trial to Assess a Policy of Women Holding their own Obstetric Records', *British Journal of Obstetrics and Gynaecology*, 94, pp. 612–19.

Farrant, W., 1980, 'Importance of Counselling in Antenatal Screening', *Mims Magazine*, 15 June 1980.

—— 1983, 'Prenatal Screening: Overlooking Women's Needs', *Maternity Action*, 9, pp. 4–5.

—— 1985, 'Who's for Amniocentesis? The Politics of Prenatal Screening', in H. Homans (ed.), *The Sexual Politics of Reproduction* (Aldershot, Gower Press).

Fitzpatrick, R., 1984, 'Satisfaction with Health Care', in R. Fitzpatrick *et al.* (eds.), *The Experience of Illness* (London, Tavistock).

Garcia, J., 1981, 'Findings on Antenatal Care from Community Health Council Studies' (National Perinatal Epidemiology Unit, Oxford).

—— Corry, M., MacDonald, D., Elbourne, D., and Grant, A., 1985*a*, 'Mothers' Views of Continuous Electronic Fetal Heart Monitoring and Intermittent Auscultation in a Randomised Controlled Trial', *Birth*, 12, pp. 79–85.

—— Anderson, J., Vacca, A., Elbourne, D., Grant, A., and Chalmers, I., 1985*b*, 'Views of Women and their Medical and Midwifery Attendants about Instrumental Delivery Using Vacuum Extraction and Forceps', *Journal of Psychosomatic Obstetrics and Gynaecology*, 4, pp. 1–9.

Graham, H. and McKee, L., 1980, *The First Months of Motherhood* (Health Education Council Monograph 3; London, The Health Education Council).

Grant, A., Elbourne, D., Valentin, L., and Alexander, S., 1989. 'The Effect of a Policy of Routine Formal Fetal Movement Counting on the Risk of Antepartum Late Death among Normally Formed Singleton Fetuses: A Multicentre Randomised Controlled Trial', the *Lancet*, 2, pp. 345–9.

Griffiths, Sir Roy, 1983, *NHS Management Inquiry Report* (London, DHSS).

Hampstead Health Authority, 1987, 'A Report of Women's Satisfaction with the Maternity Services in the Hampstead Health District'.

Hart, J. Tudor, 1971, 'The Inverse Care Law', the *Lancet*, 1, pp. 405–12.

Jacoby, A., 1987, 'Women's Preferences for and Satisfaction with Current Procedures in Childbirth', *Midwifery*, 3, pp. 117–24.

Joffe, M. and Grisso, J. A., 1985, 'Comparison of Antenatal Hospital Records with Retrospective Interviewing', *Journal of Biosocial Science*, 17, pp. 113–19.

Jones, L., Leneman, L., and Maclean, U., 1987, *Consumer Feedback for the NHS: A literature review* (London, King Edward's Hospital Fund).

Kidderminster Community Health Council, 1978, *Is the Baby All Right?* (A Survey of Maternity Care Undertaken in Kidderminster Health District in Conjunction with the Social Services Unit, University of Birmingham).

Kitzinger, S., 1975, 'Some Mothers' Experiences of Induced Labour'. Submission to the DHSS from the National Childbirth Trust.

—— 1987, *Some Women's Experiences of Epidurals: A Descriptive Study* (London, National Childbirth Trust).

Locker, D. and Dunt, D., 1978, 'Theoretical and Methodological Issues in Sociological Studies of Consumer Satisfaction with Medical Care', *Social Science and Medicine*, 12, pp. 283–92.

McIntosh, J., 1987, 'Some Working Class Perspectives on Childbirth: A Study of 80 Primigravidae' (Department of Child Health and Obstetrics, University of Glasgow).

Macintyre, S., 1981, *Expectations and Experiences of First Pregnancy* (Occasional Paper 5, University of Aberdeen).

Martin, C., 1987, 'Monitoring Maternity Services by Postal Questionnaire: Congruity between Mothers' Reports and their Obstetric Records', *Statistics in Medicine*, 6, pp. 613–27.

Martin, E. M., 1986, 'Consumer Evaluation of Human Services', *Social Policy and Administration*, 20/3, pp. 185–99.

Martin, J. and Monk, J., 1982, *Infant Feeding 1980* (London, HMSO).

Mason, V., 1989, *Women's Experience of Maternity Care—A Survey Manual* (London, HMSO).

Maternity Services Advisory Committee, 1982, *Maternity Care in Action*, i. *Antenatal Care* (London, HMSO).

Nelson, M. K., 1983, 'Working-Class Women, Middle-Class Women and Models of Childbirth', *Social Problems*, 30, pp. 284–97.

New Generation, 6/4, Dec. 1987 (National Childbirth Trust).

Oakley, A., 1979, *Becoming a Mother* (Oxford, Martin Robertson).

—— 1980, *Women Confined: Towards a Sociology of Childbirth* (Oxford, Martin Robertson).

O'Brien, M., 1978, 'Home and Hospital: A Comparison of the Experiences of Mothers Having Home and Hospital Confinements', *Journal of the Royal College of General Practitioners*, 28, pp. 460–6.

Parents Magazine, 'Birth in Britain', 92, Nov. 1983.

Porter, M. and Macintyre, S., 1984, 'What Is, Must be Best: A Research Note on Conservative or Deferential Responses to Antenatal Care Provision', *Social Science and Medicine*, 19, pp. 1197–200.

Riley, E. M. D., 1977, 'What do Women Want? The Question of Choice in the Conduct of Labour', in T. Chard and M. Richards (eds.), *Benefits and Hazards of the New Obstetrics* (London, Spastics International Medical Publications).

Shaw, I., 1985, 'Reactions to Transfer out of a Hospital Birth Centre: A Pilot Study', *Birth*, 12, pp. 147–50.

Social Services Research and Intelligence Unit, Portsmouth Polytechnic, 1985, *Women's Experience of Antenatal Care* (A Report of Research Conducted in Collaboration with Portsmouth and South-East Hampshire CHC; SSRIU Occasional Paper 12).

Stimson, G. and Webb, B., 1975, *On Going to See the Doctor* (London, Routledge and Kegan Paul).

West Birmingham Community Health Council, 1984, 'Women Waiting: Antenatal Services in West Birmingham'.

14

Pressure Groups and Maternity Care

Lyn Durward and Ruth Evans

GROUPS working for better maternity care cover everything from pre-conception care to services for the sick new-born. Not all of these would define themselves as pressure groups. Self-help groups, in particular, have burgeoned in the last ten years, and many local and national groups, such as those which make up the Miscarriage Association and the Caesarean Support Network, exist primarily to provide mutual support and information to individual parents. Yet virtually all such groups also see it as part of their purpose to use public advocacy to improve practice amongst those who fund, plan, and organize services for their interest group. For the purposes of this chapter, maternity-care pressure groups are defined as all those whose aims include the promotion of improvements in services for parents-to-be, new parents, and new-born babies.

The ways in which pressure groups relate to existing maternity services, and their relationships with the wider social world, is seen most clearly from a review of their history (see Chapters 1 and 5). As Jane Lewis describes in Chapter 1, their roots lie in the early feminist movement and in the beginnings of the organization of working women. It was not until the 1950s that pressure groups developed which had maternity as their primary focus. That decade saw the establishment of both of the major consumer groups working in this area today: the National Childbirth Trust (NCT) (see Kitzinger, Chapter 5); and the Association for Improvements in Maternity Services (AIMS). These two groups grew up around particular concerns about the ways in which NHS maternity care was developing, and its treatment of pregnant women and mothers. Initially the new groups lobbied for very specific changes in service provision, but as the organizations matured, they increasingly sought to ensure that these services matched women's needs and wishes. A specific focus which was, in the next thirty years, to spawn many more campaigning groups, including the Active Birth Movement and the Society to Support Home Confinements, was the degree to which medical technology dictated mothers' and babies' experience of childbirth.

By contemporary standards, however, both the NCT and AIMS have a wide brief in maternity care. The NCT, for example, is probably best known for its ante-natal classes; but its interests are wide, encompassing breast-feeding support and support for mothers with disabilities. This flexibility has contributed to its continuing strength, enabling it to incorporate new interest groups rather than seeing them break away as separate organizations. Similarly, AIMS, which has a more public pressure-group image and which is not involved in teaching, has campaigned on new issues deriving from advances in technology, such as ultrasound screening and the adequacy of anaesthesia during Caesarean operations.

The 1970s and 1980s saw the development of many new groups, including the Foundation for the Study of Infant Deaths, the Stillbirth and Neonatal Death Society (SANDS), Baby Life Support Systems (BLISS), and the Pre-eclamptic Toxaemia Society, which all seek to represent the interests of specific groups of parents and babies. These reflect both changes in medical technology, particularly neonatal intensive care, and increasing concern about baby deaths at a time when still-birth and infant death rates were falling rapidly. They demonstrate, too, a growing belief in specialized pressure groups as a means of achieving change. A notable feature was the emergence of a number of pressure groups set up by, and for, black and ethnic-minority women using the maternity services. These are mainly local health groups, formed to enable women, especially non-English speaking women, to understand and use the maternity services, and to encourage the providers of these services to allow for the needs and wishes of women from minority communities (see Phoenix, Chapter 15). At their most effective, groups such as

Tower Hamlets Maternity Services Liaison Scheme, and City and Hackney Multi-Ethnic Women's Health Project act as powerful advocates for their interest group. The separate development of these black and ethnic-minority groups reflects the failure of the major maternity pressure groups to acknowledge their needs and to function effectively as their representatives.

The Maternity Alliance, established in 1980, took a different direction from most existing groups, having a broader remit and bringing together a wide range of interests relating to maternity. By including maternity benefits and rights, as well as health care, in its key concerns, the Maternity Alliance recalls the earliest pressure-group activity in maternity care, demonstrating the re-emergence of poverty and the needs of working mothers as major issues in a climate of growing female employment and increasing dependence on low wages and on benefits.

The Diversity of Pressure Groups

The development of pressure groups reflects scientific and social change. With technical advances in maternity care has come a pathological model of pregnancy, while the improved techniques of assisted reproduction have variously increased and reduced women's control over their own fertility. The growth of a multi-ethnic population has created differing cultural and language requirements, and the increasing number of married women employed outside the home and of people in poverty has demanded new employment legislation and income maintenance provision. In response to these changes, new pressure groups have been formed, and existing groups have modified their aims and ways of working.

The diversity of interests and service priorities represented by pressure groups is matched in range by the size, structures, operational modes, and aims of the organizations. For, whilst all pressure groups serve as forces for change, the methods by which they seek to influence services are very diverse. The single unifying factor is that they operate under the umbrella of the 'voluntary sector'.

The voluntary sector can be defined as that group of organizations and services not given specific responsibilities under statute, yet not including private services run for profit or private gain, or trade unions. It spans national, regional, and local organizations, as well as loose groupings of individuals undertaking unpaid work. It is made up of voluntary organizations (incorporated and unincorporated), charities (e.g. BLISS), self-help groups (e.g. Meet-a-Mum Association), and pressure groups (e.g. Maternity Alliance)— terms which are not mutually exclusive, but which indicate the functional priorities of individual organizations. In the history of any one organization, its priorities and structure may change to reflect changes in membership or public policies, in medical practice and knowledge, or even in funding sources.

Voluntary organizations are not, however, to be equated with *volunteer agencies* or *volunteer staff*; although voluntary organizations may encompass volunteering, they will remain voluntary organizations even if some members are paid, or if they receive money from public funds—an issue discussed in the final section of this chapter. However, they are usually *managed by volunteers* through a committee structure, and they form part of public provision, delivered through organizations directly accountable to their members and funders. In the case of charities, accountability is also regulated by the Charity Commission; similarly, companies are accountable to Company House.

The distinguishing feature of voluntary organizations, whatever their aims, size, management structure, membership, and finance, is that they function as *advocacy agencies*. Voluntary organizations exist, above all, to represent, promote, and support the needs and requirements of a particular group of users of the services. In the broadest sense of the term, advocacy can be defined as the process of demanding, supporting, or initiating change or redress. In other words, they act as pressure groups.

Pressure Groups as Advocacy Agencies

There are four key functions of advocacy: personal, professional, public, and practical; and these apply to maternity as well as other fields. The priorities of particular pressure groups will determine both the balance of these advocacy roles and the sectors served.

With *personal advocacy*, pressure groups will endeavour to provide individuals with information on the options available to them in law, and—if necessary—negotiate on their behalf, for example with a hospital or social security office. Personal advocacy encompasses face-to-face contact with clients, as well as employing other agencies and the media to get the message across.

Through its entirely volunteer branch network, AIMS deals with hundreds of enquiries each year from women requiring information about maternity care. AIMS illustates the flexibility of voluntary organizations to adapt to changing circumstances. Its formation in 1960, when home confinements were common, was largely inspired by a body of women demanding the right to hospital births; in the 1980s, with home confinements constituting less than 1 per cent of all deliveries, AIMS now focuses its campaigning thrust on *choice* in the place of birth, including the right to home confinements. It is largely owing to organizations like AIMS and the Society to Support Home Confinements that women are now aware that health authorities have a *legal obligation* to provide a midwife for a home birth.

Personal advocacy can include providing information through many different routes. The Maternity Alliance, for instance, distributes some 80,000 leaflets every year giving parents information about benefits, rights at work, and pre-pregnancy health, as well as answering thousands of individual enquiries and advising journalists and other organizations seeking information for their members.

The Spastics Society, the Association for Spina Bifida and Hydrocephalus (ASBAH), and the Royal Society for Mentally Handicapped Children and Adults (Mencap) are examples of large disability agencies whose primary role is to provide services for groups with particular needs, each incorporating the important subsidiary function of supplying information on the *preventive* aspects of maternity care. They, along with smaller charities such as the Sickle Cell Society, have sophisticated information units offering professional expertise on screening and counselling for congenital and hereditary handicapping conditions which complement the work of mainstream maternity groups.

Similarly, agencies concerned with fertility and reproductive rights, such as the Family Planning Association (an agency which provided a national network of family planning clinics until these were taken over by the NHS in the 1970s, and which now plays an important role in training and education about family planning), Brook Advisory Centres (specializing in contraception and counselling services for young people), and the Women's Health and Reproductive Rights Information Centre (a collective with a small staff team), all provide men and women with advice and information on the range and efficacy of pre-pregnancy services.

Professional advocacy involves taking up issues on behalf of individuals, and pursuing them through formal administrative complaints procedures, tribunals, and the courts. Small organizations, without legal expertise and largely dependent on volunteer support, are less well equipped to provide this form of advocacy than specialist agencies (although AIMS, which negotiates with health authorities on behalf of individual women, proves a notable exception). In addition, many other pressure groups which include aspects of maternity care within their overall aims will provide complementary advocacy expertise where it relates to their own campaign objectives. The Child Poverty Action Group (CPAG), the Legal Action Group, Action for Victims of Medical Accidents, the National Council for Civil Liberties, the Joint Council for the Welfare of Immigrants, the National Council for One-Parent Families, the Family Rights Group, and the Patients' Association all employ specialized staff-teams which represent clients involved in complaints filed variously with health authorities, the parliamentary ombudsman, the Health Service Commissioner, and Social Security and Employment tribunals.

Individual casework is just one element of a pressure

group's activity. Seeking change at a broader level is equally important, and this *public advocacy* is often achieved through campaigns at national, regional, or local level. These will range from mass campaigns such as Maternity Emergency (see below), to consumer participation in district service planning. The NCT, for example, now has extensive representation on district health authorities' (DHAs) Maternity Services Liaison Committees, which were established in most DHAs following the recommendations of a government committee (Maternity Services Advisory Committee 1984).

Maternity Emergency, launched in 1986 in defence of maternity benefits and rights, was one of the biggest campaigns in recent years. It is a useful example to examine, because it was planned as a broadly based initiative on a single issue. The campaign was run for a limited period and employed a variety of strategies. Maternity Emergency aimed to increase awareness amongst MPs, the media, and the public of the importance of maternity rights for working parents, of universal maternity benefits which recognize the common needs of parents, and of adequate additional benefits for those in the greatest need. The spur to the campaign was the threat to already inadequate provisions contained in government white papers. Maternity Emergency won the support of over 200 organizations, including the major women's organizations, the health professions, and trade unions. Supporters were mobilized to promote the campaign through hundreds of parliamentary questions, letters to MPs, articles in local papers, and through local petitions, meetings, and events organized by its regional network. The campaign culminated in a mass rally at Central Hall, Westminster in 1987, where a Charter for Working Parents' Rights was issued which could form the basis of continued lobbying.

Mass lobbying is one aspect of public advocacy. The other is campaigning for changes in services at local level. This is undertaken both by local branches affiliated to national pressure groups, such as NCT branches, AIMS groups, and birth centres, and by self-help community groups under the wing of the burgeoning movement of community health. Their aim is to develop constructive relationships with the statutory authorities in order to influence those responsible for maternity care at local level. Though the pattern of collaboration between the voluntary and statutory sectors is varied and uneven, there is a common approach in local lobbying which centres on conducting surveys of service-users, participating in planning and consultative bodies, and setting up informal working groups.

Channels have been established during the past decade which give statutory force to the representation of women's interests in the development of local maternity services. This enables voluntary bodies to influence the joint planning process alongside statutory bodies. Voluntary organizations are entitled to seek nomination by their regional health authority for one of the eight generalist seats on their district health authority. Following the Health and Social Services and Social Security Adjudication Act (1983), three voluntary representatives now sit on Joint Consultative Committees. District planning teams for maternity services may also invite representation from voluntary bodies (although this is rarely done), and the formation of district Maternity Services Liaison Committees (see above) provides for voluntary-sector representation amongst the membership. In addition, there is, of course, the Community Health Council, the major statutory forum for the consumer voice within the NHS. Here, the voluntary sector is entitled to one-third of the seats on any Council and may co-opt their representatives on to maternity services sub-committees.

The formation of local links between voluntary and statutory sectors is therefore an important adjunct to mass campaigning. Where these two forms of public advocacy at national and local level result in a common cause with clear objectives, a tension is created which will, over time, lead professionals to re-examine their attitudes and practices. This is clearly demonstrated in the *cause célèbre* of obstetrician Wendy Savage, recently suspended from practice for eighteen months for alleged negligence. The subsequent inquiry was largely centred on Savage's liberal approach to the management of labour—in particular, her belief that a woman's needs and wishes should, within the confines of safety, be accorded paramount respect in the delivery of care. With full media coverage given to the supporting evidence of eminent

professional colleagues who had been called as witnesses to
the inquiry, the debate on the liberal management of
childbirth assumed a national significance. Formerly, maternity
pressure groups worked alongside professionals in an effort to
change practice. Here, care-givers joined forces with local
women in defence of liberal maternity care. Nevertheless,
voluntary involvement at local level is largely dependent upon
the willingness of the providers to enter into dialogue with
women and their representatives. And translating this into
good practice is another thing altogether.

It is here that the fourth and final component of the
advocacy model comes into play, that of *practical and exemplary
advocacy*. Practical advocacy involves providing for needs
which are not currently met by statutory services. Exemplary
advocacy highlights imaginative, innovative approaches to
service provision through voluntary action. Both forms are
undertaken independently as alternatives and complements to
statutory health and social services. The list of initiatives is
inexhaustible, spanning services provided by national organizations and their branches, to the hundreds of local community-
health action groups covering everything from residential
establishments and day centres to self-help mother and
toddler groups or befriending schemes for black and ethnic-
minority women. The Tower Hamlets Maternity Services
Liaison Scheme, for example, was founded in 1981 to offer
information and advice before, during, and after pregnancy to
local Asian and Afro-Caribbean women. Originally set up in
response to the dissatisfaction expressed by some of these
women about the quality of care they received, the scheme
developed into a team of community health workers funded by
Tower Hamlets Inner Area Programme to support women
using the maternity services. The range and impact of
community ante-natal health initiatives are well documented
(Allen and Purkis 1983; Maternity Alliance 1985; Community
Projects Foundation and the Scottish Health Education
Group 1988).

Practical and exemplary-advocacy schemes recruit thousands
of individuals on a volunteer or salaried basis to provide some
kind of service. Between them they cover every aspect of
maternity care from family planning and pre-conception care

to ante-natal services, childbirth, and the post-natal period. Some provide clinical expertise and counselling (FPA and Sickle Cell Society), some provide classes (the NCT), others provide support networks and befriending schemes (Caesarean Support Group, Miscarriage Association), day centres and schools (Mencap, Spastics Society), whilst still others provide equipment (Toy Libraries Association, BLISS, Pre-School Playgroups Association). The voluntary sector in Britain has traditionally performed a catalytic and innovative role as a provider of services, and this is clearly demonstrable in relation to groups working alongside the maternity services. Whilst this is their distinctive contribution, it is important that voluntary organizations are not seduced into accepting unrealistically low levels of public funding to provide services on the cheap. (We shall return to this theme in our concluding section.)

The Impact of Pressure Groups

Pressure groups working in maternity care have achieved some notable successes. Although few would identify themselves overtly with the wider feminist movement, women's health groups and maternity pressure groups have made a substantial contribution to informing and empowering women in their relationships with the providers of services. By educating women about their rights, about the services available to them, and about their own bodies, pressure groups have not only produced a formidable active membership of their own, but they have influenced wider perceptions about the normal relationship which exists between pregnant women and health professionals. Among the effects of these changing perceptions can be seen the growing willingness to negotiate the pattern of a woman's labour, and the decline in such unpopular practices as routine shaving and enemas.

Direct examples of changes in policies relating to maternity care, maternity benefits, or maternity rights which can be attributed to pressure groups are harder to find. The Maternity Emergency Campaign, for example, succeeded in raising public awareness of the erosion of mothers' benefits and employment rights, and promoted the first parliamentary bill to establish a statutory right to paternal leave—introduced by Harry Cohen MP in February 1987. It failed, however, to change government policies in the short term, though the impact on opposition parties' thinking may pay dividends in the longer term.

At the level of hospital practice or health authority policy, even the newest groups might claim some success, even if it is only that health professionals have agreed to acknowledge the problems which the particular group addresses—by referring potential clients to the group for counselling, for example, or by inviting a speaker from the group to talk to local health workers. More substantial achievements of voluntary-group pressure include the acceptance of fathers' presence during labour and delivery, and the provision by health authorities of link-workers to act as advocates and interpreters for women from ethnic-minority communities. Success is rarely immediate or complete, however, and even these two improvements in service provision are not available everywhere to women who need them, or are not available in a sufficiently flexible form (for example, acceptance of a woman's chosen supporter in labour where this is not the father).

In general, maternity pressure groups have been more interested in changing practice in the clinic and on the labour ward than in influencing legislation. Of those which took a broad political view, the Women's Co-operative Guild achieved enormous gains for mothers and babies through their campaigns for ante-natal and infant care, and for maternity benefits to be paid to the mother. On the other hand, their natural successor, the Maternity Alliance, which campaigns on many similar issues, has been forced into a defensive position in its lobbying for maternity benefits, rights, and care which are adequate and acceptable to all mothers. This might simply indicate that the Guild was more effectively organized. But the Guild, along with many other organizations, was working in a climate of government which sought to extend protection and support for the relatively powerless members of society, including women and children. This view is no longer fashionable among legislators, and the present trend is to let everyone, weak and strong together, fight for themselves. It may be that the climate in which groups are working has as much to do with their success as any aspect of their organization, though changing the climate can, of course, be one of their tasks. George and Wilding (1984) argue that pressure-group activity can raise awareness of an issue and lead to the re-examination of provision. It is no accident, perhaps, that so many specific pressure groups have sprung up in the 1970s and 1980s, when governments of all political persuasions have sought swingeing cuts in expenditure. The financial squeeze on Health Service expenditure has occurred at a time when advances in medicine have raised women's expectations of the quality and range of available maternity care.

Pressure groups in maternity care operate under the same constraints and within the same limits as other pressure groups (Hall *et al.* 1975). Their successes may be due in some part to the fact that consumers and professionals have often shared the same goals. Their failures may be because most of them are composed of groups of women, whose main qualification is that they are mothers. They thus come into the category which George and Wilding (1984) described as the 'ignorant if opinionated laity'. It should come as no surprise that they are relatively ineffective at a time when highly organized, professional groups like trade unions are also failing to influence policy.

Modern governments *do* consult with a wide range of pressure groups. But this can enable them to ignore demands more easily unless the groups present a united front. The problem is not entirely overcome by the creation of formal alliances. For instance, the Maternity Alliance includes a diversity of opinions among its membership of seventy national organizations, and it may occasionally formulate a policy to government which contradicts the views of a member organization also involved in a consultation.

The well-established groups probably no longer believe, if they ever did, that one day they will achieve their aims and then disappear. Some groups, like SANDS, might argue that their self-help function is, in any case, best performed by a voluntary organization. The pressure-group roles of trying to persuade health authorities to improve their procedures and practices following a neonatal death, trying to improve health professionals' training, and trying to promote good practice are also likely to be continuing, since services must constantly adapt to changing knowledge and changing needs. Larger pressure groups with a broader focus are even less likely to go out of business because they see their aims achieved. The record of, in particular, the NCT and AIMS points to the need for flexible and adaptable organizations which can take on new issues in maternity care.

Towards the Future

Britain's maternity services are complemented by voluntary activity by many agencies using a variety of approaches. This benefits the consumer, giving more choice, more specialization, and more experimentation. However, the balance between health authorities, local authorities, voluntary organizations, and informal carers requires constant scrutiny to ensure that decisions take account of the interests of users.

Successive governments (as well as many health authorities and local authorities) have promoted a pluralistic approach in service delivery. They recognize and reward voluntary organizations for having skills in specialist areas which they lack. Voluntary organizations tap different resources (finance, people, client-contact); they stimulate volunteer involvement; they encourage different management styles, enabling excluded people to administer their own services; and they experiment and work across bureaucratic boundaries. The voluntary sector now *employs* more than 160,000 people, and receives £1.5 billion from government and another £3.5 billion from other public and private sources. The DHSS alone spends some £30 million per annum to fund the core administrative costs of voluntary agencies ranging from the Maternity Alliance to Contact-A-Family, and the Association for Spina Bifida and Hydrocephalus to BLISS.

The picture of partnership is not, however, quite as straightforward as it may appear. While a consensus exists on the good works performed by the voluntary sector, its shape, concerns, and future directions are issues around which the consensus begins to break down. For although these figures represent an undeniable financial commitment, the government seems less able to accord the voluntary sector an equality of partnership in the responsible management of services.

Voluntary organizations are subject to insecurity of funding, interminable wrangles over small amounts of money, and lengthy delays in approval of grants. Delays in processing applications—and it is not uncommon for grants to be settled half-way through the relevant financial year—have extremely damaging consequences for voluntary organizations. Not only is time wasted pursuing applications, but effective forward planning is undermined, and there are serious morale problems when staff contracts cannot be renewed or redundancy notices have to be issued.

This failure of the government departments providing funds to groups of the kind discussed in this chapter to encourage responsible management by voluntary agencies is a symptom of the underlying ambivalence of the government towards the voluntary sector. It betrays an implicit philosophy that voluntary organizations are necessary partners in service planning and provision—necessary but unequal. The necessity for *involving* voluntary organizations in the planning of services centres on the political capital to be gained from accountability. The necessity for their *participation* in service provision focuses on a straightforward cost-benefit analysis!

In other words, the apparent political consensus on the voluntary sector resolves itself into two basic and fundamentally different views: the first highlights the primacy of the volunteer, self-help, and 'Victorian values'. The second comes from a tradition of community activism, innovation, and the primacy of welfare values. With the Conservatives in office for a third successive term, the political importance of the voluntary sector is bound to increase further. Any attempts to roll back the boundaries of the state inevitably mean a higher profile for the voluntary sector. For those organizations whose primary role is to provide a *service function*, with campaigning of secondary importance, the reality of welfare pluralism, or a mixed public sector, requires close attention. There remains a very thin dividing line between initiating, developing, and promoting examples of good practice and actually providing essential bread-and-butter services.

It is incumbent upon all voluntary agencies undertaking this form of activity to ensure that careful monitoring and evaluation mechanisms are built into their operations which will safeguard and sustain their integrity as exemplary models of provision. Further, they need to guard against efforts to use them, individually and collectively, as token consumer representatives in order to legitimize practices over which they have no real control.

The growing pattern of consultation and collaboration between the providers of services and voluntary organizations over the past decade is another remarkable development which owes much to the changing political climate in Britain. Only fifteen years ago it would have been inconceivable to think of the Royal College of Obstetricians and Gynaecologists and other professional groups sharing the platform with groups like AIMS. Undoubtedly, much of the credit for this new dialogue must go to the maternity lobby, but it has to be remembered that partnerships are often forged in times of adversity. The overtures of professional associations to consumer opinion, coinciding with cut-backs in health and social services expenditure and persisting health inequalities, is partly provoked by the realization that pressure groups play a key role in defending and safeguarding existing resources. Nevertheless, such partnerships are derived from a mixture of motives, and are of mutual advantage to each party. Pressure groups benefit by becoming more respectable and hence influential, even though they may have to moderate some of their more radical aims. The professions, in turn, gradually become more radical, though this may require changes in well-established policies and practices. In some cases, separate activist groups are set up. For example, the Association of Radical Midwives has a membership of over 1,000, that is about 4 per cent of practising midwives in the United Kingdom.

In the field of maternity research, there have been similar shifts in the relationship between voluntary and professional organizations. Some voluntary groups, particularly those concerned with specific medical problems, were set up with the promotion of research as one of their major aims. Their membership often includes some health professionals, and the kind of research which they fund is frequently decided by an advisory group of professionals. Since 1971, for example, the Foundation for the Study of Infant Deaths has sponsored more than 100 research projects on the recommendation of its scientific committee. The views of professionals about the role of pressure groups in research has largely been influenced by their relationships with funding groups of the kind described. There is little evidence that researchers have consulted pressure groups about the questions that need to be asked or the best ways of addressing them. Some pressure groups have tackled the problem of who decides what research should be done by carrying out their own studies—from literature reviews to surveys of their members. The NCT's survey of post-natal infections in a self-selected sample of their members is one example (NCT 1988). Studies of this kind are usually carried out on a shoe-string budget and may suffer from methodological problems, such as the use of unrepresentative samples. Nevertheless, they have aired many important issues previously ignored by the main funding agencies and those whose research interests are partly determined by career prospects. Few pressure groups have had the self-confidence or, perhaps, the skills to fund and carry out major pieces of research themselves. But groups are constantly looking for evidence to guide their priorities for action, and this has led them to seek a more active role in deciding what research is needed, and to examine the nature of their collaboration with research professionals. Individual examples of collaboration can be found, such as the involvement of lay advisers in the work of the National Perinatal Epidemiology Unit and the National Birthday Trust Fund, but the relationship is far from equal.

   The latest development in the story is the setting-up of an informal grouping—Consumers for Ethics in Research (CERES)—to look at consumer representation on ethics committees, guidelines for ethical research, and ways of influencing the research agenda. There is a risk that as consumer organizations become more significant in size, numbers, and activities, and as they work more closely with statutory bodies, they will be asked to rubber-stamp research projects or policies rather than being consulted as equal partners. If pressure groups are to retain their unique value as consumers and producers of services, it is essential that they do not surrender their independence and their critical perspective on maternity services. They may need to guard against too great a dependence on either professional bodies or, financially, on government departments.

To conclude, whilst voluntary organizations form an independent and complementary component of the public sector, their efficacy depends on a properly funded, well-managed, and high-quality statutory sector. We have seen how pressure groups are in a very good position to press for change and improvements in maternity services. They are free, essentially, to explore lack of services, or malpractices, or to campaign for and demand new services or changes to existing services. They also often point the way to change by providing innovative schemes. Yet this will only be effective if they work with a vigorous statutory sector which can take on and develop those new ideas which have been shown to work. The art is to ensure that voluntary organizations are established as full partners in service development, but without the responsibility of work which properly belongs to the statutory services. Voluntary organizations can never be more than an adjunct, albeit an important one, to statutory maternity services.

References

Allen, R. and Purkis, A., 1983, *Health in the Round: Voluntary Action and Antenatal Services* (London, Bedford Square Press).

Community Projects Foundation and Scottish Health Education Group, 1988, *Action for Health* (London, Community Projects Foundation, and Edinburgh, Scottish Health Education Group).

George, V. and Wilding, P., 1984, *The Impact of Social Policy* (London, Routledge and Kegan Paul).

Hall, P., Land, H., Parker, R., and Webb, A., 1975, *Change, Choice and Conflict in Social Policy* (London, Heinemann).

Maternity Alliance, 1985, *Multi-Racial Initiatives in Maternity Care* (London, Maternity Alliance).

Maternity Services Advisory Committee, 1984, *Maternity Care in Action*, ii. *Care during Childbirth* (London, HMSO).

National Childbirth Trust, 1988, *Postnatal Infection* (London, National Childbirth Trust).

15

Black Women and the Maternity Services

Ann Phoenix

WOMEN'S experiences of maternity care are not uniform, but are differentiated by class (Reid 1983) and race. Working-class women and black women (more of whom are working class than middle class) are likely to receive less favourable treatment than middle-class women or white women (Cartwright 1979; Larbie 1985). This less favourable treatment is partly because the maternity services (as social institutions) reflect the racial discrimination (and class privilege) that is institutionalized in British society.

Since most obstetricians and midwives are white (Pearson 1985a), it is not surprising that some of them have racially discriminatory attitudes which become apparent in their interactions with pregnant and newly delivered black women. This is not the whole story, however. Racial discrimination in the maternity services is not simply a matter of a few individual practitioners engaging in discriminatory behaviour. Discrimination is structured into the practices of the maternity services.

This chapter is concerned with the relationship between black women and the maternity services. 'Black' is used here to refer to people of Asian and of African (including Afro-Caribbean) origin. Using the term 'black' to refer to this diverse range of people indicates that black women's experiences of the maternity services are mediated by racial discrimination. This does not deny the importance of the varied cultural practices that women have. Rather, it emphasizes the common experiences of the maternity services that black women share as a result of racial discrimination.

The author would like to thank Ronny Flynn, Marie Claude-Foster, Ann Oakley, and Barbara Tizard for their helpful comments.

The chapter will start by considering the ways in which racial discrimination is institutionalized in the maternity services. It will then discuss the particular problems that black women face within the maternity services, and will conclude by looking at the attempts that have been made to improve the services provided to black women.

The Linking of Reproduction and Racism

The maternity services are permeated with ideologies about which women make the most suitable mothers. This is most apparent when the prescriptions associated with these ideologies are violated. For example, Macintyre (1976) found that doctors were less willing to agree to abortions for married women than for single women, and felt that single women would automatically be displeased about being pregnant. Marital status is of crucial importance in reproductive ideologies. The social construction of married women is such that they *should* want to have children, while single women should not (Busfield 1974; Antonis 1981). Age is also important in reproductive ideologies. Mothers should be old enough for it to be clear that they are adults (Murcott 1980). 'Teenage mothers' are thus socially constructed as undesirable.

In western societies, childbearing and child-rearing are expected to be an individualistic and private enterprise. Reproduction is treated as if it were solely the product of personal desires. Yet in reality many societies are concerned to influence the quantity and quality of children produced. Children are therefore social products as well as individual ones: 'The eugenic loop of argument that traces one generation's problems simultaneously backwards and forwards via the state of the pregnant mother and the quality of antenatal care she receives, is a telling example of a prime concern for national health. A desire for a nation to be fit and healthy focusses and refocusses on the quality of its offspring.' (Murcott 1980: 18.) The desire to exercise control over fertility is most apparent during those periods when women's social position is changing. For example, there has been a steady increase in the proportions of children born to single (rather than married) women in Britain. Government statements about the undesirability of 'single parent households' are themselves attempts to regulate the circumstances into which children are born.

Overt statements about regulating the health of the nation through the control of women and reproduction are less publicly acceptable than they were at the turn of the century (Bland 1982). Despite changes in emphasis, however, concerns about regulating reproduction are still commonplace. For example, Beveridge's desire to sterilize the unemployed did not receive widespread support in the middle of this century. But pressures for pregnant women to attend ante-natal clinics and to accept pre-natal screening are current examples of eugenic concerns, as are debates about sterilizing the mentally handicapped and discussions on the new reproductive technologies (Reid, Chapter 16; Stanworth 1987).

Although eugenic policies and beliefs are now unacceptable, concerns about 'race' and reproduction have not disappeared. As the British economy has gone into recession, there has been a shortage of the kind of unskilled and semi-skilled jobs traditionally filled by black workers. At the same time, increasingly restrictive immigration laws have reduced the numbers of black people entering Britain. Those already here, however, have continued to reproduce. For those who fear that black people and their alien cultures will 'swamp' white society and 'British' cultures, both the immigration of, and reproduction by, black people have given cause for concern.

It is now relatively uncommon for women to have more than two children. The average number of children for each British-born woman is currently 1.7 (OPCS 1988), which is below population-replacement level. Yet there are still popular beliefs that it is antisocial to have 'too many children'; and black women are stereotyped as having many more children than white women (Lawrence 1982).

In reality, both black women and white women are now having fewer children than they did fifteen years ago. Women born in the Caribbean now produce an average of 1.8 children, while Indian-born women (Indian people being the majority of Asian people in Britain) currently have an average of 2.9 children (OPCS 1988). Although accurate figures are not available for British-born black women (the majority of black women of childbearing age in Britain), it is unlikely that they have a higher fertility rate than overseas-born black women. Most black women in Britain, therefore, are neither having large numbers of children, nor many more children than their white peers.

Whatever their origins, black people are socially constructed as 'not belonging' to British society (Seidel 1986), and hence as having no right to 'have too many children' who will compete for scarce resources with white British people. For those who believe that black women bear 'too many' children, it makes sense to try to reduce the black birth-rate wherever possible. In Britain the differential treatment of black and white fertility has neither the sanction of law, nor social acceptability. Attempts to reduce black women's fertility rate are therefore necessarily covert.

Although they are less visible than policy decisions, reproductive ideologies also have a regulatory function. They serve to restrict the categories of people who it is generally believed *should* be producing children, and hence they help to regulate the circumstances into which children are born. It is in the maternity services that this regulatory function can most readily be put into practice. Women *can* be (and sometimes are) referred to abortion clinics when they make their first ante-natal visit. After childbirth, hospitals can liaise with social services and adoption agencies with regard to the process of adoption; women can be sterilized; and they can be advised not to have any more children. Most women are given contraceptive 'advice' before they leave hospital post-natally, and some are either prescribed contraceptives, or are actually given them, before they leave hospital.

The intersection of this stereotyping of black people as having too many children and attempts to regulate the production of children is well illustrated by the health education messages provided specifically for black women. More health education leaflets on contraception have been translated into Asian languages than on any other health issue (Brent Community Health Council 1981).

The Social Construction of Black Women as 'At Risk'

The maternity services thus provide an opportunity for the regulation of women's childbearing. The main obstetric rationale for this regulation is linked to the assessment of risk factors. Many British and American obstetricians use a risk-scoring system of social and medical factors to predict which women are likely to have obstetric problems. In several of these assessments, 'race' (meaning blackness) is deemed to be a risk factor. Thus, women can be considered to be at risk of, for example, low birth weight simply because they are black (see e.g. Institute of Medicine 1985). This has resulted from the elision of two sets of disparate observations. Firstly, it has been well documented that children born with the lowest birth weights tend to experience more perinatal complications than heavier babies. Secondly, there is evidence that black women have lighter babies than white women.

However, there may well be different cut-off points for risk from low birth weight in black and white populations: 'Black infants born at less than 2,500 grams have long been recognized to have better rates of survival in the neonatal period than low birthweight white infants of similar birth-weights.' (Institute of Medicine 1985: 56.) Including all preg-nant black women in a generalized 'at risk' category, therefore, is not helpful to those who need to assess whether obstetric intervention is likely to be necessary. Using blackness as an indicator of risk is also discriminatory, in that it provides a reason for concern about all black women's—but not all white women's—pregnancies. Furthermore, there is little evidence that commonly used risk factors are useful in predicting real risk, since they produce a high rate of false negatives and of false positives. In general, therefore, it is difficult to justify the blanket use of the category 'black' as a risk factor.

Evidence from Britain and the USA does suggest that black infants have a higher perinatal mortality rate than white infants (Maxwell 1982; Macfarlane and Mugford 1984). There may be regional differences in the perinatal mortality rates of children born to black women. For example, a study of

Asian women in East London found 'no increase in perinatal or infant morality over the general population in the same borough' (McEnery and Rao 1986). A Bradford-based study, however, found that 'the perinatal mortality rate for Asian babies born in Bradford . . . was persistently higher than for babies born to United Kingdom mothers' (Lumb *et al.* 1981). However, the differential between the perinatal mortality rates of babies whose mothers were born in the United Kingdom (which include black as well as white women), and those whose mothers were born in the Indian sub-continent, Africa, or the Caribbean is decreasing.

In 1980, only the infants of black women born in Pakistan had much higher perinatal mortality rates than the children of British-born mothers (26.3 per 1,000 as opposed to 13.3 per 1,000). The children of mothers born in the Caribbean, India, Bangladesh, and Africa had perinatal mortality rates which were roughly comparable to (being just slightly above) the national average for social classes IV and V (Ahmed and Pearson 1985). Most black women are not 'at risk' of poor obstetric outcome, therefore, but are nonetheless included in this category. Since this inclusion is on the basis of colour alone, it is in effect racially discriminatory.

There is a high correlation between 'race' and class in western societies, with the majority of black people coming from the working classes. In the minority of instances where there is poor perinatal outcome, therefore, it is necessary to question whether it is blackness *per se*, or the poor socio-economic circumstances of many black people, which is responsible.

Medical Professionals and Obstetric Control

In addition to providing the site and rationale for the regulation of women who *bear* children, the maternity services are staffed by professionals who consider that their roles should include the regulation of who *rears* children and in what circumstances. Farrant (1985) found that most (75 per cent) of the consultant obstetricians she interviewed would

only give amniocentesis if women consented in advance to abort a fetus found to have a genetic abnormality. Fetal screening was not, therefore, perceived as a way of enabling women to make informed decisions (after counselling) about whether or not to keep genetically abnormal fetuses. Instead, obstetricians wanted to use amniocentesis to ensure that only 'normal children' were born.

Similarly, MacIntyre (1976) found that doctors made decisions about whether or not women should be given abortions on the basis of their assessments of the pregnant women's relationships with their male partners rather than on the women's own accounts of why they wanted abortions.

In deciding which women they would prefer to have (or not to have) further children, obstetricians and other practitioners in the maternity services influence current thinking about which women make suitable mothers, and how many children it is acceptable for them to have. In other words, they not only reproduce, but they also produce, reproductive ideologies in such a way that societal power-relations of 'race' and class are maintained (see Henriques *et al.* 1984, for a description of how this process works).

As members of society, medical practitioners (most senior members of whom are white) are subject to social constructions of black women as producing too many children. They are likely, therefore, to have a negative orientation to black women who start to have children early in their reproductive careers, and to those who return to hospital for a third or subsequent child. Larbie (1985: 19) illustrates this in a quote from a young black woman: 'This sister said to me: "You black people have too many babies". As far as I was concerned, I wasn't "You black people", I was me. You don't forget something like that. Even now it makes me angry to think about it . . .'.

There are few studies of black women's experience of the maternity services in Britain, and sterilization, abortion, and contraceptive statistics are not broken down according to colour. There are, however, persistent reports of black women being offered (and some of them given) abortions and sterilizations that they did not want, as well as injections of depo-provera to which they had not given their consent

(Mama 1984, Sheffield Black Women's Group 1984; Bryan et al. 1985; Pearson 1985b; Stanworth, 1987).

The absence of official British statistics on 'sterilization abuse' does not affect the point being made here. As social institutions staffed by members of society, the maternity services reproduce already existing negative social values about black women's fertility. By virtue of their ability to comment on (and in some instances control) women's future fertility, they also actively produce ideas about which characteristics 'good' mothers should have. It is the intersection of these two factors—the negative social construction of black mothers, and the regulatory function of the ante-natal and post-natal clinics—that institutionalizes racial discrimination within maternity-service provision.

The negative social construction of black women's child-bearing is likely to involve black women in interactions with medical practitioners who see them as potentially 'problem' parents. Disapproval is likely to be .worse for those black women who are young and/or poor, and/or have children already. White working-class women may also be subject to disapproval of their childbearing. However, the prevalence of stereotypes about black women's fecundity means that black women are likely to experience discrimination within the maternity services specifically *because they are black*.

Black Women's Experience of the Maternity Services

This chapter is predominantly concerned with black women's experience of the maternity services as 'patients'. But many black women are also employed within the National Health Service; their jobs tend to be at the lowest levels of the Health Service, and they are more likely to be ancillary and maintenance staff or State Enrolled Nurses than midwives or obstetricians. This is not merely accidental or because qualified black people do not apply for higher-level jobs. The St George's medical school and various health authorities have been shown to have discriminated against black applicants for jobs or training (Pearson 1985a; Radical Statistics Health

Group 1987; CRE 1988). Black people do not have equal
access to employment within the National Health Service.
The context in which black women use the maternity services
is thus one in which there are few senior black personnel, and
some senior white staff are not keen to employ black staff at
anything other than the most basic levels.

Much of what black women experience in ante-natal clinics
and on post-natal wards is common to all women. Long
waiting times, insensitive internal examinations, and inadequate explanations about the progress of the pregnancy or
the procedures used are cited as problems by both black and
white respondents (Oakley 1979; Larbie 1985). However, at
each stage of the ante-natal procedure black women can
experience additional problems as the result of direct or
indirect racial discrimination.

The quotation used in the last section is an example of
direct discrimination. The nursing sister's statement seems to
have been designed to make the young black woman reporting
the incident feel uncomfortable. The use of procedures to limit
black women's fertility without their consent is also direct
discrimination, as is the informal practice observed in one
London hopital of using air-freshener after certain Asian
women had been in the reception area. Most of these actions
would not be condoned officially, because they are illegal.
(The exception is the practice of recording blackness as an
automatic risk category.)

However, checking black women's immigration status
before allowing them maternity care *is* officially sanctioned by
law, in that National Health Service (NHS) care is only
available free of charge to British citizens and certain other
categories of people (like EEC residents and overseas students).
Anyone suspected of not having a legitimate right to NHS
treatment can be asked for proof of their entitlement. The
discretion that this allows Health Service personnel means
that in practice 'it is Black people who are most often required
to prove citizenship, in case they are "foreign"' (Mama 1984).
This is directly discriminatory, in that pregnant women may
be required to prove their entitlement simply because they are
black, while white North Americans, South Africans, Europeans,
Australians, etc. are less likely to be asked for similar proof.

Indirect discrimination is harder to identify. It may be unintentionally produced by health staff personnel, and not recognized as racial discrimination. It is here that the contradictions inherent in the social construction of black people within the maternity services become apparent. Midwives and obstetricians claim to provide a universal service to pregnant and newly delivered women. That is, the service they provide is claimed to be 'colour blind', with race making no difference to treatment (Pearson 1985*b*). At the same time, the social construction of black people as alien to British society fosters beliefs that black women are different from white women. Thus, black women are perceived to be culturally different from white women, and to have different fertility patterns and customs.

Underpinning these two approaches are two separate and contradictory philosophies relating to black people. These are:

(*a*) an assimilationist approach

(*b*) a culturally pluralist approach

Each of these approaches individually has proved unsatisfactory in the maternity services.

(*a*) *Universality of Provisions: An Assimilationist Approach*

When significant numbers of black people came to Britain in the 1950s and 1960s it was assumed that they would assimilate to British society and institutions. It was not considered necessary for society to make any adaptations. British social institutions were felt to be adequate already, and to be sufficiently open and accessible. Any difficulties black people encountered with various institutions were considered to reflect their own shortcomings, and they were not expected to make any demands on society.

The assimilationist approach is frequently discussed as if it fell into general disfavour in the 1970s. Those who argue this, suggest that once the cultural distinction between black and white people had been recognized, it was clear that black people would never totally assimilate. But assimilationist approaches did not disappear; they are still current in many institutions. In the maternity services, the colour-blind approach—that equal provision is made for all women,

irrespective of colour—is an example of assimilationism.
Black women were expected to use a pre-existing service, and
to make no particular demands upon it.

The insistence of universality of provision, regardless of
race, can itself be racially discriminatory. Black women may
not be given appropriate, specific treatment when necessary.
For example, all new-born babies are now routinely tested for
phenylketonuria (PKU), which has a very low incidence (at
about 1 in every 10,000 births (Prashar *et al.* 1985)) but is more
common in white than in black populations. By way of contrast, diseases like sickle cell anaemia and beta-thalassaemia,
which are more common but mainly occur in black populations,
are not routinely screened for (Pearson 1985b; Prashar *et al.*
1985; Constantinides 1987). In this instance, universality of
provision simply means making available to black women that
provision which has been specifically geared to white women's
needs, while ignoring black women's needs.

It is estimated that in Britain about 1 in every 200 babies of
Caribbean origin, and 1 in every 100 babies of West African
origin are born with sickle cell disease (Prashar *et al.* 1985).
Each year an estimated fifty babies are born with sickle cell
disease and sixteen are born with beta-thalassaemia major
(Constantinides 1987). Beta-thalassaemia mainly affects people
with ancestry in the Mediterranean, the Indian sub-continent,
and South-East Asia (Constantinides, unpub.). Sickle cell
anaemia and thalassaemia are now well-understood diseases
(Constantinides 1987). It is not surprising that the difference
in policy towards them and towards PKU causes 'the black
and ethnic minority communities [to] therefore rightly feel
discriminated against and allege that there is racism within
the National Health Service' (Prashar *et al.* 1985).

Left untreated, both sickle cell disease and beta-thalassaemia
major are potentially life-threatening, but with increasingly
sophisticated medical techniques the quality of life for those
who suffer from them can be improved, provided treatment is
started early. 'Management of both . . . [can be] burdensome,
expensive and life long' (Modell 1987). However, the carriers
of both diseases can be detected cheaply and easily with a high
degree of accuracy. All pregnant women of Afro-Caribbean
origin in Britain are already routinely screened for sickle cell

disease in case they require anaesthesia; they are not, however, routinely given counselling if they are found to be carriers or to have the disease (Prashar *et al.* 1985).

In order to prove that it takes black people's health as seriously as it does white people's, the NHS clearly needs to introduce routine screening for sickle cell anaemia and thalassaemia. The question then arises as to how this should be done. Should it be selectively geared to those populations which have the highest incidence, or comprehensively provided? In answer to the first question, pregnancy and neonatal screening are not mutually exclusive. If a pregnant woman is found to be either a carrier of, or to have, a haemoglobinopathy (like sickle cell anaemia or thalassaemia), then the father of the child, if available, can also be screened. If either the father is not available, or both partners are found to be carriers or sufferers, the potential parents need to be counselled and offered fetal screening, with the possibility of abortion or early prophylactic treatment of infants who have either disease. **But there is a major difficulty with fetal screening and abortion of fetuses found to have sickle cell anaemia. For,** while the prognosis for infants with beta-thalassaemia major is well known, there is a great deal of variability in the ways in which sickle cell anaemia affects those who have it (Prashar *et al.* 1985). **Because of this, the Sickle Cell Society has expressed** concern that some black women are being encouraged to have abortions without proper counselling (Anionwu 1987).

The question of whether screening should be comprehensive or not requires some consideration of Britain's black population. Black people of Afro-Caribbean origin are increasingly forming marital and cohabiting unions with white British people. About a third of the under 30s age-group are estimated to be in such unions. In addition, most people of Afro-Caribbean origin who are of childbearing age have been born in Britain (OPCS 1988). Clearly, it is going to become increasingly difficult to establish pregnant women's origins (and hence to assess whether they are at risk for haemoglobin-opathy) by using simple colour cues, or by asking where their parents were born. Even in the Caribbean, a minority of people of Afro-Caribbean heritage do not have any visible African ancestry.

Some hospitals with a high number of black and ethnic-minority maternity patients have recognized this, and screen all pregnant women for thalassaemia as a matter of course. Since such a procedure is both cheap and simple (Modell 1987), it seems sensible to operate comprehensive screening. Comprehensive screening is also preferable to selective screening, in that it avoids stigmatizing black women by treating them as if they were exotic specimens singled out for special attention.

In practice, then, the claim of universal provision, with its habit of catering for white infants' needs more than for black infants' needs, has been based on an assimilationist philosophy which is racially discriminatory in the way in which it operates.

(b) *Cultural Pluralism and 'Special Needs'*

The philosophy of universal provision often coexists with the presumption that black women have 'special needs' within the maternity services. When it was recognized that black people were not simply going to be assimilated into white society, cultural pluralism gained popularity. In cultural pluralism, all people, black and white, are recognized as having equally valid cultures.

This is a more progressive view than the assimilationist one. Yet, because the power-relations between black and white people are not questioned in cultural pluralism, the provision that was already being made for the white population was taken for granted as 'normal'. As a result, black people (in the maternity services and other institutions) were perceived to have extraordinary needs, requiring special provision. Cultures were not in fact treated as equal in practice.

The 'special needs' approach in the maternity services is invidious, in that it suggests that black women's needs are extraordinary, and that the satisfaction of those needs is likely to make extra demands on the maternity services. Black women are thus constructed as presenting problems for the maternity services. It follows from this that there is likely to be some resentment at their failure to make the necessary effort to accommodate themselves to the maternity services.

Thus, for example, receptionists become irritated with black women of Asian origin whose names they consider to be confusingly similar or hard for them to pronounce and remember (Pearson 1985b). Such contact between receptionists and Asian maternity patients serves to heighten receptionists' perception of Asians as alien to British culture and disruptive of the smooth running of ante-natal clinics. Similarly, black women who do not speak or understand much English, who do not want to be examined by a male doctor, who bring several relatives to clinics or the labour room with them, and who do not want to eat standard hospital food tend to be viewed with impatience.

In such instances, it is easy for white hospital staff to conclude that the things they find inconvenient about black women are cultural in origin. However, in reality, many women, black and white, do not like hospital food; many women find it difficult to understand what the medical staff say to them; and it is now well documented that many women do not like having internal examinations, particularly from male doctors. For example, in her study of women becoming first-time mothers, Ann Oakley says: 'Apprehension about internal examinations was very commonly mentioned by women in their accounts of medical care.' (Oakley 1979: 297–8.) The following quote from a 28-year-old white woman interviewed by Oakley illustrates this: 'To tell you the truth it was so embarrassing that I wouldn't want to go there again . . . [Did it hurt?] It did hurt. I held his hand . . . it was very bad . . . I didn't think there was a need for all this—when you're having a baby to have such an examination?' (Oakley 1979: 44–5.)

Moslem women are reported to be very concerned to maintain body modesty for cultural reasons. Yet other factors sometimes overrule such cultural conventions. West Birmingham Community Health Council (1984) found that a third of the Moslem women they interviewed had no preference about being examined by a female doctor. Similarly, in her small-scale study, Currer (1987) found that Pathan women (most of whom are very strict Moslems) did not necessarily want a female doctor to examine them in pregnancy. There are thus definite overlaps between black and white women's feelings about being examined by male doctors.

The focus on Asian or Afro-Caribbean cultures as a source of problems for the maternity services is based on the presumption that all 'Asian' women and all 'Afro-Caribbean' women share unitary cultures. This presumption takes no account of the various religions, languages, and life-styles of black women. The propensity to see black women as being 'all the same' is not only inaccurate, but also racially discriminatory, in that it can mask individual black women's needs.

For example, Torkington (1987) describes an incident reported to her while she was carrying out her study of the health-care needs of racial minorities, where 'a Muslim woman was left in a hospital for two days without food'. The ward staff knew that she was not eating the hospital food, but presumed that she was being brought in meals by her family. In fact, her husband was away and nobody had visited her in hospital. Torkington suggests that if the hospital staff had not been blinkered by their stereotype of Asian women as having large, supportive families who bring them in meals, they would have noticed this particular women needed to be provided with food that she could eat.

Stereotypes of Asian women's 'low' pain threshold can mean that their responses to pain in childbirth are greeted with irritation and not taken seriously (Brent Community Health Council 1981). Similarly, assumptions about Afro-Caribbean women 'just popping them out like peas' can predispose medical staff to categorize women of Afro-Caribbean origin as physically more geared to childbearing than white women, and so requiring less support and sympathy.

The belief that black women's behaviour can most readily be explained by reference to their supposed cultural origins can also obscure the similarities between black and white women. For example, women's right to have their infant's father with them during childbirth was a hard-won advance in obstetric practice. In many hospitals, however, it has ossified into practice in such a way that it is no longer just an available right, but is deemed to be essential. Many hospitals consider male partners to be the most desirable companion for women in delivery rooms (see Barbour, Chapter 11), yet many women would in fact prefer to have a female friend or relative with them. If Asian women do not have their male partners

with them in labour, this tends to be perceived as a further indication of the 'repressive' culture under which Asian women are stereotyped to live (Brent Community Health Council 1981). On the other hand, white women who are not accompanied by their male partners during labour are likely to be considered as individually (rather than culturally) deviant. Conversely, women of Asian origin whose children's fathers are present during birth are likely to be presumed to have abandoned their 'Asian culture', because heterogeneity within black groups is not recognized.

Cultural practices are not simply divided along colour lines. Instead they are the result of a complex interrelationship of such factors as class, geographical locality, and historical period. Black people (like white people) have a diversity of cultural practices. In addition, black people and white people of similar class backgrounds are likely to share certain beliefs and cultural practices. Yet, because black people are socially constructed as inferior to white people, features perceived to be representations of their cultures are negatively stereotyped as strange and exotic, and hence devalued. Behaviour patterns that are disliked or felt to be inconvenient are treated as if they were due to group differences rather than individual preferences. Thus, there is a predisposition within the maternity services to see black women as the cause of any identified problems. The possibility that it may be the procedures themselves that generate these problems is not usually considered.

Cultural beliefs and practices have important influences on women's lives, and are therefore relevant to maternity-service provision. Obstetric staff do need to learn about and, where necessary, accommodate to, the maternity practices of their local population. This accommodation does not necessitate a cultural relativism, the uncritical acceptance of every possible maternity practice. But black people are no more culturally homogeneous than white people are. It should never be presumed that there is a simple one-to-one correspondence between a woman's place of origin, colour, and/or religion and the maternity practices in which she wishes to engage. In addition, many black women and white women come from the same sort of backgrounds. Their shared class and gender

mean that they are likely to have many similar beliefs and experiences. Colour does not necessarily differentiate women's requirements of the maternity services.

Cultural practices are dynamic rather than static. Women (both black and white) change their customs over time to fit in with new knowledge, the areas in which they live, etc. It would be counter-productive for maternity staff to feel that anything they learn about some black women's maternity practices will continue to be relevant indefinitely. Attempts to ensure that black women are adequately catered for within the maternity services have so far been inadequate because most have trivialized black women's experiences by reducing them to cultural stereotypes.

Recent Responses

Black Women's Responses

Over the last two decades black women in Britain have set up groups to campaign for an improvement in their treatment within the National Health Service. While many of these have been general health groups or women's groups, many of the issues they have campaigned around have concerned aspects of practice within the maternity services. Their approach to these issues has been three-pronged. Some groups have concentrated on getting those health issues that only affect black women dealt with; some have been geared to the prevention of abuses of black women; others have been broad-based campaigning and information organizations.

An example of the former is the Organization for Sickle Cell Anaemia Research, set up in Britain in 1975. This has campaigned for the screening of pregnant women of African origin, and raised funds for research into sickle cell anaemia. A related example is the survey of screening and counselling facilities for sickle cell anaemia conducted by the Runnymede Trust (Prashar *et al.* 1985). An example of an organization which aims to stop abusive practices is the Campaign against Depo-Provera, the use of which involved white women as well as black women. Poor white women and poor black women

were being given Depo-provera either without their knowledge or without being counselled about the potential side-effects (Rakusen 1981; Bryan *et al.* 1985). An example of a broad-based campaigning organization is the Black Health Workers' and Patients' Group. This was established in 1981 and campaigns around a wide range of issues affecting black people. It also publishes a bulletin.

Semi-Official Responses

Campaigns led by black people have tended to take as their starting-point the fact that the existence of racial discrimination is responsible for inequities in health-care provision between black women and white women. More official responses have not necessarily been based on this premiss. The Asian Mother and Baby Campaign, for example (funded for four years from 1984 by the Department of Health and Social Security and the Save the Children Fund), has produced material about racism in the maternity services. Its primary concern, however, has been to provide Asian mothers with basic information about maternity care and child care. The unspoken assumption seems to be that it is the Asian women who are responsible for the problems they are stereotyped to pose for the health services:

Problems under scrutiny lose their reference to patients' race and class positions while they highlight their cultural elements. Thus, the reformist intentions of the Campaign tend to collude, at the ideological level, with an image of a 'Black pathology' although they represent a genuine attempt to challenge personal racism. (Rocheron 1988: 5.)

The Asian Mother and Baby Campaign, cited Asian mothers as attending antenatal clinics only late on in pregnancy. There seemed no attempt to counter the stereotypes that judged that this was because Asian women were submissive, unreliable and not able to cope with situations in which they had to speak English ... We found that the major reason for the non-attendance ... was due to up to a four month backlog in notifying pregnant women of their antenatal clinic appointments. (Lone 1987: 6.)

The suggestion that late attendance is frequently outside women's control is confirmed by a survey of 150 patients

conducted by West Birmingham Community Health Council:
'On the basis of this survey's findings one can say that in the
majority of cases late booking at the hospital was the result of
factors beyond the women's control, and the late booker
cannot be considered a reluctant receiver of ante-natal care.'
(West Birmingham Community Health Council 1984: 19.)
The West Birmingham findings suggest that a greater
proportion of women would attend ante-natal clinics early in
pregnancy if booking procedures were efficiently co-ordinated.
Hospitals and general practitioners, therefore, have as important a role as pregnant women in ensuring that women
attend ante-natal clinics sufficiently early for routine pre-natal
diagnosis.

Training in Health and Race (TIHR) provided practical
resources for opposing racism in the Health Service. It was
funded by the Health Education Council between 1982 and
1986. At a time when many people had not considered issues
of health and race, it devoted a lot of energy to finding ways of
countering racism in maternity care. Despite this orientation,
it too gave a disproportionate amount of attention to black
women's late attendance at ante-natal clinics (Pearson 1985b).
TIHR did not mention the possibility of black women
receiving ante-natal appointments late. In addition, it left
three important questions about late attendance at ante-natal
clinic unasked: firstly, whether class is a relevant factor, in
which case late booking is equally relevant to white women;
second, whether factors like lengthy waiting times deter more
black women than white women; thirdly, and most importantly,
whether late attendance matters, given the absence of
evidence of a causative relationship between late attendance
at ante-natal clinics and poor perinatal outcome. In all these
issues, class may be a more relevant factor than race in
explaining late attendance at ante-natal clinics. It may also
have been worth pointing out that most women do eventually
attend ante-natal clinics regularly, despite the fact that they
do not enjoy their experience of it.

TIHR publications are good at pointing out what bad
practice in maternity provision looks like, and in giving
examples of good practice. Yet the examples chosen sometimes
reveal the tension between treating black women as if they

present a problem to the Health Service by having 'special needs', and recognizing that the maternity services *themselves* present problems for many women. For instance, it is not clear what hospitals should do in response to the suggestion that they should make special provision for Asian women 'rubbing their hair with oil' (TIHR 1984: 8). Rather than 'special provision' being made, all that is required is that ward staff should understand that women care for themselves in a variety of ways and may need privacy in order to do so. Whether women want to apply make-up or oil their hair is irrelevant, in that neither requires special attention from ward staff.

Staff do not need to be specially trained to 'ensure a positive and well informed attitude towards minority group patients' individual needs and wishes' (TIHR 1984), but they do need to be trained to do this for all patients, whatever their class, race, or ethnicity. All pregnant women require information about hospital procedures and what is happening to them, and all need to be provided with a diet that is both nutritious and palatable. British society is multilingual and multi-ethnic. Information and nutrition need to be provided in a variety of ways, therefore. Maternity hospitals need to recognize these fundamental (not special) needs if they are to provide a satisfactory service to both black and white women. However, this recognition of the diversity of women's life-styles must take account of the diversity within, as well as between, ethnic and religious groups. Knowing that a woman is Jewish or Moslem, for example, is not sufficient indication of her attitudes and desires. Women's beliefs and practices have to be established rather than presumed.

Maternity Service Responses

Individual health authorities and hospitals have introduced changes in their maternity practices that are designed to recognize that black women have been receiving less favourable treatment than white women. For example, some authorities have provided translators for women who find it difficult to communicate in English. A few hospitals have also introduced clerking procedures which deal appropriately with all the

naming systems used by women who attend clinics (Pearson 1985*b*). Some authorities have translated leaflets and hospital signs into a variety of languages, and some are prepared to refer pregnant women who do not speak English to appropriate classes.

The City and Hackney Multi-Ethnic Women's Health Project was the first British project to employ staff from different ethnic groups to act as advocates on behalf of black and other minority users of the maternity services (Ahmed and Pearson 1985). The success of the project has inspired others to provide similar language support and advocacy. Some Community Health Councils also provide translators for women who are not comfortable using English. There are, in addition, a few examples of hospitals routinely offering all patients a choice of a variety of foods other than standard British hospital fare. Some medical practitioners have also made attempts to understand the issues involved in race and health.

These innovations are all welcome signs that the maternity services are prepared to try to fulfil their legal obligation to provide a genuinely universal service. However, many of these changes are piecemeal, and are designed to alleviate particular perceived problems. For example, many NHS 'ethnic advisers' (the first of which was appointed in Haringey in 1985) were only given two- and three-year contracts (McNaught 1987). They are unlikely to be able to implement substantial, well-founded changes anywhere in the Health Service.

Without an underlying and continuing commitment to tackling racism, black women will continue to be seen as 'the problem' in the maternity services, and changes will be token rather than fundamental. The provision of translators, for example, does not necessarily mean that black women will be as well informed about maternity procedures as white women (Brent Community Health Council 1981; West Birmingham Community Health Council 1984). After all, translators cannot translate information that they are not given.

The maternity services exist within a society in which racism is institutionalized. They are therefore permeated with racial discrimination. This discrimination exists at both an institu-

tional and a personal level, and occurs in a number of ways.

Firstly, the maternity services provide a unique site for the regulation of the number of children that a woman bears. The intersection of racist stereotypes and reproductive ideologies enables the production and reproduction of negative social values about black women's fertility; and within the maternity services this can easily be (and sometimes is) translated into sterilization and contraceptive abuses. The rationale for the differential obstetric treatment of black and white women is partly provided by the categorization of blackness itself as a risk factor.

Secondly, a relatively small proportion of black people have been employed at the higher levels of the maternity services. And, thirdly, the maternity services have at the same time taken a 'colour blind' approach to service provision. This apparent equality of treatment masks inequalities of provision. Black women are less likely than white women to have their specific needs (e.g. for screening) met. It also masks the fact that many white women, particularly those who are working class, do not get their individual needs met either.

The belief that equality of provision already exists within the maternity services has led to the construction of black women as having 'special needs' and posing 'special problems' within the maternity services. These 'special needs' have usually been presumed to be the result of cultural differences and linguistic deficits.

There are obviously cultural differences between some black women and some white women. But the needs of women using the maternity services (e.g. appropriate screening techniques, food which is both religiously acceptable and palatable, and efficient and successful communication) are not 'special', they are fundamental to all women. In a multi-ethnic society these needs have to be provided in a variety of ways. Many institutions in the maternity services currently operate as if Britain were a mono-ethnic and monolinguistic society. In doing so, the maternity services are racially discriminatory; they are more likely to meet the needs of white women than those of black women. The definition of black women's relationship with the maternity services as one in

which they have 'special needs' does not acknowledge the multi-ethnicity of British society. Neither does it take account of the existence of racism, the diversity of black people's cultures, or the many similarities between black women and white women from similar class backgrounds.

The 'special needs' approach has resulted in piecemeal change within the maternity services. While some of these changes make for better service delivery, they are not sufficient to eradicate racial discrimination. Good practice requires the recognition that racial discrimination lies at the heart of black women's experience of the maternity services. Without this recognition, and without conscious attempts to counter racism, there cannot be genuinely equal maternity provision. There is an urgent need for continued discussions of how such an approach can be structured into the maternity services, and for further research on black women's experiences of those services.

References

Ahmed, A. and Pearson, M., 1985, *Multi-Racial Initiatives in Maternity Care: A Directory of Projects for Black and Ethnic Minority Women* (London, Maternity Alliance).

Anionwu, E., 1987, Interview on *File on Four*, BBC Radio 4, 15 Dec. 1987.

Antonis, B., 1981, 'Motherhood and Mothering', in Cambridge University Women's Group (ed.), *Women in Society: Interdisciplinary Essays* (London, Virago).

Bland, L., 1982, '"Guardians of the Race" or "Vampires upon the Nation's Health"? Female Sexuality and its Regulation in Early Twentieth-Century Britain', in Whitelegg, E. *et al.* (eds.), *The Changing Experience of Women* (Oxford, Blackwell).

Brent Community Health Council, 1981, *Black People and the Health Service* (London, Brent Community Health Council).

Bryan, B., Dadzie, S., and Scafe, S., 1985, *The Heart of the Race: Black Women's Lives in Britain* (London, Virago).

Busfield, J., 1974, 'Ideologies and reproduction', in Richards, M. (ed.), *The Integration of a Child into a Social World* (Cambridge, Cambridge University Press).

Cartwright, A., 1979, *The Dignity of Labour?* (London, Tavistock).

Commission for Racial Equality, 1988, *Medical School Administration: Report of a Formal Investigation into St George's Hospital Medical School* (London, CRE).

Constantinides, P., 1987, 'Health Care Services for Populations at Risk for Genetically Determined Disease', *New Community*, 13/3, pp. 359–66.

—— unpublished, 'Genetics and Genealogies: Social Aspects in the Delivery of Health Care'.

Currer, C., 1987, 'Immigrant Mothers: The Nature of the Challenge for Child Health Care in Britain', Seminar presented at the Thomas Coram Research Unit, 4 Nov. 1987.

Davis, A., 1981, *Women, Race and Class* (London, The Women's Press).

Farrant, W., 1985, 'Who's for Amniocentesis? The Politics of Prenatal Screening', in Homans, H. (ed.), *The Sexual Politics of Reproduction* (Aldershot, Gower).

Henriques, J. *et al.* 1984, *Changing the Subject* (London, Methuen).

Institute of Medicine, 1985, *Preventing Low Birthweight* (Washington, National Academy).

Larbie, J., 1985, *Black Women and the Maternity Services* (London, TIHR).

Lawrence, E., 1982, 'Just Plain Commonsense: The "Roots" of Racism', in Centre for Contemporary Cultural Studies (ed.), *The Empire Strikes Back: Race and Racism in 70s Britain* (London, Hutchinson).

Lone, R., 1987, 'Asian Women and Health', Women's Health Information Centre *Newsletter*, 7 (Spring).

Lumb, K. M., Congdon, P. J., and Lealman, G. T., 1981, 'A Comparative Review of Asian and British-Born Maternity Patients in Bradford, 1974-8', *Journal of Epidemiology and Community Health*, 35, pp. 106-9.

McEnery, G. and Rao, K. P. S., 1986, 'The Effectiveness of Antenatal Education of Pakistani and Indian Women Living in this Country', *Child: Care, Health and Development*, 12, pp. 385-99.

Macfarlane, A. and Mugford, M., 1984, *Birth Counts: Statistics of Pregnancy and Childbirth* (London, HMSO).

Macintyre, S., 1976, 'Who Wants Babies? The Social Construction of Instincts', in Barker, D. and Allen, S. (eds.), *Sexual Divisions and Society: Process and Change* (London, Tavistock).

McNaught, A., 1987, *Health Action and Ethnic Minorities* (London, Bedford Square Press).

Mama, A., 1984, 'Black Women, the Economic Crisis and the British State', *Feminist Review*, 17, pp. 21-36.

Maxwell, J., 1982, *The Prevention of Prematurity: A Strategy to Reduce Infant Mortality in the District of Columbia* (Washington, Greater Washington Research Centre).

Modell, B., 1987, 'The Haemoglobinopathies', in King's Fund Forum, *Screening for Fetal and Genetic Abnormality* (London, King's Fund).

Murcott, A., 1980, 'The Social Construction of Teenage Pregnancy', *Sociology of Health and Illness*, 2/1, pp. 1-23.

Oakley, A., 1979, *From Here to Maternity: Becoming a Mother* (Harmondsworth, Penguin).

Office of Population Censuses and Surveys, 1988, *Social Trends 18* (London, HMSO).

Pearson, M., 1985a, *Equal Opportunities in the NHS* (Leeds, TIHR).

—— 1985b, *Racial Equality and Good Practice Maternity Care* (London, TIHR).

Prashar, U., Anionwu, E., and Brocović, M., 1985, *Sickle Cell Anaemia: Who Cares? A Survey of Screening and Counselling Facilities in England* (London, Runnymede Trust).

Radical Statistics Health Group, 1987, *Facing the Figures: What Really*

is *Happening to the National Health Service?* (London, Radical Statistics).

Rakusen, J., 1981, 'Depo-Provera: The Extent of the Problem', in Roberts, H. (ed.), *Women, Health and Reproduction* (London, Routledge and Kegan Paul).

Reid, M., 1983, Review article, 'A Feminist Sociological Imagination? Reading Ann Oakley', *Sociology of Health and Illness*, 5/1, pp. 83–94.

Rocheron, Y., 1988, 'The Asian Mother and Baby Campaign: The Construction of Ethnic Minorities' Health Needs', *Critical Social Policy*, 22, pp. 4–23.

Seidel, G., 1986, 'Nation and "Race" in the British and French New Right', in Levitas, R. (ed.), *The Ideology of the New Right* (Cambridge, Polity Press).

Sheffield Black Women's Group, 1984, 'Black Women: What Kind of Health Care Can we Expect in Racist Britain?', in Kanter, H., Lefanu, S., Shah, S., and Spedding, C. (eds.), *Sweeping Statements: Writings from the Women's Liberation Movement 1981–83* (London, The Women's Press).

Stanworth, M., 1987, 'Reproductive Technologies and the De-construction of Motherhood', in Stanworth, M. (ed.), *Reproductive Technologies: Gender, Motherhood and Medicine* (Cambridge, Polity Press).

Torkington, N. P. K., 1987, 'Racism and Health', Women's Health Information Centre, *Newsletter*, 7 (Spring).

Training in Health and Race, 1984, *Providing Effective Health Care in a Multiracial Society* (London, TIHR).

West Birmingham Community Health Council, 1984, *Women Waiting: Ante-Natal Services in West Birmingham* (Birmingham, West Birmingham Community Health Council).

16

Pre-Natal Diagnosis and Screening: A Review

Margaret Reid

TODAY screening during pregnancy has become an issue of central and sometimes controversial importance for both parents and practitioners. New findings in the field of detection of genetic disorders are reported with apparent frequency in the media, while scarcely a day passes without one British newspaper carrying an item relating to the broader theme of the relationship between genetics and reproduction. Despite the promise of some of the new developments, it remains the case that screening can only detect a small proportion of handicapping conditions, albeit a relatively important group. While the future goal of many may be primary prevention of handicap, the routines of pre-natal screening and diagnosis are entrenched in today's maternity care. It is the purpose of this chapter to review this fast-growing and sometimes contentious aspect of maternity practice.

Screening, according to one authority, is 'the identification, among apparently healthy individuals, of those who are sufficiently at risk of a specific disorder to justify a subsequent diagnostic test or procedure, or in certain circumstances, direct preventive action' (Wald 1984: 537). What happens next is dependent in part upon the state of medical science. Simple anaemia, once diagnosed, can be treated: the HIV virus, once diagnosed with a highly accurate test, may lead to action but not effective treatment. Screening is not simply a technical procedure, however; it is concerned with a complex

I would like to thank the editors for their comments on earlier drafts, and Sally Macintyre for making some papers available.

interaction of issues, some clinical, others psychological, ethical, and social. The principle actors involved in effective screening differ widely in their roles, yet all are crucial to the outcome. At one end of the spectrum, geneticists are attempting something that was science fiction only decades ago, the mapping of the gene field through the scientific discipline of molecular genetics. As recently as 1956 came final agreement on the number of chromosomes each individual possesses—forty-six; three years later, the first published work appeared identifying Down's syndrome as resulting from an extra chromosome 21 (hence its other name of Trisomy 21) (Kevles 1986). Today it is known that 1 in every 150 live new-born children is chromosomally abnormal. Geneticists talk of gene-mapping, although at present they have identified only about 5 per cent of our genes, and mapped only 1 per cent to a particular chromosome or chromosomal region (Evans 1986). The obvious eugenic undertones of such an enterprise are recognized, although it is difficult to anticipate the ways in which such developments may ultimately be used.

At the other end of the spectrum we find the genetic counsellor, who is present when science confronts men and women in what is often a highly emotional situation. As a 'communication process', genetic counselling has developed as a result of the need to discuss with parents the detailed implications of identifying genetic conditions. Debates within the field exist as genetic counsellors struggle to find ways of presenting the alternative outcomes to their clients which will allow families to make the decision with which they remain happiest.

Given the potentially broad remit of pre-natal screening, this chapter will deliberately take a narrow focus. We shall be less concerned with the scientific debates and with the field of genetic counselling. Instead, after reviewing the screening and diagnostic tests that are currently available during pregnancy, we shall consider the social and moral implications of new developments; finally, we shall look briefly at what may be available for the pregnant woman of the 1990s.

Screening: Past Times

The routine of ante-natal screening which forms the core of modern, medical ante-natal care began around the turn of the century, although tests continued to be added to the basic routine over the decades. As will be evident, while many of the screening tests were developed in the early part of the century, the majority of the diagnostic tests are products of recent years.

Little detailed information is available on ante-natal routine before the 1930s, when care became more standard. Abdominal palpation was pioneered by Pinard in 1889. Vaginal examination was only carried out very occasionally, usually with the patient sedated or even anaesthetized (Oakley 1984). Routine vaginal examination came much later. The recognition of different blood groups occurred in 1907, although again, the routine screening of one of blood's components, haemoglobin, was not established until much later. It seems that by the 1930s the basic procedures of ante-natal screening included weighing, palpation, checking the lie and presentation of the fetus, blood pressure, and urine testing. Further tests (such as blood tests) were added later, and some of the 'basic' tests were carried out more frequently during the pregnancy (Oakley 1984). More recently, urinalysis has been extended to include stress tests (placental function tests) to check for possible intra-uterine growth retardation (IUGR), while in the last decade fetal activity has been monitored through the simple addition of fetal kick charts.

X-rays offered the first insight into the uterus at the turn of the century, and became routine by the 1920s. Long after they had fallen out of favour, in the 1970s, ultrasound became the accepted way of viewing the fetus. Used routinely now to screen for gestational age, ultrasound is also a diagnostic test for certain fetal abnormalities, such as neural tube disorders. It is also used as guidance during amniocentesis and chorionic villus sampling (CVS), a new technique pioneered in China in the mid-1970s and in the West in the 1980s. In 1967 amniocentesis was first used in Britain for the pre-natal diagnosis of chromosomal disorders. In 1972–3 alpha feto-

protein (AFP) testing was introduced in Britain (somewhat later in America). It was found that AFP testing, used in conjunction with amniocentesis, produced a more reliable result. Amniocentesis is now used both as an adjunct to AFP testing, and as a test in its own right.

In the 1980s, over 200 mainly fetal conditions can be detected by newer tests which involve drawing off fetal or maternal fluids (blood or tissue, for example). Most of these are not screening tests, in that they are not routinely applied to pregnant women (with the exception of AFP testing in some areas), but are more correctly titled 'diagnostic' tests, available to particular individuals designated as being at high risk for that condition. However, the boundaries of screening and pre-natal diagnosis are not clear-cut, and, indeed, this chapter will continue to consider both kinds of test.

Screening and Diagnosis in the 1980s

The routine of ante-natal screening tests remains very much as it is used to be, although questions continue to be raised about the efficacy, value, and, in some cases, the safety of some tests. Information about uterine growth gained from the vaginal examination is now seen by some as being more accurately assessed from ultrasound tests, and in some regions in Britain the vaginal examination is now little practised (although obstetricians in some other countries continue to place value on it). The test for weight gain is now under scrutiny; in this instance, obstetricians question the interpretation of findings. Whereas in the past, weight gain was viewed as a sign of potential problems in the pregnancy, and therefore careful weighing was carried out at each check-up, nowadays it is recognized that there is a wide variation in the range of normal weight gain, and that little additional information may be gained through regular weighing (Hytten 1980; Varma 1984). In Britain recent articles have also questioned the value of screening for bacteriuria (Campbell-Brown et al. 1987), while there continues to be a debate over the best test for intra-uterine growth retardation (e.g.

MacKenzie *et al.* 1986), and the value of ultrasound for measurement of gestational age (e.g. Pearce and Campbell 1987). While this clinical debate continues, another body of literature began to contribute to our knowledge of screening. In the last two decades there has been an increasing awareness of the effect of psychological and social factors on health and behaviour, an awareness brought about in part by social science studies of consumers' views of their medical experiences. The field of birth was well represented in these studies, and this work contributed to a hard-fought campaign for greater rights for women during their labour and delivery which has created an environment in which women may have more influence over the birth of their babies. Now, new developments in screening procedures have begun to shift consumer attention back to pregnancy and screening, and the fast-growing literature again addresses the consumer experience.

British studies of women's attitudes towards the experience of pregnancy and birth (e.g. Breen 1975; Graham and McKee 1979; Oakley 1979, 1980; Macintyre 1981; Perfrement 1982) included in their sections on ante-natal care a little about women's knowledge of routine screening procedures. The researchers were mainly interested in looking at the degree to which these tests were accepted and understood, but found that they had become so absorbed into the routine of ante-natal care, and the results of such tests were so rarely given, that many women were not even aware that they *were* undergoing tests (Macintyre 1978; Boyd and Sellars 1982). However, one study suggests that this awareness might change during pregnancy. Perfrement asked a sample of seventy-five pregnant women early in pregnancy to name regular medical checks. Only 38 per cent of the women mentioned at least two checks and the reasons for them. Later in pregnancy this figure had increased to 80 per cent (Perfrement 1982).

This lack of comprehension of the tests is evident in other studies. Macintyre, for example, studied fifty first-time pregnant women, and asked them about giving samples. Her research concludes that while women gave blood and urine samples regularly, 'None ever refused to give or queried the need for samples of blood or urine, although most disliked

providing samples and did not know their purpose.' (Macintyre 1981: 135.) Vaginal examinations were still routine, yet Perfrement (1982), one of the few researchers to ask about these, noted that early in pregnancy over half of the sample (55 per cent) could either only give one reason for the internal examination or did not know why it was being carried out at all. By contrast, Draper and her colleagues found that the majority of women asked to fill in a fetal kick chart were given a clear explanation of how to do this, and were aware of the reasons for filling it in (Draper, Field, and Thomas 1984).

Research has shown that women would like to know more about the tests involved in routine ante-natal screening, and would like to be given their results (Macintyre 1981; Perfrement 1982). Doctors, on the other hand, tend to give general reassurance about the test rather than a proper explanation, a situation which women found less than satisfactory. However, there was more likelihood of an explanation when routine tests were used for non-routine purposes (Macintyre 1981; Perfrement 1982; Draper et al. 1984).

Ultrasound as a pre-natal test is interesting, as it constitutes both a screening test applied at around sixteen weeks to quite a lot of pregnant women, and it may also be used as a diagnostic test. There is currently controversy over ultrasound, and statements have come from both the USA and from Britain concerning its efficacy and safety as a *routine* screening test (NIH 1984; RCOG 1984). These reports have resulted in further debate, to which—interestingly, as an indication of the power of consumers in the 1980s—consumer organizations have added their contributions (Shearer 1984).

Studies of women's reactions to ultrasound have shown that it confirms a woman's pregnancy even before she herself may have felt the baby (Milne and Rich 1981; Hyde 1986). Women also report finding the experience anxiety-allaying (Milne and Rich 1981; Hyde 1986) (although we shall argue later that in some circumstances seeing the baby at this stage could be a negative as well as a positive feature). However, Hyde noted (as did Stewart (1986)) a varied response to ultrasound, with not all women finding the experience reassuring. While Petchesky (1987) also acknowledges that many women like

having an ultrasound test, she argues that their class, age, sexual preference, reproductive history, and, of course, whether or not they want the baby are important variables affecting how women 'see' the baby, and their overall experience of ultrasound. Hyde underlined the importance of good feedback for women during the experience, and suggested that low feedback from the technician could actually be negative or harmful (Hyde 1986).

Amniocentesis is increasingly used to test for such conditions as chromosomal disorders and inborn metabolic errors of the fetus (including Tay-Sachs disease). Estimates of the risk of the procedure vary, but if an experienced obstetrician carries out the amniocentesis using modern ultrasound techniques, the chances of causing a miscarriage are said to be as low as 0.5 per cent (Leschot, Verjaal, and Treffers 1985). The test is carried out between sixteen and twenty weeks of pregnancy, and consists of inserting a long needle into the uterus, with the use of ultrasound for guidance, and drawing out from the amniotic sac a small amount of fluid which contains some fetal cells. Processing the test (which involves growing the cells in a culture) takes up to four weeks, making the result available between nineteen and twenty weeks.

The social experience and aftermath of amniocentesis have perhaps been studied more than any other diagnostic test. Overall, women report that, unlike ultrasound, undergoing amniocentesis is a less immediately reassuring experience. Katz Rothman, for example, reported that a few of her sample of sixty women had a repeat test because of problems in the initial collection of the fluid (Katz Rothman 1986). Women are worried about pain or about potential harm to the baby (Beeson and Golbus 1979; Katz Rothman 1986). The test is said to be relatively painless, although a few women did report experiencing pain from the procedure (15 per cent of one sample (Finley *et al.* 1977)). Like ultrasound, however (Hyde 1986), it has been suggested that anxiety can be reduced if the woman is able to take a companion in with her (Draper *et al.* 1984), and if the test is carried out by a sensitive operator whose attitudes towards the woman, and the time taken over the procedure, make her feel relaxed (e.g. Boyd and Sellars 1982). Knowledge about the test is variable, and certainly not

all women know of the risks attached to the procedure (e.g. Farrant 1985).

We have seen that diagnostic tests are only usually applied to those who have undergone some form of screening (even if it is only the fact of being over the age of 35 which has placed the woman in a high-risk category). But a distinction needs to be made within this group of women undergoing diagnostic tests. In an important paper on the topic, Farrant (1985) notes the difference in women's reactions depending upon whether the diagnostic test was required because of a known risk (e.g. a previous affected baby), or was done as 'a bolt from the blue', that is, because routine screening indicated signs of a possible disorder in the pregnancy. Farrant's study of 135 London women who had undergone amniocentesis for neural tube defects indicated that while both categories of women were pleased to have the tests available, those who had been identified as 'at risk' through routine AFP screening found the experience much more distressing (Farrant 1985). Others have taken as their sample, women with no previous history of neural tube defects (i.e. the group Farrant had identified as being at high risk), and measured the women's stress before amniocentesis. They showed how stress increased before the test and only decreased when the (negative) results were known (e.g. Robinson, Hibbard, and Laurence 1984). However, an Italian study (Michelacci *et al.* 1984) of forty women undergoing amniocentesis argued that those undergoing the test for genetic indications showed *higher* levels of psychological stress than those being tested because of their age. They also showed that while stress may fall after amniocentesis, the level rose again in the third trimester for all their sample.

It has been argued elsewhere that the reduction in stress depends upon the way in which the patient is informed of the result; those who are not told anything, on the grounds that 'no news is good news', remain much more anxious (Fearn, Hibbard, and Robinson 1982). (In fact, a wealth of studies comment on the poor procedures for information- and result-giving). Genetic counsellors are still learning the best ways to present information to families, and a number of authors now suggest that for many parents counselling advice is only the

first step in a long process of decision-making about the future of the pregnancy (Lippman-Hand and Fraser 1979).

One alternative test which may lead to less dependence upon amniocentesis is the development of chorionic villus sampling (CVS). CVS can be carried out at around eight to twelve weeks, and is used to diagnose chromosomal ab-normalities and inherited disorders, and to make gene probe tests to detect haemoglobinopathies, muscular dystrophy, haemophilia, Huntington's disease, and others, but *not* neural tube defects. The procedure involves aspiration of a small sample of chorionic villi, the tissue developing around the placenta, from which chromosomal analysis can be performed. Unlike amniocentesis, the result can be known within a few days.

The advantages over amniocentesis are obvious. If problems are diagnosed, the technical procedure of aborting a fetus at ten weeks by vacuum aspiration is simpler and more acceptable to both the mother and the practitioner than a possible second-trimester abortion. Women could make the decision to abort long before they actually feel the baby, or even 'see' it through ultrasound. At eight or nine weeks a woman would not be obviously pregnant, and if the couple do decide to abort, it could remain a less public decision. If the woman is at high risk, and the fetus is found to be normal, then she can enjoy the remainder of her pregnancy safe in that knowledge (although it can never be forgotten that the diagnosis is only for certain identifiable disorders). Current drawbacks to the procedure are that the precise risks are not known, and unnecessary decisions to abort are sometimes made after the test (a percentage of fetuses spontaneously abort within these early months) (Wyatt 1985).

At the time of writing, CVS is undergoing randomized multicentred trials run by the MRC (although the test is currently offered in a number of centres outside the trial). While the outcome of the trial is not yet known, consumer demand has already been tested, albeit hypothetically. Several studies have asked women to choose, hypothetically, between amniocentesis and CVS (Lippman *et al.* 1985; McGovern, Goldberg, and Desnick 1986; Bryce, Bradley, and McCormick, 1989). In the first of these studies, detailed information about

each test was given to a sample of women aged over 35 who were scheduled for amniocentesis. Approximately half the women chose amniocentesis, and half CVS; the known risk favoured choosing the former, while the timing and the nature of the test favoured the latter. If the risk were established to be the same in both, 82 per cent of the women said that they would prefer CVS (Lippman *et al.* 1985). Findings in the other studies were very similar.

Availability, Access, and Use

In Britain and America genetic disorders are known to occur in 3 to 5 per cent of all births, and chromosomal disorders in at least 0.5 per cent (Kevles 1986). However, a number of studies from Britain and elsewhere show that a far smaller proportion of the population than those who are actually at risk undergo appropriate pre-natal screening and diagnosis. It is estimated in the U.S.A. that in 1979–80 'only half the women who were deemed medically appropriate for amniocentesis underwent the procedure, and it was being peformed on only 10 per cent of a comparable group within Britain' (Kevles 1986: 291–2). This suggests a gulf between the scientific discovery of a test and its practical availability to, and use by, the appropriate population. In order to understand why this is so, we must consider a number of interacting issues.

The first point underlined by international studies is that there is considerable variation in the national availability of different tests. A study across EEC countries shows that women in Britain may undergo fewer tests than many of their European counterparts, for whom an array of different screening and diagnostic tests have been cited as 'routine' (Heringa and Huisjes 1988). In Belgium, not only are women subject to a considerably larger number of screening tests, but some undergo the same tests more than once during the pregnancy (the Wassermann test for syphilis, for example). Testing for hepatitis B virus is routine in Belgium and Italy, but less common elsewhere; rubella testing is routine in Britain and a number of other EEC countries, but is only

recommended in Greece and Denmark (Heringa and Huisjes 1988).

The availability of some tests may be geographically variable even within one country; AFP testing, for example, is more common in Britain than in some European countries, but it is subject to regional differences in Britain and elsewhere (e.g. in Sweden (Schnittger and Kjessler 1984) and America (Hook and Schreinermachers 1983), amongst others). The explanation which may at first present itself is that the variation largely depends upon the incidence of the condition, in this case neural tube defects, which themselves appear to have a variable geographical distribution. But while it is true that some conditions are more common in certain areas and populations (Constantinides 1987), this is only part of the story. The apparent arbitrariness of the minimum maternal age (anything from 32–40 years of age) at which screening for chromosomal disorders becomes routine within different areas in Britain suggests in itself that other—more social and political—explanations have a bearing on the availability of tests. One reason for variation between Britain and Belgium is provided by the overall structure of their respective health services. In Belgium, state hospitals are paid per test, and there is therefore considerable pressure on hospitals to adopt as routine a large number of screening tests. Physician behaviour affects referrals in both private and state-run health systems. In the USA there is evidence of over-testing of patients; fear of litigation may encourage doctors to practise cautious medicine. Research has also emphasized that physicians' knowledge about the test is important for a percentage of client referrals (Lippman-Hand and Cohen 1980), as well as the type of practice in which they are based (Leighton Read *et al.* 1983).

Other interrelated issues are accessibility and usage. Here the explanations move further into the realms of behaviour, knowledge, and attitudes—of professionals as well as consumers. In Britain the incidence of sickle cell anaemia and thalassaemia is known to be high amongst those from (or with parents or grandparents from) the Mediterranean, the Indian sub-continent, West Africa, or the Caribbean. Uptake of screening services varies, however. In certain communities in

London the uptake of screening services for beta-thalassaemia has been good (Modell and Mouzouras 1982); this may be the result of a combination of awareness from the at-risk group itself, helped by a good health education programme, a cultural pattern of marriage within the community, and the presence of an individual enthusiast. Community health programmes have been successful; the public health programme organized by the WHO, for example, resulted in a huge international reduction of thalassaemia births (Kuliev 1986). However, screening must extend beyond the limited population of pregnant women, since these programmes depend upon carrier-detection of the disease within families (especially for recessive inherited diseases).

Aside from community-wide programmes, middle-class (or middle-income) women generally have greater 'social access' to health care and, in this case, to the available screening and diagnostic tests than the large category of working-class (or lower-income), socially disadvantaged, black, rural, and older women (e.g. see Adams *et al.* 1981; Davies and Doran 1982; Chamberlain 1984). While this relates to the ability to pay in countries such as the USA, the uneven and late usage of ante-natal care is well documented even with state-financed health care, where diagnostic tests may be (theoretically) more available to all (Garcia 1982). One of the findings of a study by Knott and his colleagues was the low take-up of amniocentesis amongst Asian women, some of whom did not appear to have even received counselling on the topic (Knott, Penketh, and Lucas 1986).

The timing of pre-natal screening tests is important. In their Welsh study of AFP screening, Roberts and his colleagues found that 30 per cent of their large sample of women were not screened for AFP. They acknowledged that the lateness of women being booked into the hospital ante-natal clinic was due to slow administration and the general practitioners themselves, but part of the problem was women's initial delay in going to their general practitioners (Roberts *et al.* 1983). CVS requires a woman to go to her GP by the time she is eight weeks pregnant, a date which at present would exclude many from the test (especially multiparous women and those who, for a variety of reasons, do not wish to acknowledge the pregnancy). Good pre-natal and even pre-pregnancy information is always important, but especially in this situation.

There is currently discussion in Britain about the anonymous screening of all pregnant women for the HIV virus (see e.g. *The Times* 23 Jan. 1988). While the Wassermann test has been practised without query for many years (essentially anonymously, since very few women knew they were being tested for syphilis), the recent AIDS debate has rekindled many of the more general issues associated with the introduction of full-scale, anonymous screening. These include the possibility of creating anxiety through false positives (although it is said that the test for HIV virus has a high degree of sensitivity and specificity), the invasion of privacy, and the social consequences of informing someone unsuspecting that their test is positive.

Social and Moral Dilemmas: 'Screening is Sometimes Used as a Substitute for Thinking'

This chapter has not yet dealt in any detail with the problems facing couples when they come into contact with pre-natal screening. These are often problems with a strong social and moral component which force the couple, and the family, to make decisions with lifelong impact. The imperfections of science merely add to the stress. Thomas (1986) notes that while few tests have 100 per cent accuracy, a growing number are at least 90 per cent accurate. However, there is always the fear of false positives—the result being read inaccurately as positive and the woman being told in error that a problem exists with the fetus. Although there has been considerable interest in assessing the reliability of the many tests, there is little written about the social consequences of false positives (or false negatives). Not surprisingly, the one study traced (Burton, Dillard, and Clark 1985) reports on the high anxiety level for such women, which only decreases after further explanation and counselling.

There are many other examples where the test fails to yield results. It may be that the fluid collected during the test was insufficient, became contaminated, or, in the case of amniocentesis, there was a culture failure. Recessive sex-linked diseases in which the females are carriers while the male develops the condition, pose yet other problems. For many such conditions pre-natal diagnosis can detect only the sex of the fetus, but not (as yet) whether the male child has inherited the condition. Recently, however, DNA techniques (particularly following CVS) can produce more accurate information about, for example, haemophilia and Duchenne's Muscular Dystrophy.

One of the critical issues inherent in any discussion of screening concerns abortion. Fletcher (1983) has argued that this is the most controversial issue surrounding pre-natal diagnosis, and certainly a number of unspoken assumptions regarding abortion lie behind many of the screening procedures. Let us take ultrasound, for example. During the ultrasound examination, the mother lies back watching the screen while the operator identifies the baby with the equipment, and then shows the moving picture of the fetus to the mother. If the mother has not yet felt the baby, this may be her first introduction to her child as a live entity; yet, ironically, the test may identify malformations or serious deformities which suggest that life outside the uterus is not viable.

Research has brought to light the difficulties that the mother may experience in undergoing ultrasound. While for some it may mean the chance to bond earlier with their babies, others are forced (especially if ultrasound is used nonroutinely) to identify with a baby that they may have to consider aborting (Silvestre and Fresco 1980; Katz Rothman 1986). Whether or not to have an abortion following amniocentesis is one of the most difficult decisions a woman may have to face (Nielson 1981; and others), and one can only guess that the use of ultrasound does not help this choice. The dilemma seems to encapsulate the double-edged status of such tests, which both save lives but also make decisions about life more difficult to make.

This topic is sensitively dealt with by Katz Rothman (1986). In her study of sixty women undergoing amniocentesis she emphasizes the difficulties faced by women who wish to suspend their 'bonding' with the fetus until after the results of their amniocentesis. She confirms that some women manage to create this state of 'suspended animation', ignoring signs of quickening, and repressing thoughts of the baby—maintaining the pregnancy as tentative until the test outcome is known.

Pre-natal diagnosis personalizes the decision about abortion. Thus, a difference exists between someone wishing an abortion after pre-natal diagnosis, and someone wishing an abortion for 'social' reasons—because they were under age or did not want a baby at this stage in their lives. In the latter example, the decision to abort represents a general wish not to have a baby. In the former instance the decision to abort becomes a personal one. It is not that the couple want an abortion, but that they wish to abort *this particular fetus*. Hubbard puts it slightly differently: 'It is one thing to abort when we don't want to be pregnant and quite another to want a baby but decide to abort the particular fetus we are carrying in hopes of coming up with a "better" one next time.' (Hubbard 1984: 334.)

The understanding that abortion *should* follow amniocentesis is at times made explicit in the literature ('Of course most centres take care to ensure a commitment to abortion if the outcome of the test should be abnormal before arranging amniocentesis' (Muir Gray 1984: 528)), as well as being shown through research. Some of the women in Farrant's sample reported being pressurized to go through with an abortion even though they had changed their mind since their pre-test agreement (Farrant 1985). This study underlined the contradictory views of abortion held by obstetricians, some of whom oppose it on social and psychological grounds while supporting it for fetal diagnosis. Farrant and others question the potential decision-making of pre-natal diagnosis: is it a choice if the woman is pressurized into having an abortion after amniocentesis?

The package of 'pre-natal diagnosis with selective abortion' presents the latter as the solution to the clinical problem. Jerome Lejeune, the scientist who discovered the abnormal chromosomal count which creates Down's syndrome, is vehemently opposed to abortion being seen as the 'cure' for Down's syndrome: 'Amniocentesis and abortion injure the practice of medical science,' he writes. 'They have transformed the traditional goal of medicine from a cure to an attack on the patient. Young medical-genetic students ask me these days why I continue to work on Trisomy 21—after all, Down's fetuses can be discarded. I think of Trisomy 21 as a symptom of disease. The students think of it as a symptom of death.' (Lejeune, quoted in Kevles 1986: 287.) Others, from very different motives, have shared the same sentiment, arguing that attention is thus detracted from primary prevention and from concern about environmental and occupational health hazards which may carry a genetic risk.

At least some of the difficulties to do with bonding and ultrasound at sixteen weeks could be bypassed if and when CVS is introduced routinely. However, while CVS may appear to solve some difficulties (late-trimester abortions, for example), it continues and intensifies other issues raised by amniocentesis. There is now evidence that couples are using pre-natal diagnosis for sex selection (sex identification being an essential part of chromosomal analysis). The reports range from occurrences in America (*Hospitals* 16 Sept. 1985) to a recent British report of the same problem (the *Independent* 4 Jan. 1988), when it was suggested that it was Asian and Middle-Eastern women with a preference for boy babies who were abusing pre-natal screening tests in Great Britain. All of the reports condemned the practice, and suggest that legislation would be needed to ban sex disclosure. Abortion for a fetus of the wrong sex may be difficult to obtain on the NHS, but in the private sector and in other countries where the consumer has strong buying power (as in the USA), sex selection may well become one of the many choices facing the middle-class client. A report from MIDIRS notes that the use of CVS was curtailed in China, where it was abused as a test for sex selection (MIDIRS 1986).

Choice is, of course, a middle-class option, no less in childbirth than elsewhere in life. But, as some point out, choices are socially created and socially constrained (Katz Rothman 1984). First, they are socially created by the technology available at the time and place. Today, women over the age of 40 can 'check' on the fetus pre-natally with amniocentesis, and Swerts found that the availability of pre-natal diagnosis played a major role in the decisions of families who already had a child affected by Down's syndrome or with a neural tube defect (Swerts 1987). This kind of choice is socially constrained, however; while middle-class couples can choose, and see their choices through to fruition, others have less choice and far less resources with which to fulfil their wishes. In the USA for example, working-class (lower-income) women can only choose what is open to them; abortion is not always on offer, while hysterectomies are covered by social insurance (Hubbard 1984).

Choice is not only constrained by money, but also by lack of knowledge and by social conventions. This is most clearly seen in the issue of disability. Couples report considerable problems in accepting the birth of an abnormal baby; they experience guilt at the imperfectness of the child. Given the state of medical science, some may tend to accept their lot and raise the child, while others may send the child to an institution. Writing forcibly on the matter, Saxton (1984) argues that choice depends upon how the options are presented. Contemporary society has both stereotyped and limited perceptions of disability; the disabled child is seen in very negative terms as unfulfilled, suffering, and unable to take on responsible adulthood. The 'choice' of whether or not a woman would wish to abort her disabled fetus is weighted against the fetus. Unfortunately, pre-natal diagnostic tests do little to help these social constructions of normality; in fact, they undermine the 'disabled' view of normality by emphasizing the genetic differences of these babies. A recent British meeting on the topic underlined this concern over the increasing stigmatization of disabled people and their families, and the possible impairment of services for the disabled (Kings Fund Forum Consensus Statement 1987). And while many would continue to maintain that abortion should be available on demand, one could also argue that its liberal availability will ultimately encourage a divided society, split between the 'perfect' and those whose abnormality was not picked up pre-natally and who are not born 'perfect'.

Recent advances in the field of medical genetics create other dilemmas. Families with one affected child are now being given the opportunity to have their next child tested *in utero*. While for some this may be a relief, for others, and for those children already born with the condition, it may present difficulties; for the child, especially, may come the realization that they might not have been born had their parents been given this choice (Black and Furlong 1984). Because of this, the impact of screening and diagnostic tests should be considered in the context of the whole family rather than simply in terms of the mother or the couple. In fact, studies of family building after the birth of a child affected with cystic fibrosis (Evers-Kiebooms 1987), Down's syndrome (Boon 1986), and Down's syndrome and neural tube defects (Swerts 1987) all found there to be a subsequent reduction. However, Swerts's couples noted the positive influence of genetic counselling with regard to family building.

Since the 1980s it has been possible to identify more inherited diseases. Some of these are rare, and may affect only a small percentage of the population. Others, such as the finding of the marker for sickle cell anaemia, touch more lives than we may know. Huntington's disease, an autosomal dominant disease which affects both sexes with lethal outcome, has an average onset age of 41 years. With the identification of the gene for this disease, a screening test can now discover with 95 per cent accuracy whether a fetus is affected, and, indeed, blood tests can identify whether any member of the family carries the gene or not. While one interpretation of this is undoubtedly progress, such knowledge creates considerable stresses for families who, prior to this scientific discovery, lived knowing only that they were 'at risk'. Bird (1985) quotes one study which suggests that the rate of suicide for those newly diagnosed or suspected of Huntington's disease is 4–14 times higher than that of the general population. Such knowledge could also result in exclusion from jobs, and problems with life- and house- insurance. The issue now facing at-risk families is whether or not to find out for certain (Evers-Kiebooms 1987). Thus, for certain families, pregnancy may be the first time they have thought about their own genetic history.

The Future

Looking into the 1990s one can begin to make a number of predictions; partly speculation, but in part guided by the achievements of science over this decade. In the broad field of reproduction, there is speculation over such possibilities as male pregnancy (Kent 1986), the choice of an 'in-body or an out-body' pregnancy (Hubbard 1984), and gene surgery and cloning becoming a matter of routine. It may be that sex selection becomes normal practice, and that couples will sue their geneticist if their infant is born female or has fair hair, instead of the dark-haired boy they requested.

There is evidence from a case in hearing in 1988 that fetal rights are becoming an important issue in the USA, shifting the emphasis from the pregnant women to the primacy of the fetus. Some women writers have long argued that reproductive technologies represent a male desire to control women's unique ability to reproduce (e.g. Corea 1985; Overall 1987; Stanworth 1987), and that the controversy over fetal rights is yet another example of how such technologies may be turned against women. While there is considerable discussion on the topic at the moment, no one line has emerged as the feminist stance, nor is consensus likely to be achieved. Screening tests are, it is widely argued, an extension into pregnancy of the medicalization of childbirth. Yet the issues are complex, for reproductive technology (such as amniocentesis) may be used in a way which benefits many women, but at the same time creates further problems for others (see Feldman 1987 for a useful analysis).

The 1970s and early 1980s were a time for establishing some choices in birth; the 1990s will bring a change of focus from the birth to the pregnancy itself. In future, concern will not be with long queues and short consultations (albeit symptomatic of deeper problems), but rather with the many choices offered by pre-natal screening and diagnostic tests. Writing from the forefront of molecular genetics, Evans (1986) suggests that the day will soon come when detailed diagnosis for recessive diseases will be routine in pre-natal care. And from gene identification it is a short step to the further development of gene surgery—mending genes *in utero*.

It is likely that the use of screening tests will continue and, indeed, will be extended well beyond their pre-natal use. In decades to come we may well learn more about our genetic inheritance, accepting a greater intrusion into our biology through increased population-screening programmes for such recessive-inherited diseases as cystic fibrosis. It has already been suggested that pre-pregnancy tests are to be on the agenda of tomorrow's young people. What are regarded as the miracles of science today will no doubt become the everyday choices of tomorrow.

320 *Margaret Reid*

References

Adams, M., Finley, S., Hansen, H., Jahiel, R., Oakley, G., Sanger, S., Wells, G., and Wertelecki, W., 1981, 'Utilization of Prenatal Genetic Diagnosis in Women 35 Years of Age and Older in the United States, 1977–1978', *American Journal of Obstetrics and Gynecology*, 139, pp. 673–7.

Beeson, D. and Golbus, M., 1979, 'Anxiety Engendered by Amniocentesis', *Birth Defects: Original Article Series*, 15/5c, pp. 191–7.

Bird, S., 1985, 'Presymptomatic Testing for Huntington's Disease', *Journal of the American Medical Association*, 253/22, pp. 3286–91.

Black, R. B. and Furlong, R., 1984, 'Impact of Prenatal Diagnosis on Families', *Social Work in Health Care*, 9/3, pp. 37–50.

Boon, A. R., 1986, 'Family Building in Parents with Down's Syndrome Children', *Journal of Epidemiology and Community Health*, 40, pp. 154–60.

Boyd, C. and Sellers, L., 1982, *That's Life Survey of the British Way of Birth* (London, Pan).

Breen, D., 1975, *The Birth of the First Child: Towards an Understanding of Femininity* (London, Tavistock).

Bryce, R. L., Bradley, M. T., and McCormick, S. M., 1989, 'To What Extent Would Women Prefer Chorionic Villus Sampling to Amniocentesis for Prenatal Diagnosis?', *Paediatric and Perinatal Epidemiology*, 3, pp. 137–45.

Burton, B. K., Dillard, R. G., and Clark, E. N., 1985, 'The Psychological Impact of False Positive Elevations of Maternal Serum Alpha-Feto-Protein', *American Journal of Obstetrics and Gynecology*, 151, pp. 77–82.

Campbell-Brown, M., McFadyn, I., Seal, D., and Stephenson, M., 1987, 'Is Screening for Bacteriuria in Pregnancy Worth While?', *British Medical Journal*, 294, 1579–82.

Chamberlain, J., 1984, editorial, 'The Benefits and Costs of Prenatal Diagnosis', *Revue d'Épidémiologie et de Santé Publique*, 32, pp. 85–7.

Constantinides, P., 1987, 'Health Care Services for Populations at Risk for Genetically Determined Disease', *New Community*, 13/3, pp. 359–66.

Corea, G. (ed.), 1987, *Man-Made Women: How New Reproductive Technologies Affect Women* (Indiana, Indiana University Press).

Davies, B. and Doran, T., 1982, 'Factors in a Woman's Decision to Undergo Genetic Amniocentesis for Advanced Maternal Age', *Nursing Research*, 31, pp. 56–9.

Draper, J., Field, H., and Thomas, H., 1984, *An Evaluation of a Community Antenatal Clinic* (Cambridge, Hughes Hall).

Evans, H. J., 1986, 'Molecular Genetics: What Is it and What Is its Impact on Current and Future Medical Practice?', *Health Bulletin*, 44/6, p. 319–29.

Evers-Kiebooms, G., 1987, 'Decision Making in Huntington's Disease and Cystic Fibrosis', *Birth Defects: Original Article Series*, 23/2, pp. 115–49.

Farrant, W., 1985, 'Who's for Amniocentesis? The Politics of Prenatal Screening', in H. Homans (ed.), *The Sexual Politics of Reproduction* (London, Gower).

Fearn, J., Hibbard, B. M. and Robinson, J. O., 1982, 'Screening for Neural-Tube Defects and Maternal Anxiety', *British Journal of Obstetrics and Gynaecology*, 89, pp. 218–21.

Feldman, R., 1987, 'The Politics of the New Reproductive Technologies', *Critical Social Policy*, 7/1, pp. 21–39.

Finley, S. C., Varner, P., Vinson, P., and Finley, W., 1977, 'Participants' Reaction to Amniocentesis and Prenatal Genetic Studies', *Journal of American Medical Association*, 238, pp. 2377–9.

Fletcher, J. C., 1983, 'Ethics and Trends in Applied Human Genetics', *Birth Defects: Original Article Series*, 19/5, pp. 143–58.

Garcia, J., 1982, 'Mothers' Views of Antenatal Care', in Enkin, M. and Chalmers, I. (eds.), *Effectiveness and Satisfaction in Antenatal Care* (London, Spastics International Medical Publications, Heinemann).

Graham, H. and McKee, L., 1979, *The First Months of Motherhood* (Report on a Health Education Council Project concerned with women's experiences of pregnancy, childbirth, and the first six months, *Medical Care*, 4, University of York).

Heringa, M. and Huisjes, H., 1988, 'Prenatal Screening: Current Policy in EC Countries', in Huisjes, H., Buekens, P., and Reid, M. E. (eds.), *Antenatal Screening: Current Policies in the EC and Evaluation* (Supplement to the *European Journal of Obstetrics, Gynaecology and Reproductive Biology*, 28, pp. 7–49.

Hook, E. B. and Schreinermachers, D. M., 1983, 'Trends in Utilization of Prenatal Cytogenetic Diagnosis by New York State Residents in 1979 and 1980', *American Journal of Public Health*, 73/2, pp. 198–202.

Hubbard, R., 1984, 'Personal Courage Is Not Enough: Some Hazards of Childbearing in the 1980s', in Arditti, R., Klein, R. D., and Minden, S. (eds.), *Test-Tube Women: What Future for Motherhood?* (London, Pandora Press).

Hyde, B., 1986, 'An Interview Study of Pregnant Women's

Attitudes to Ultrasound Scanning', *Social Science and Medicine*, 22/5, pp. 587–92.

Hytten, F. E., 1980, 'Weight Gain in Pregnancy', in Hytten, R. E. and Chamberlain, G. (eds.), *Clinical Physiology in Obstetrics* (Oxford, Blackwell).

Katz Rothman, B., 1984, 'The Meaning of Choice in Reproductive Technology', in Arditti, R., Klein, R. D., and Minden, S. (eds.), *Test-Tube Women: What Future for Motherhood?* (London, Pandora Press).

—— 1986, *The Tentative Pregnancy* (New York, Viking).

Kent, R., 1986, 'The Birth of the Male Pregnancy', *New Society*, 76, 9 May 1986, pp. 7–9.

Kevles, D. J., 1986, *In the Name of Eugenics: Genetics and the Uses of Human Heredity* (Harmondsworth, Pelican).

Kings Fund Forum: Screening for Fetal and Genetic Abnormality, 1987, *Consensus Statement* (London, King Edward's Hospital Fund for London).

Knott, P. D., Penketh, R. J. A., and Lucas, M. K., 1986, 'Uptake of Amniocentesis in Women Aged 38 Years or More by the Time of the Expected Date of Delivery: A Two-Year Retrospective Study', *British Journal of Obstetrics and Gynaecology*, 93, pp. 1246–50.

Kuliev, A. M., 1986, 'Thalassemia can be Prevented', *World Health Forum*, 7, pp. 286–90.

Leighton Read, J., Stern, R., Thibodeau, L., Gear, D., and Klapholz, H., 1983, 'Variation in Ante-Natal Testing over Time and between Clinic Settings', *Journal of the American Medical Association*, 249, pp. 1605–9.

Leschot, N. J., Verjaal, M., and Treffers, P. E., 1985, 'Risks of Midtrimester Amniocentesis: Assessment in 3000 Pregnancies', *British Journal of Obstetrics and Gynaecology*, 92/8, pp. 804–7.

Lippman, A., Perry, T., Mandel, S., and Cartier, L., 1985, 'Chorionic Villi Sampling: Women's Attitudes', *American Journal of Medical Genetics*, 22, pp. 395–401.

Lippman-Hand, A. and Fraser, F., 1979, 'Genetic Counseling: The Post Counseling Period, i. Parents' Perceptions of Uncertainty', *American Journal of Medical Genetics*, 4, pp. 51–71.

Lippman-Hand, A. and Cohen, D., 1980, 'Influence of Obstetricians' Attitudes on their Use of Prenatal Diagnosis for the Detection of Down's Syndrome', *Canadian Medical Journal*, 122, pp. 1331–6.

McGovern, M. M., Goldberg, J. D. and Desnick, R. J., 1986, 'Acceptability of Chorionic Villi Sampling for Prenatal Diagnosis', *American Journal of Obstetrics and Gynecology*, 155, 25–9.

Macintyre, S., 1978, 'Obstetric Routines in Antenatal Care', in

Davis, A. (ed.), *Relationships between Doctors and Patients* (London, Saxon House).

Macintyre, S. 1981, *Expectations and Experiences of Pregnancy: Report of a Prospective Study of Married Primagravida* (Institute of Medical Sociology, Occasional Paper 5, University of Aberdeen).

MacKenzie, W. E., Ashford, S., McNamara, A., Elliot, V., Millar, D., Innes, M., and Wild, S., 1986, 'An Assessment of Combined Symphysial-Fundal Height Measurements and Qualitative Amniotic Fluid Volume for the Antenatal Detection of Intra-Uterine Growth Retardation', *Journal of Obstetrics and Gynaecology*, 6, pp. 248–50.

Michelacci, L., Fava, G., Trombini, G., Zielezny, M., Bovicelli, L., and Orlandi, C., 1984, 'Psychological Distress and Amniocentesis', *Gynaecological and Obstetric Investigations*, 18/1, pp. 40–4.

MIDIRS, 1986, *Chorionic Villus sampling: A Review* (Midwives Information and Resources Service Information Pack, 1, Mar. 1986).

Milne, L. S. and Rich, O. J., 1981, 'Cognitive and Affective Aspects of the Responses of Pregnant Women to Sonography', *Maternal–Child Nursing Journal*, 10, pp. 15–39.

Modell, B. and Mouzouras, M., 1982, 'Social Consequences of Introducing Antenatal Diagnosis for Thalassemia', *Birth Defects*, 18/7, pp. 285–91.

Muir Gray, J. A., 1984, 'Needs of the Community', in Wald, N. J. (ed.), *Antenatal and Neonatal Screening* (Oxford, Oxford University Press).

National Institutes of Health Consensus Development Conference, Consensus Statement, 1984, 'The Use of Diagnostic Ultrasound Imaging in Pregnancy', (Bethesda, Maryland, National Institute of Health).

Nielson, C., 1981, 'An Encounter with Modern Medical Technology: Women's Experiences with Amniocentesis', *Women and Health*, 6, pp. 109–24.

Oakley, A., 1979, *Becoming a Mother* (Oxford, Martin Robertson).

—— 1980, *Women Confined: Towards a Sociology of Childbirth* (Oxford, Martin Robertson).

—— 1984, *The Captured Womb* (Oxford, Blackwell).

Overall, C., 1987, *Ethics and Human Reproduction: A Feminist Analysis* (Boston, Allen and Unwin).

Pearce, J. M. and Campbell, S., 1987, 'A Comparison of Symphasis-Fundal Height and Ultrasound as Screening Tests for Light for Gestational Age Infants', *British Journal of Obstetrics and Gynaecology*, 94/2, pp. 100–4.

Perfrement, S., 1982, *Women's Information on Pregnancy, Childbirth and Babycare* (Centre for Medical Research, University of Sussex).

Petchesky, R. P., 1987, 'Artificial Insemination, In-Vitro Fertilisation and the Stigma of Infertility', in Stanworth, M. (ed.), *Reproductive Technologies: Gender, Motherhood and Medicine* (Cambridge, Polity Press with Blackwell).

Roberts, C. J., Elder, G., Laurence, K., Woodhead, J., Hibbard, B., Evans, K., Roberts, A., Robertson, I., and Hoole, M., 1983, 'The Efficacy of a Serum Screening Service for Neural-Tube Defects: The South Wales Experience', The *Lancet*, 337, pp. 1315–18.

Robinson, O., Hibbard, B. M., and Laurence, K. M., 1984, 'Anxiety during a Crisis: Emotional Effects of Screening for Neural Tube Defects', *Journal of Psychosomatic Research*, 28/2, pp. 163–9.

Royal College of Obstetricians and Gynaecologists, 1984, *Report of the RCOG Working Party of Routine Ultrasound Examination in Pregnancy* (London, RCOG).

Saxton, M., 1984, 'Born and Unborn: The Implications of Reproductive Technologies for People with Disabilities', in Arditti, R., Klein, R. D., and Minden, S. (eds.), *Test-Tube Women: What Future for Motherhood?* (London, Pandora Press).

Schnittger, A. and Kjessler, B., 1984, 'Alpha-Feto Protein Screening in Obstetric Practice', *Acta Obstetrica Gynaecologica Scandinavica*, Supplement 119, pp. 25–31.

Shearer, M. H., 1984, 'Revelations: A Summary and Analysis of the NIH Consensus Development Conference on Ultrasound Imaging in Pregnancy', *Birth*, 11, p. 1.

Silvestre, D. and Fresco, N., 1980, 'Reaction to Prenatal Diagnosis: An Analysis of 87 Interviews', *American Journal of Orthopsychiatry*, 50/4, pp. 610–17.

Stanworth, M. (ed.), 1987, *Reproductive Technologies: Gender, Motherhood and Medicine* (Cambridge, Polity Press with Blackwell).

Stewart, N., 1986, 'Women's Views of Ultrasonography in Obstetrics', *Birth*, 13, pp. 39–43.

Swerts, A., 1987, 'Impact of Genetic Counselling and Pre-Natal Diagnosis for Down's Syndrome and Neural Tube Defects', *Birth Defects: Original Article Series*, 23/2, pp. 61–83.

Thomas, S., 1986, *Genetic Risk: A Book for Parents and Prospective Parents* (Harmondsworth, Pelican Books).

Tyler, A., 1987, 'Genetic Counseling in Huntington's Chorea', *Birth Defects: Original Article Series*, 23/2, pp. 85–95.

Varma, T. R., 1984, 'Maternal Weight Gain in Pregnancy and Obstetric Outcome', *International Journal of Gynaecology and Obstetrics*, 22, pp. 161–6.

Wald, N. J., 1984, 'Conclusions', in Wald, N. J. (ed.), *Antenatal and Neonatal Screening* (Oxford, Oxford University Press).

Wyatt, P. R., 1985, 'Chorionic Biopsy and Increased Anxiety', The *Lancet*, 2, pp. 1312–13.

17

How Obstetrics Might Change:
Wendy Savage Talks to Robert Kilpatrick

Wendy Savage

SINCE 1977 Wendy Savage has been Senior Lecturer and Honorary Consultant in Obstetrics and Gynaecology at the London Hospital. A long dispute with some of her colleagues about the nature of obstetric practice and medical power culminated with her suspension from medical practice in April 1985 for allegedly being a 'danger to her patients'. Her fight to clear her name received very wide public support, not least among the women for whose care she had been responsible and their general practitioners. She was fully exonerated by a public inquiry and was reinstated in July 1986. These events are described in *A Savage Enquiry: Who Controls Childbirth* (London, Virago Press, 1986).

RK: I would like to begin with an obvious question: why did you become an obstetrician and what were your expectations about such a career?

WS: When I was a student I liked obstetrics best. I think a lot of students do like obstetrics best, because it is one of the few times you are allowed to do something. I did my house jobs and then I went to the States to do research, which I enjoyed. Later I became what is known as a General Duty Medical Officer in West Africa. I did everything. At the end of that year I decided that I really did want to do obstetrics and gynaecology; not because of any great feminist input, or because I thought that the system was wrong and I wanted to change it, but because I found it the most interesting branch of medicine. It has a combination of medicine and surgery, and it's not all about death and disease. It's very positive because you are around at the time of birth, which is such a fantastic experience. And I was impressed by the way that women dealt with it all.

RK: Was there anything in your training as a medical student that led you to question the medical profession's control of pregnancy and birth?

WS: I think my questioning began when I saw how women dealt with childbirth. When I had finished working in Africa, I certainly had reached the position that birth was a dangerous event. The skills that I had learnt were those which made you think that you could predict which woman was not going to make it, and needed a Caesarean section quite early on in labour. I came back and worked at the Royal Free Hospital. It was just after the abortion law had changed, and so I had also questioned the teaching about abortion in Africa, because it just seemed crazy that women were killing themselves with self-induced attempts at abortion when we could have done it safely. When I spoke to my bosses about it, they said, that is the law and there is nothing you can do about it. I think one of the things that made me sceptical about the medical profession was the discrepancy between what those people said and what they did.

RK: Do you mean the doctors?

WS: Yes. The senior doctors.

RK: Do you think that you have been led to criticize the present state of maternity care in Britain because you are a woman obstetrician?

WS: Well I think that has something to do with it, yes. But I do not think it is the whole story, because there are many women obstetricians who do not challenge the system. It is more that I am not particularly a conformist, and somehow I never really felt inside the system. So I somehow retained this scepticism.

RK: I wonder if there is something about the career structure of obstetrics that produces conformity?

WS: I think it has become very narrow, yes. Getting my membership of the Royal College of Obstetrics and Gynaecology was a sweat, because I did a one-in-two job[1] and my youngest was 6 months old. I had four children, builders in the house, and on alternate weekends I went to the hospital on Friday at 8.00 a.m. and did not come home until 6.30 p.m. on Monday.

RK: You are tiring me just telling me!

WS: When you look at people who get into obstetrics, they are not necessarily those who really one would want to go into obstetrics, but the ones that can stand the training as organized. They are not necessarily the ones that I would have chosen. When I look at the good students, that I would like to see going into obstetrics, they are not usually doing that.

RK: What is a good student?

WS: They do not accept all they are told uncritically, just like a lot of sponges, and also they can relate to people.

RK: Do you think that the system weeds out a lot of good people?

WS: A lot of them are very sensitive, but I think that the training distances them from patients, and being a house officer is the final killer. You think about it, the torture by sleep deprivation [*laughs*]. It is quite surprising that any of them come out of it as reasonable people!

RK: How do you think medical education should be changed?

WS: Well, you would have to change the medical profession itself. I think that in our society we have reached a point where we should seriously question whether the structures that have built up over the last hundred years are what we need for the next century. For example, we should take far more mature students. The idea that somebody slogs away at school from the age of 5 to 18, then goes straight into a five-year course, having never had any experience outside of that environment, is absurd. Most students go into this really distorting environment, where until very recently, as young men, they have been surrounded by a large number of young women in training, but all at the lesser levels in the

[1] A 1-in-2 rota involves working for alternate days and nights and alternate weekends.

hierarchy—the nurses, physiotherapists, dieticians, and radiographers. It is a double hierarchical system, in which the medical student is at the bottom of the pecking order of doctors but high up in the pecking order of the hospital, which is organized on gender lines. Medical students learn very early on, if they are at all politically astute; they discover that the way to succeed is to keep their mouths shut and not ask disturbing questions. Once they get to their clinical years, they realize that this includes intellectual questioning. In the pre-clinical years they are allowed to ask intellectually disturbing questions, but once they get on to the wards, the people who are teaching them do not take kindly to students asking about the basis on which decisions are made. In the United States, students do a degree course, which can be a liberal arts degree, and then go off to do their medical course. Whereas here, as you know, medical students spend almost all their five or six years in scientific and medical training. Despite this, there is not much difference in the practical abilities of American doctors compared to British doctors. So, clearly it is not necessary to cram people full of physics and chemistry and biochemistry and physiology right from the age of 18. You can do other things, and I think that in itself would be more liberating. However, what you find is that the powerful professors are very sceptical about subjects like sociology: 'What are we doing wasting our time teaching students sociology when they ought to be learning about cancer', is a common attitude.

RK: I wonder, in the case of obstetricians, how the training might influence their perceptions of childbirth?

WS: Training takes place in hospital, and so students do not know what normal labour is. And the only time in their careers when they will sit with a woman in labour is when they are a student. The general belief is that you advance in your profession by taking part in research, not sitting with women in labour. Research, whilst laudable in itself, takes people away from doing more practical things, so that you have a danger that professors of obstetrics will be heavily research-orientated but not much good at the practical sphere and do not spend as much time actually with women as in the past.

RK: But are not most babies in Britain delivered by midwives?

WS: Yes. And so the time that you learn about normal—or at least spontaneous delivery—is when you are a student. You are supposed to have observed at least fifteen labours in order to take your exam in London, and it is much the same in the other medical schools. The deliveries have to be normal ones, but there is a tendency for people to call the students to 'the interesting things', like Caesars, and so the students' perception of what birth is all about is distorted to the abnormal. Once they become a house officer they do not sit with women having normal labours, they are called when something goes wrong. And then as registrars they do intervene when something goes wrong, and as consultants they only go into the labour ward when something is seriously wrong. The view that people like myself take, that pregnancy is not an illness and everything is normal until it is seen to go wrong, is seen as dangerous because it is said that we will not intervene early enough. I believe that for the majority of obstetricians, because their training is so distorted by only seeing women labouring in hospital where the climate is alien for many women, and because they are trained to deal in abnormal obstetrics, they genuinely believe it is because of their own efforts that the perinatal mortality has declined.

RK: What has led you to see things in new ways?

WS: Once a woman at Charing Cross Hospital said to me that my advice to her to have pethidine had been the wrong advice. Now, I think that had somebody said that to me earlier in my career, I probably would not have been able to accept it, because I was insecure then and I might well have reacted defensively. But later, because I had been running my own practice in New Zealand, I was able to listen to what she said, and I realized that I was wrong. Subsequently I came to work for Peter Huntingford, who was very perceptive and a brilliant teacher. I have never forgotten an occasion when I went into the labour ward where a woman was pushing. It was clear to me that she was pushing ineffectively and she was going to need assistance with her delivery. When we had left her, I said to Peter: 'Why aren't we doing a forceps?' And he said to me: 'She's not ready to give up yet.'

RK: Are you willing to say that it is safer to have a baby at home?

WS: It is safer in the sense that you are more likely to achieve a normal delivery and have a normal labour. And if you have a normal delivery and a normal labour, you are more likely to have a healthy baby.

RK: What are the advantages and drawbacks of home delivery?

WS: The advantages are that you are in your own place, and you are in charge there, so that the professionals who come in are visitors. It is your territory not their territory, and you are not subjected to the rules of an institution. It is also an advantage that you are looked after by a midwife and a GP that you know. Of course, with the way that domiciliary midwives are organized these days, that does not always happen, and you may have someone you do not know. But at least you will have a midwife who is likely to believe that birth is a natural process, and who has come to terms with her own anxiety about the uncertainty of childbirth. The third advantage is that you do not have to move when you are in labour. If you look at animals, they go and make themselves a little dark hole and make it ready for birth, and then lie down. They do not move around.

RK: And in hospital the woman is moved from the ward into the delivery room.

WS: . . . she has to go from her home, in a car or ambulance, sometimes driving miles and miles to go into an admitting room, then perhaps a first-stage room, and later a second-stage room. Even if it is not like that, it is the environment. They are ugly, most hospitals . . . They are not soft, welcoming places are they? They have harsh fluorescent lights, they are noisy, the phone rings, people walk in and out of the room.

RK: Would you, except in emergency cases, abandon hospital completely?

WS: Well, I think that a woman has to give birth in the place where she feels safest. Because our society has this enormous belief in science and technology—which has been in many ways so successful—and because the lack of success of medicine is not given much prominence in our media, a hospital may seem safer than home to many women. I think that, coupled with the advice that obstetricians have been giving women for the last twenty years at least—that the only way to achieve successful birth is to attend clinics regularly, to hand over your body to the professionals, and deliver in a place where, if something goes wrong, it can immediately be dealt with—has led to many women wanting to go to hospital. I think it would be wrong to force women to make a decision to have their babies at home. To change this we would need to start education in the schools. As Shirley Prendergast and Alan Prout have reported [Chapter 7], children at school are shown birth from a doctor's point of view, all very medical. The girls were frightened, and the boys made coarse jokes to hide their feelings. That kind of education in schools obviously needs to change.

RK: Where should we be going from here?

WS: We need women to challenge the power of the obstetrical establishment, and that really is a full-time job, isn't it? To organize people to see what has to be done.

RK: What alliances have you found to be useful in this struggle?

WS: The pressure groups like the Association for Improvements in the Maternity Services (AIMS) and the National Childbirth Trust (NCT): but in a way, NCT is not so much a pressure group as a group of women who want to do things their own way, and they have had modest successes in doing that. Whereas AIMS is more of a pressure group: it recently celebrated its twenty-fifth birthday but is still little known. I think what we need is GAIMS, which is Grandmothers' [*laughs*] Association for Improvement in Maternity Services. Grandmothers are not so involved with children any more, and what is more there are ten million of them between 45 and 65. There is also the Association of Radical Midwives, and they have done well. But you see the whole structure of the midwifery system needs changing. It does make me feel that the only answer is revolution, and having lived through the

Biafran war, I know that is no easy option and it does not usually succeed.

RK: Well, ruling that out for the time being, can you suggest what kind of strategy the various groups of people you have mentioned would pursue to achieve the desired changes in maternity care in Britain?

WS: First of all I think we have to lay our hands on some money, because in today's society the only way that you can effectively lobby is to spend money in holding events and getting yourselves known.

RK: Who should be lobbied?

WS: Well, you have to get the media on your side in order to get the message across. Then you have got to lobby the politicians and the people who are in the health authorities, to point out to them that there is an alternative viewpoint from that they are given by the obstetricians and health-care planners.

RK: What strikes me about that is that the mothers have been left out.

WS: The mothers and the grandmothers would be the lobbyists. Also, we need to have a much wider debate about maternity care. In Denmark they have got a woman Minister of Health. One day some new guidelines for maternity care landed on her desk and she was not sure about them. She gave the papers to some women for comment, and they said: 'No, this is not what we want'. So there was a public debate about it, and proposals were made for changing the maternity services which were, in part, from the women and not just from obstetricians. Whether that has made any difference, I do not know. In the United States the task force on Caesarean section included representatives from women's groups, and it was they who managed to get acceptance for the idea that vaginal birth after Caesarean section was an option that should be pursued. It was endorsed by the task force and several leading obstetricians. But policies are slow to change. The power interests of obstetricians are not served by changing the system. They are the ones that control the training of the future generations of obstetricians, so you need to get in there as well and change the training of obstetricians.

RK: Perhaps obstetricians need pregnant women more than pregnant women need obstetricians.

WS: Yes; you can say to women, right, stop going to obstetricians. That has been the strategy of a few GPs.

RK: What is good ante-natal care?

WS: If a woman knows what she wants, she can go to her GP and say she wants to have her baby at home, or that she wants a domino delivery, or to go to a private obstetrician or to a particular obstetrician at a hospital she knows to be good. But the majority of women do not have that kind of knowledge. When they go to their GP, they are excited about the fact that they are pregnant. They can hardly take it in when the GP says, well I'll write a letter to the hospital for you, and they will send you an appointment for a booking visit. And so they are sucked into the system right from the beginning. Even some good GPs do not offer the woman a domino delivery, because of the competing demands on their time. The community midwifery service, because it is now part of the hospital-based service, is directed from the hospital. If the labour ward in the hospital is short of staff, what they do is pull in a community midwife to do the deliveries, and so the community midwife cannot do her own booked community deliveries. As is always the way, the high-tech hospital will take what it needs from the low-tech community service. You can see that with geriatric care and mental handicap, and fields like that. Despite these being nominated as priority areas in health for at least the last ten years, the money is not going to them, especially now with the cuts.

So, very few women really get a choice. In a very few districts there is a leaflet which sets out what the choices are for women, but these always put it in the order—hospital, domino, home.

RK: Do you think the question of individual choice can be properly addressed within the National Health Service?

WS: There is no good evidence that the NHS is unable to provide the cheapest and best service for people, as long as it has a reasonable amount of money. The Conservative Party and those who are asking for basic change in the NHS do not believe in the collective provision of care for the majority,

whereas those on the left of centre believe that we should
provide for our whole population things which are important
for the health and well-being of the nation, such as education
and health, and social security, and, I suppose, defence,
although we might argue what sort of defence. The all-party
Social Services Committee has been saying that the NHS has
been underfunded for the last eight years, and that we need a
commitment to put in a greater proportion of our gross
national product to allow the NHS to go forward.

I think there is room for looking at different ways of
delivering the care within the NHS to make it more responsive
to people's needs. We have had a sort of pseudo-democracy
since the Health Service was reorganized in 1974. Health
authorities were set up as a way of allowing people to voice
their opinions, but in fact there is very little direct way that
people can express their needs. If we ever got a Labour
government, what I would like to see them doing is setting up
health authorities which are directly elected by the people
who live in the area, and who would be accountable to the
people who elected them. Because at the present time district
health authority members are nominated by the universities
and the regional health authority, and have local councillors
who are already overburdened with the work they do on the
council, you get a system which is unresponsive to people and
their needs.

RK: In other words, you want to make medicine explicitly
political rather than implicitly so?

WS: Yes. The other thing we need to do is to change the way
that consultants and GPs are appointed, because that is all
done within the system at present.

RK: So are you saying that the ballot-box can take the place of
market forces?

WS: Yes. I feel what the government should say is, we can
afford to give the Health Service, say 7 or 8 per cent of the
gross national product, and we will tell you the amount of
money you will get for the next four or five years. Then if the
NHS required more, because of something like a major new
technological advance which is not essential but would be nice
to have, then the NHS could have a lottery, or do some fund-

raising in other ways for that particular thing. That would seem to me to be a reasonable way of adding things which are not essential. However, if something essential and unforseen occurred, like the AIDS crisis, for example, then the government could say we will put in extra money. The lack of accountability to the patient or the community, the way the NHS has been set up, makes it much too much at the mercy of a government's policy-swings. There has never been a proper accountability of doctors to the health authorities. I know that is what general management is supposed to be bringing in, but because this is happening at the same time as the NHS has been systematically starved of funds, managers are too busy trying to keep the show on the road with the least harm possible to patients, to work on administrative reform.

RK: Do you, as a doctor, consider that you are accountable to your profession? Are you accountable to your Royal College first?

WS: Well, I personally think I am accountable to my patients.

RK: Are you unusual in that respect?

WS: It is not a point I have discussed much with doctors. Perhaps there are two groups of doctors, those who are for patients and those who are for medicine, and I think that those for patients are possibly in the minority.

RK: Is there necessarily a conflict of interest there?

WS: Well, there should not have to be. If you take the ideals of medicine, there is no conflict. But it is just like the Church. The system grows up and becomes more important than the actual function, and people are busy maintaining their position in the organization.

RK: Do you think that the system that we are talking about is the way it is because it has been set up by men.

WS: Well, yes, I suppose I do. If women had been involved in the evolution of this system, I think they would have had more understanding of the emotional and psychological needs of both the doctors and the patients, and therefore they would never have set up such a ridiculous system.

RK: Would you have any advice for a young woman who intends to become an obstetrician?

WS: Well, first of all I would advise them to have a female support group to enable them to cope with the rigours of the training system. Secondly, I would advise them to think very carefully before they got married or committed themselves to a long-term relationship, given the usual view men have of a working wife. I think young women today may be more realistic about these things. For my generation, I think that most of us thought that that battle had been won, and we could work and have a family. But when it came down to it, for almost all my contemporaries the man's career came first, and the woman tended to stay at home and look after the children for at least some of their married life. I was one of the few who could actually afford to get divorced, because I had the salary of a doctor. Even as a single parent, I could afford to have proper help in the house; that is absolutely crucial.

RK: What about the role of midwives in the future?

WS: Because midwives stay with women during labour, they understand birth. And yet, because of the way we have set up the system, we have almost destroyed that for many midwives. There are something like 120,000 trained midwives, of whom only 32,000 are practising. I know that some· of those midwives did the training because they had to in order to become a health visitor, but if even half of them wanted to be midwives, why are only half of those women practising? I think that the work of Sarah Robinson [see Chapter 4] shows what some of the reasons are. Midwives cannot do what they want to do and what they have been trained to do, and they leave because the job is so unsatisfactory. We must take the midwives out of the controlled environment where they are subjected to the manager of midwifery services and the protocols of the obstetricians, which stops them from giving extra time to a woman who needs it. Some midwives have been disciplined for using their judgement. Unless we can change that and treat them like autonomous professionals, the service cannot improve. Health Service and midwifery managers must accept the fundamental anxiety about birth. The first question a woman always asks at birth is: 'Is the baby all right?' You have to learn to contain that anxiety. But what our present training system is doing, I think, is reinforcing the anxiety of both doctors and midwives, so that they are compelled to do all this checking and monitoring and thereby muck up the process for a considerable number of women.

I think midwives should be the central professional, and they should be the ones who decide when a woman needs to be referred for a medical opinion. They should decide how the ante-natal care is structured, and what protocols are necessary in labour wards. Obstetricians do not know anything about normal labour. But the majority of women are normal and healthy, and have normal, healthy babies.

RK: Why is there a tendency for midwives to leave the profession, to opt out, rather than binding together collectively and putting forward a positive programme of change.

WS: I think it is partly because the majority of midwives have been nurses first. Nurses come in at 18 straight from school into a rigidly hierarchical system. They are the bottom of the pecking order, and therefore not used to collective action. Also there has been this ladylike approach: you do not belong to unions and things like that, you do not strike. You can see all that in nursing, but it is beginning to change. After nursing, they come into midwifery training within the context of the hospital. They are keen to learn the skills, but they do not want to rock the boat because if they are seen as trouble-makers it will not be easy for them to get a job. They are at the bottom of the medical pecking order, below the registrar and the senior house officer.

It is ridiculous, the way we set it up. If something goes wrong, a qualified midwife has to call an SHO, who does not know anything about it, and who may not have done obstetrics for two or three years since he was a student. He decides whether to call a registrar, who then decides whether to operate or consult with his boss, the consultant. I thought it was very interesting that in the research about hospitals organized without the registrar-tier, that midwives grew in confidence and power (see Kitzinger, Green, and Coupland, Chapter 8).

RK: Presumably it's also true that young midwives as well as young nurses and medical students are rewarded for conforming within this system that we are discussing, and punished for rebelling?

WS: Absolutely.

RK: Can we explain the demise of domiciliary midwifery in part by the nature of the midwifery training?

WS: Yes we can, but I also think it stems back to the 1974 reorganization of the Health Service, with its laudable idea of amalgamating the tripartite system of local authority, GP, and hospital care. This stopped midwives being employed by the local authority and based in the community as independent women with their patch, and they became part of the hospital system. They were based in the hospital and went out in the community, instead of being based in the community and occasionally taking their women into the hospital. The second factor was the decline in the number of home deliveries so in 1958 one-third of women had their babies at home, by 1970 it was 11 per cent, by 1980 it was 1 per cent. Therefore, in an area like ours, with 3,000 deliveries a year, there are now between twenty-five and thirty home deliveries. With six midwifery students coming every six months, they would be lucky to see even one home delivery.

RK: So, most young midwives these days might think about the possibility of domiciliary midwifery in abstract terms, but they will not have had much direct experience of it?

WS: That is right. Many community midwives are being used as post-natal nurses. We have sixteen community midwives here, so with about thirty home deliveries, each would not have more than two in a year, so they begin to feel their skills are being lost. All their time is spent doing post-natal visits with women that they probably have never seen before who delivered in hospital. Some midwives will like that, because its a nine to five-ish job and they have got children at home, and it suits them at that time in their life. But the ones who want to do domiciliary midwifery are frustrated by being forced into this role of being a post-natal nurse. And they leave.

RK: So they are being deskilled.

WS: Yes, that is right.

RK: Can you suggest some possible scenarios for the future development of childbirth in this country?

WS: In my idealized one, midwives would be a central figure in the community, working as an independent practitioner with their own premises and equipment, in the same way that GPs do. That kind of independent-practitioner status might commend itself to Mrs Thatcher. But, of course, they would have to be paid more than at the present time. They would refer women to obstetricians if necessary. Those GPs who wished to be involved in ante-natal care would share that with the midwives. Care would be based on the principle that pregnancy is normal until proved otherwise. There would be a considerable number of women who would want their babies at home, and that hospitals might become separated into a high-tech area and a birthing centre.

RK: The last question I want to ask you is: what do you think are the major obstacles to the changes that you have been talking about?

WS: The major obstacle is that English people on the whole are resistant to change. They do not see it as a good thing in itself. Despite the fact that we think of ourselves as a democratic country, it is very difficult for ordinary people to achieve the kind of changes that they want. I think you can see that at the moment, with the Conservative Party attacks on education, welfare, and the Health Service despite the fact that the majority of people in this country believe in these institutions, and do not want them dismantled. The political power of organizations which have been set up by Parliament, such as health authorities and the statutory bodies, makes it hard to change the kind of people that get to the top in medicine. And there is the power of the medical profession itself. It seems to me that people who get to the top of systems in our country are the kind of people who are able to close their eyes to their family's emotional needs and their own emotional needs. They are interested in the pursuit of power. Even people who start off wanting to get the power in order to change the system are unlikely to emerge at the other end with their ideals and their ideas for change intact. I think those are the major things.

I see a lack of power of the women's movement in this country compared with, say, the United States. There the women's movement has had much more impact on the structures and the ability of women to rise to the top. But it has not had much effect on the basic values of society, and in order to get to the top the women have to play it the men's way. But here women are still not likely to get to the top. It seems to me that the women's movement in this country has not managed to set up a network of women who are able to achieve change in these entrenched systems, and part of that is because of the way that people will go about saying: 'I'm not a feminist, but . . .', as if being a feminist was a dirty word. Women who are getting anywhere in the system are frequently reluctant to commit themselves to the feminist movement, because it has connotations of being left-wing, and sexually outside the norm, and hating men. So we have not got a strong women's movement. Also, what women's movement we do have has not been particularly interested in birth. They channel more energy into issues such as abortion, and rape, and forced sterilization. All of these are important issues, but birth is also an important issue. There have never been howls of indignation from the women's movement about what is happening to birth. I think that is another obstacle to changing things.

RK: So the issue of maternity-care provision in Britain is, in the end, a political one?

WS: Yes.

RK: Thank you.

Index